SUSTAINING
THE
CARRIER WAR

Titles in the series:

Progressives in Navy Blue: Maritime Strategy, American Empire, and the Transformation of U.S. Naval Identity, 1873–1898

Learning War: The Evolution of Fighting Doctrine in the U.S. Navy, 1898–1945

Victory without Peace: The United States Navy in European Waters, 1919–1924

Admiral John S. McCain and the Triumph of Naval Air Power

Churchill's Phoney War: A Study in Folly and Frustration

COSSAC: Lt. Gen. Sir Frederick Morgan and the Genesis of Operation OVERLORD

The Emergence of American Amphibious Warfare, 1898–1945

U-Boat Commander Oskar Kusch: Anatomy of a Nazi-Era Betrayal and Judicial Murder

Warship Builders: An Industrial History of U.S. Naval Shipbuilding, 1922–1945

Mahan, Corbett, and the Foundations of Naval Strategic Thought

The Fall and Rise of French Sea Power: France's Quest for an Independent Naval Policy, 1940–1963

A Ceaseless Watch: Australia's Third-Party Naval Defense, 1919–1942

Genesis of the Grand Fleet: The Admiralty, Germany, and the Home Fleet, 1896–1914

STUDIES IN NAVAL HISTORY AND SEA POWER
Christopher M. Bell and James C. Bradford, editors

Studies in Naval History and Sea Power advances our understanding of sea power and its role in global security by publishing significant new scholarship on navies and naval affairs. The series presents specialists in naval history, as well as students of sea power, with works that cover the role of the world's naval powers, from the ancient world to the navies and coast guards of today. The works in Studies in Naval History and Sea Power examine all aspects of navies and conflict at sea, including naval operations, strategy, and tactics, as well as the intersections of sea power and diplomacy, navies and technology, sea services and civilian societies, and the financing and administration of seagoing military forces.

SUSTAINING THE CARRIER WAR

The Deployment of U.S. Naval Air Power to the Pacific

STAN FISHER

Naval Institute Press
Annapolis, Maryland

Naval Institute Press
291 Wood Road
Annapolis, MD 21402

© 2023 by Stanford E. Fisher III
All rights reserved. No part of this book may be reproduced or utilized in any form or by any means, electronic or mechanical, including photocopying and recording, or by any information storage and retrieval system, without permission in writing from the publisher.

Library of Congress Cataloging-in-Publication Data

Names: Fisher, Stan (Stanford E.), III, author.
Title: Sustaining the carrier war : the development of naval aviation in the Pacific / Stan Fisher.
Description: Annapolis, Maryland : Naval Institute Press, [2023] | Series: Studies in naval history and sea power | Includes bibliographical references and index.
Identifiers: LCCN 2022037588 (print) | LCCN 2022037589 (ebook) | ISBN 9781682478479 (hardcover) | ISBN 9781682478479 (ebook)
Subjects: LCSH: Aircraft carriers--United States--History--20th century. | Aircraft carriers--Flight decks--United States. | United States. Navy--Aviation--History--20th century. | United States. Navy--History--World War, 1939-1945. | World War, 1939-1945--Naval operations, American. | World War, 1939-1945--Aerial operations, American. | CYAC: World War, 1939-1945--Campaigns--Pacific Area. | BISAC: HISTORY / Wars & Conflicts / World War II / Pacific Theater | HISTORY / Military / Naval
Classification: LCC V874.3 .F57 2023 (print) | LCC V874.3 (ebook) | DDC 359.9/4350973--dc23/eng/20220920
LC record available at https://lccn.loc.gov/2022037588
LC ebook record available at https://lccn.loc.gov/2022037589

♾ Print editions meet the requirements of ANSI/NISO z39.48–1992 (Permanence of Paper).
Printed in the United States of America.

31 30 29 28 27 26 25 24 23   9 8 7 6 5 4 3 2 1
First printing

To the *Professionals* of HSL-49, Detachment FOUR;
the *Nomads* of HSL-46, Detachment SEVEN;
and the *Bruisers* of HSL-46, Detachment TWO.

Contents

LIST OF ILLUSTRATIONS	xi
ACKNOWLEDGMENTS	xiii
Introduction	1
Chapter 1. Progress and Shortcomings	14
Chapter 2. Expansion, Turf Wars, and Estimates	27
Chapter 3. Establishing the Trade Schools	47
Chapter 4. Paradigm Shift	74
Chapter 5. Specialization of Labor and Timing the Delivery	112
Chapter 6. Supplying a Throwaway Culture	152
Conclusion	205
NOTES	215
BIBLIOGRAPHY	237
INDEX	241

Illustrations

Figures

Figure 1.1. Navy Fighter Engine Horsepower	25
Figure 4.1. Group I NATTC Activities	82
Figure 4.2. Group II NATTC Activities	83
Figure 4.3. Group III NATTC Activities	85
Figure 4.4. NATTC Group IV Activities as of December 15, 1944	86
Figure 6.1. Aviation Personnel vs. Aircraft Carriers over Time	171
Figure 6.2. Aviation Personnel vs. Fighter Aircraft (VF) over Time	171

Tables

Table 2.1. BuAer Enlisted Aviation Personnel Estimate, 1937	43
Table 2.2. Aviation Enlisted Personnel on Active Duty	44
Table 3.1. Summary of Enlisted Personnel by Month	62
Table 3.2. Current and Planned Capacity of Trade Schools as of November 29, 1941	64
Table 3.3. Length of Curriculum by School and Rating	69
Table 4.1. Enlisted Technical Schools as of September 1942	78
Table 4.2. Officer Technical Schools, September 1942	79
Table 4.3. Sample SECNAV Approved Additional Ratings, September 28, 1943	93
Table 4.4. SECNAV Approved Aviation Ratings, 1941 and 1945	94
Table 5.1. Aircraft Strength per Aircraft Carrier Class	114
Table 5.2. Average *Essex*-Class CV Air Group Complement	115
Table 5.3. AROU-5 Summary of Engine Overhauls, July 1943–February 1945	145
Table 6.1. USN Aviation Personnel and Matériel on Hand, 1940–45	170
Table 6.2. Average Unit Aircraft Prices, Navy F4F vs. F6F, January 1944	173
Table 6.3. Semiannual Value of Navy Fighter Aircraft Deliveries to June 1945	176

Table 6.4. Cost of Equipping a Carrier Air Group, 1929 and 1944   184
Table 6.5. Aircraft Distribution for Carriers, June 1944   199
Table 6.6. U.S. Carrier Aircraft Losses in Combat and Noncombat Operations   200
Table 6.7. Losses by Carrier Aircraft on Combat Mission by Cause of Loss   201

Acknowledgments

This book is the culmination of two and a half decades of my own naval service and over a century of naval aviation as a whole. It is a story that has been written by all naval aircrews since the Navy first began its fascination with operating aircraft from ships more than a century ago. Every aviator, officer or enlisted, understands the significance of competent aircraft maintenance and the invaluable asset that is the aircraft technician, better known as the "maintainer." The men and women who serve our country as aircraft technicians and flight deck crews are the reason U.S. naval aviation is unparalleled in its success and capability. Whether it's air-to-air, strike, anti-submarine, counter-piracy, reconnaissance, search and rescue, command and control, logistics, or the myriad of other missions we fly, none of it would be possible without a competent maintenance team. This book is testament to the dedication, determination, and diligence of every sailor or Marine that has ever turned a wrench, fixed a gripe, completed a daily or turnaround inspection, refueled, spotted, or pulled chocks since Eugene Ely first launched from the USS *Birmingham* in 1910.

As for this book, there have been many along the way who deserve recognition and my sincerest gratitude for assisting me in this endeavor. First, I must credit Dr. Jon T. Sumida, my doctoral advisor at the University of Maryland, College Park, for suggesting the subject of this book as a focus for my dissertation. As we discussed the idea throughout the fall of 2015, it became apparent that no one had researched or written on the topic and it was a story that needed to be told. The fact that so much has been written on carrier aviation without any discussion of how maintenance was performed or how the Navy created one of the largest skilled labor forces in history is unfathomable. As a former pilot and squadron maintenance officer, it quickly became personal to me. Under Jon's attentive and analytical eye, the project grew into a defendable dissertation, and ultimately this book. In addition to Jon, I must acknowledge my entire dissertation committee: David Rosenberg, Holly Brewer, Colleen Woods, and Meredith Kleycamp, who asked the hard questions and provided sage advice to help me deliver a manuscript that was academically and historically sound.

Dr. Hal Friedman, who graciously mentored me throughout the entire process, deserves similar credit. Hal's thoughtful feedback and expert critique on every chapter has been invaluable to me and this book would not have been possible without it. Jim Bradford, who took a chance on me when he first got wind of my work at the 2019 U.S. Naval Academy's McMullen Naval History Symposium, is the reason my research made the transition from dissertation to book. Jim's guidance and tutelage throughout the last three years has been vital to making this book project a success. I should also acknowledge the archivists and historians at the Naval History and Heritage Command and at the National Archives in College Park, Maryland. Without their support and research guidance, this book never would have been possible. My colleagues at the United States Naval Academy History Department also deserve my gratitude. They have been supportive, encouraging, and inspiring as I finished my manuscript while also introducing me to the rewards of teaching and mentoring midshipmen. I would be remiss if I did not recognize those who took the time to mentor and personally recommend me for the Navy's Permanent Military Professor program a decade ago: David "Decoy" Dunaway, John "Buzz" Nolan, Gary Mayes, Jeff Bartkoski, Jack Barry, Darnell Mondane, and Miles Yu. Without their endorsements and support, I would have never even embarked on this journey. And Kathy Finneran, who has been editing my papers since elementary school, continued to do so throughout my dissertation. Her willingness to check grammar and diction in every single sentence and provide feedback via copious spiral notebooks means the world to me. Who else but a mother would do that? Thanks, Mom.

As anyone who has ever written a book can tell you, it is always the author's family who sacrifices the most due to the hundreds of hours or more spent researching and writing instead of attending to the daily duties of home. Joshua, Seth, and Chloe, please know that anything worth doing in life, is worth doing well. Dad is far from finished writing books, but now that the first one is complete, I can spend more time editing your papers! Aren't you lucky? Thank you for being my biggest fans and believing in me. And April, as the wife of a naval aviator for over two decades, you understand as much as anyone—*if not more*—the valuable role that good maintenance plays in bringing us home from each sortie and every deployment. Your support, steadfastness, and unconditional love throughout this entire process has been awe inspiring and given me the freedom to make this book a reality. Thank you.

> **"With God all things are possible."**
> —**Matthew 19:26 (NIV)**

Introduction

Before the United States entered World War II, the might of the Navy's Pacific Fleet was characterized by the battleship rather than the aircraft carrier. Yet after December 7, 1941, the realization that carrier-based naval aviation was a force to be reckoned with soon challenged the hegemony of the battleship fleet. The Japanese attack on Pearl Harbor sank four of the U.S. Navy's eight battleships, and the remaining four suffered catastrophic damage. The U.S. Pacific Fleet's order of battle was significantly altered in just a few hours. However, its carriers were all at sea that morning, far away from the devastation encircling Ford Island. The Japanese had demonstrated the awesome power of the aircraft carrier in a single morning. The United States was forced to accept that change was coming to its naval forces, whether it was prepared for it or not. The next four years would be a proving ground for the U.S. Navy's carrier aviation forces. Much more would be tested than just the will of the pilots and admirals. Aircraft maintenance and the training of its skilled labor force, the aircraft technicians, would become critical to the success of the Navy in its war against the Japanese—both at sea and at home. The U.S. Navy did not evolve into the most powerful carrier navy in the world solely on its ability to quickly procure thousands of airplanes and more than one hundred aircraft carriers. Nor was it solely the production of thousands of courageous naval aviators that carried this mantle. Rather, it was the combination of these things augmented by behind-the-scenes aircraft technicians, or "maintainers," who kept the carrier fleet combat ready and its planes in the air that led the United States to victory over Japan in the Pacific.

The ability of the U.S. Navy to fight a protracted war throughout the Pacific Ocean in World War II was not solely the result of technology, tactics, or admiralship—naval aviation maintenance played a major role in the U.S. victory over Japan. Naval aviation leadership throughout the period between the world wars focused on the improvement of technology and tactics rather than training a new—and in the event of war, necessarily large—cohort of enlisted personnel. Aircraft maintenance was an afterthought for much of the era because of the small number of carriers and aircraft. When the United States realized a two-ocean naval war was imminent and a drastic increase in the size of its aviation fleet was ordered, the Navy was forced to reconsider its earlier practices and forge new polices and processes. The naval air war against Japan did not achieve sustained success until enough American aircraft technicians were in place to support the fast carrier task force doctrine. The U.S. Navy was not ready to fight a protracted war at sea until its carrier aircraft technicians were trained and in place.

Between 1941 and 1945, the U.S. Navy expanded its aircraft carrier operations to levels unimaginable only a few years earlier. During the interwar period, the Navy had grappled with how to best utilize its small fleet of aircraft carriers. A strong carrier navy gave a nation-state the ability to project power anywhere on the planet. The U.S. Navy did its best to make this a reality, but unfortunately throughout the interwar period, naval leadership focused more on the weapons of naval aviation than on the skilled labor that would become necessary to support a protracted naval war of attrition.

There were a few individuals, however, who recognized the Navy's lapses in planning for the future of naval aviation and did something about it. In World War II, carrier aviation would become much more than new airplanes, ships, or tactics—the role of the enlisted aviation technician, flight deck crew, and aircrew, combined with aircraft, carriers, tactics, and policy made victory in the Pacific a reality. This book focuses on one of these heretofore ignored groups: the aviation technicians.

Introduction

There is a significant but overlooked problem in historical accounts of the development of American carrier aviation: the majority of scholarly and popular writing on this subject has attributed the victory of the U.S. Navy in the Pacific war primarily to the superiority of American technology and tactics. It has been argued that these advantages were based on the massive production of carriers and aircraft, and the excellence of American naval leaders and pilots. That assertion is valid up to a point, but not a complete explanation. The waging of carrier warfare against a formidable opponent such as the Japanese navy involved intense operations over unprecedented distances in harsh weather and for a protracted period of time. The viability of the carrier as the primary strike force of the fleet was thus dependent upon the work of the large numbers of skilled technical maintenance personnel who kept its airplanes flying.

In order to meet the labor needs of an aircraft carrier-centric fleet, the U.S. Navy would have to reconsider personnel and training policies that had been in effect throughout the interwar years. How naval aviation managed the rapid growth in technical personnel beginning a year before Pearl Harbor is a story that stands on its own, but it can be linked to larger issues. Connecting the technical training of enlisted naval aviation technicians with their efforts to maintain naval aircraft in good working order, and the evolution of naval aviation maintenance policies throughout the Pacific war illustrates the point that logistical factors had a significant influence on operational outcomes in conjunction with actual combat.

For most of the interwar period, the effectiveness of naval aviation was limited by the small number of carriers and the low performance of aircraft. Battleships remained the main fighting arm of the fleet, with carriers relegated to a supporting role. Until the 1930s the primary role of naval aircraft had been scouting, air defense of the battle group, and spotting for naval gunfire. Carrier aircraft had little in the way of strike (air-to-ground) capability due to the limited horsepower of engines and weapons technology of the time. The Navy had explored various carrier attack scenarios in the Naval War College's fleet problems (wargames) in earnest beginning in 1929. However, these were simulated exercises that did not utilize live ordnance, so results were academic at best.

Live operations were limited by the number of U.S. aircraft carriers in existence.

Until 1935, the U.S. Navy operated with just three aircraft carriers. Within the Navy's Bureau of Aeronautics (BuAer) and the Bureau of Navigation (BuNav), there was little concern with meeting the skilled labor requirement for aviation activities. This was due in part to the small contingent of aviation technicians necessary to manage the even smaller fleet of airplanes, which numbered in the hundreds for most of the decade. Annual reports from the chief of BuAer make note of 754 aircraft on hand in 1934 and only 958 in 1936.[1] The United States' arsenal of both land- and ship-based aircraft never rose above 1,000 until 1937.[2] Thus, the approximately 10,000 sailors assigned to aviation since the beginning of the decade had seemed sufficient in a peacetime navy.

The management of BuAer's enlisted workforce was accomplished within the confines of smaller divisions. Officers, mainly pilots, were given priority and attention in the process of personnel assignments, whereas enlisted personnel were shuffled around internally as needed. One account recalls that there was a "complete lack of individual attention" given to the enlisted aviation technician by BuAer leadership.[3] It was not until 1940 that Rear Adm. John Henry Towers, chief of BuAer, acknowledged the fact that the impending shortage of aviation technicians would be detrimental to the strength of the fleet. Even though BuAer had begun to make changes to the distribution and training of aviation ratings in 1940, the lack of foresight kept the labor force of the Navy's air arm from reaching substantial strength for another two years.[4]

BuAer implemented its most effective changes in the training system for aviation technicians a year before entering the war. These efforts eventually restructured naval aircraft maintenance, technical training, and administration. New schools and training commands were formed to absorb the massive influx of personnel. Maintenance policies and procedures were adapted to meet the challenges of carrier naval warfare. Efficiency at aircraft overhaul and repair facilities became critical, as did supplying the fleet with either replacement parts or entirely new airplanes.

This book is essentially a chronicle of how an institution adapts to meet changing needs over time. The structure and size of the enlisted labor force of U.S. naval aviation changed dramatically between 1939 and 1945. During the preceding interwar years, very little concern was given to the importance of the naval aircraft technician. However, BuAer made great strides in aviation technology and tactics in the fifteen years since its first aircraft carrier, the USS *Langley* (CV 1), began full scale aircraft operations. Yet, consideration on how best to meet the future labor requirements of aircraft maintenance were routinely ignored or overlooked. The small contingent of aircraft carrier forces at the time did not necessitate significant changes to the status quo. Production of carriers and aircraft did not reach its zenith until two years into the war. This delay allowed naval aviation to expand the size of its skilled labor force and aircraft technicians, at the same time that industry was ramping up production of ships and airplanes.

I cannot say definitively whether or not shortages in skilled labor from 1940 to 1943 had significant effects on the U.S. Navy's ability to conduct carrier operations in the Pacific. The concurrent deficiency in the historical literature on naval logistics and matériel has made such an argument impossible to prove or disprove. But a counterfactual question is worth considering: had the U.S. carrier forces been at full strength in 1942 and 1943 (ships, planes, and pilots) would the Navy have been able to sustain combat operations in the Pacific with the quantity and quality of maintenance personnel it possessed?

After 1943, the supply of aircraft technicians was sufficient to support the growing fleet of carrier task forces. As industry produced more airplanes and aircraft carriers, the technical schools of the newly commissioned Naval Aviation Technical Training Command (NATTC) delivered a steady stream of trained maintainers. As the balance of power in the Pacific began to shift toward the United States in late 1943, the numbers of aviation technicians swelled, along with the pilots, airplanes, and ships. It was at this point that the strength of the fast carrier task forces, which have been given so much credit for their role in the Pacific War, were able to realize their potential and change the course of the war.

A careful analysis of the matériel and manpower buildup over the course of the war in terms of raw numbers illustrates the enormous challenge that this posed for the administrative leadership of the U.S.

Navy. On December 31, 1940, the Navy recorded an inventory of 245 fighter aircraft, 442 dive-bombers, and 112 torpedo bombers, a total of only 799 carrier-based airplanes. Until this point, the nearly six thousand naval aircraft technicians the United States had in its ranks had been sufficient. During the previous year, there was an effort to increase the number of enlisted technicians, along with pilots and new aircraft. Until the USS *Essex* (CV 9) was launched in late 1942, the combined total aircraft capacity of all 8 U.S. carriers in commission was a little over 600. What personnel planners could not know was that by August 31, 1945, the Navy would boast 14,748 fighters, 4,771 dive-bombers, and 5,181 torpedo bombers available for combat operations—an increase of thirty times the total size of carrier-based airplanes available just five years earlier.[5] Additionally, on V-J Day in 1945 the Navy reported an operational inventory of twenty-eight fleet carriers, and seventy-one escort carriers.[6] The size of this armada offered a capability to operate an air force of more than four thousand carrier-based aircraft at one time.[7]

Quantifying this in terms of aviation fuel, the U.S. Navy purchased 566,000 barrels of aviation fuel during the last six months of 1940 to supply a half-year's flight hours. During the second half of 1942, that acquisition jumped to 3.22 million. By 1944, the number reached 16.89 million. In the first six months of 1945, naval flight operations required 27.08 million barrels of aviation gasoline.[8] With regard to aviation personnel, a year after the attack on Pearl Harbor, the number of enlisted men assigned to aviation activities was ten times that of July 1940. By the end of the war, the Navy reported nearly 250,000 enlisted personnel serving in its air arm.[9]

Managing an expansion of this proportion was no small feat, and one might assume a very attractive subject for naval historians. Yet the opposite is the case. Exactly how the Navy dealt with the surge of men and machines after 1940 has been completely overlooked in World War II studies of naval aviation warfare. Twentieth-century naval histories tend to be voluminous in accounts of matériel and operations but shallow in administrative studies. In other words, the majority of World War II naval historians have spent their time focused on what the Navy did, but not how such efforts and actions were sustained. This book offers a long overdue and much needed corrective.

Herein, I identify and examine the vocational processes and policies that the Navy enacted in attempt to meet the skilled labor demands of carrier aviation. Historians have failed to ask serious questions regarding how the Navy obtained a highly skilled labor force to support wartime levels of aircraft operations at sea and ashore. Necessary questions—for example, how did the carrier's aircraft squadrons maintain a high degree of readiness during long periods of sustained combat operations? What were the stressors on aircraft readiness while embarked on the carrier and how did the Navy combat them? What impact did the availability of skilled labor of aviation mechanics have on the war at sea? How did the Navy train enlisted aviation mechanics—have not been asked. Present and past authors have, however, delivered ample studies on navy pilots, flight training, tactics, admiralship, and technology. Thus, I remain well clear of any serious discussion of such topics, unless they pertain to the role of the aircraft technician or contribute to an understanding of aircraft maintenance at sea. When discussing combat operations, the focus is mainly on the war in the Pacific, rather than the Atlantic. This is due simply to the fact that the vast majority of U.S. aircraft carrier operations were carried out in the Pacific Ocean, not in the Battle of the Atlantic.

This book is a study in untilled but nevertheless important ground. Ultimately, I aim to provide greater insight and a better understanding of how a modern U.S. Navy adapted its training and personnel to meet wartime demands. Increased matériel acquisition, changing defense policies, culture shifts, and surges in manpower requirements do not occur in a vacuum. This work examines the story of that which happened at the lower to mid-levels of naval aviation operations. One could almost consider it a "bottom-up" view of naval aviation in World War II. Just as the aircraft mechanic often works below the flight deck in the hangar of an aircraft carrier, this book works below the top-level histories of romantic images of fighting admirals, daring pilots, great battles, and triumphant technological innovation.

Combing the historiography of World War II naval history, one is hard pressed to find any significant studies on the subject of the aircraft technician or naval aviation maintenance. There are a few references to the aircraft technician among the oversized annals of naval aviation that hold places on the office coffee tables of commanding officers and admirals. However, I have found that the most informative material on the interwar and wartime naval aviation maintenance is found in the Naval History and Heritage Command's collection of 175 unpublished administrative naval histories of World War II. These manuscripts, which encompass nearly 300 bound volumes, were prepared by historical units of the U.S. Navy beginning in 1943 and considered complete in 1959. In particular, those of the Deputy Chief of Naval Operations for Air (DCNO, Air) and the Bureau of Aeronautics contain the most relevant information to the topic of aviation maintenance and personnel. Smaller, even more discreet individual unit histories and reports that were submitted to the Naval History Office or other upper echelon commands within the Department of the Navy throughout the war and following are full of valuable information relating to aviation maintenance. In combination, the data within these volumes presents the best picture of what the Navy was facing in terms of shortages in manpower and lack of training at the outset of the war. They also deliver a fascinating account of the responsive changes the U.S. Navy made over the first three years of the war. A. R. Buchanan's *The Navy's Air War*, a book-length manuscript published in conjunction with the official histories, spends a considerable amount of time on the importance of aircraft maintenance and the technician. Unfortunately, it falls short by not delivering a complete picture of the Navy's shortcomings in the lead-up and entry into the Pacific war.[10]

To date, there is no authoritative source that addresses the overarching question of how the Navy managed the buildup and training of its skilled labor force of aircraft technicians nor how this affected fleet operations. However, compiling the accounts and data from the aforementioned documents—as well as other primary source materials such as U.S. Navy manuals, postwar operational studies, operational reports, congressional hearings, and the personal accounts of life as an aircraft technician—have provided me with a clearer understanding behind the policy decisions before, during, and after the war.[11] This book addresses this subject in earnest, and it does so with the archival evidence to support.

Historians Jon T. Sumida and David A. Rosenberg have argued that twentieth-century navies have been shaped by "matters related to machines, men, manufacturing, management, and money."[12]

Comprehensive histories of U.S. naval administration—other than the aforementioned—are scarce. Operational or "battle histories," as characterized by popular military historians such as John Keegan, are plentiful.[13] But as Sumida and Rosenberg have suggested, a truly comprehensive history is unattainable without addressing the relationship between the administrative and the operational. It is not my intention to weave a counterargument into the canon of World War II naval history, but to add yet another layer to the already complex saga.

This book is generally organized chronologically, yet occasionally the subject material requires a brief topical study first and turns back to an earlier focus. Chapter 1 serves as an introduction to the state of naval aviation after the commissioning of the Navy's first aircraft carrier, the *Langley*.[14] U.S. naval aviation in the interwar period only generated a moderate level of interest compared to other naval weapon systems due to the small number of carriers and the limited performance of aircraft. Battleships remained the main fighting arm of the fleet, with carriers relegated to a supporting role. The limitations of the Washington Naval Treaty of 1922 restricted overall tonnage of capital ships and limited new construction. The next two U.S. carriers, the *Lexington* and the *Saratoga*, were reconfigured battle cruisers already under construction when the treaty was signed. Until 1935, the Navy operated with just three aircraft carriers.[15]

By the outbreak of war in December 1941, the U.S. Navy had managed to commission four more large fleet aircraft carriers (CV), plus one escort carrier (CVE). The smaller design of the new carriers and the lapse of the Washington and London Naval Treaty accords in 1937 allowed for the additional vessels. Due to this increase, the Navy's aircraft operating strength on board carriers would more than double to approximately six hundred. This was an impressive surge in capability, but not one that caused great concern with regard to maintenance manpower.

Chapter 2 takes a closer look at the status of fleet aircraft maintenance and technical training at the end of the interwar period. The labor force required for the small contingent of naval aircraft at shore and at sea had been sufficient since the days of Rear Adm. William Moffett and the creation of the Bureau of Aeronautics. However, with the threat of a second world war and naval aviation looking to be a major player in that conflict, personnel and training requirements were thrust to the forefront of war preparations.

Rear Adm. John H. Towers, chief of the Bureau of Aeronautics from 1939 to 1942, recognized the need for more pilots and aviation officers, but he missed signals that training enlisted technicians for the Navy's aviation labor force was equally important. In his defense, most of the Navy's leadership also overlooked the enlisted component of preparing to fight an air war at sea as pilot training and aircraft acquisition received most of their attention. It was not until President Franklin D. Roosevelt authorized a massive increase in the naval aircraft inventory in 1940 that Towers began considering changes in personnel administration to meet the oncoming challenges.

In the latter part of 1941, BuAer's repetitive calls for assistance resulted in the Navy modifying its recruitment policies and implementing more Naval Reserve activations for aviation personnel. Yet, even as these revisions filled in the gaps surrounding overall numbers of enlisted aviation technicians, quantity only solved half of the problem. The fleet needed highly skilled technicians that could maintain new airplanes and who also were capable of contending with constantly changing aircraft technology. Quantity by itself was not enough to do the job. The quality of its aviation labor force was equally important as the United States entered World War II.

Chapter 3 acknowledges that in 1940 BuAer recognized the need to change its training system for aviation technical ratings. The expansion that naval aviation was undergoing created the need for a more robust and technically advanced training program for the aviation labor force. Administrative changes in how BuAer managed the technical training program afforded the Navy the opportunity to open multiple vocational technical schools. These trade schools were responsible for quickly producing high numbers of trained technicians ready for the fleet.

The need to establish standards for prospective students, as well as the curricula, forced BuAer to reform its processes. It consolidated a national network of technical trade schools into four primary locations. BuAer also contracted with industry partners who offered specialized schooling for naval technicians at their factories as a supplement to the Navy trade schools. Students were admitted into the trade and factory schools based on standardized testing scores. Over a period of just four years, BuAer transformed a twenty-year-old nonstandard process of on-the-job technical training into a massive network of standardized schools structured to educate a technical workforce numbering one-quarter of a million men and women.

The focus of chapter 4 is the establishment of the NATTC. NATTC was responsible for creating the most technologically advanced labor force the world had ever seen. The first year of World War II proved to be a much bigger burden on BuAer and the Bureau of Naval Personnel (BuPers) than was expected.[16] The continued personnel challenges since Naval Aviation's period of expansion was authorized in 1940 were being met on paper, but the raw numbers were misleading. The number of trained aircraft technicians graduating from naval trade schools was slowly erasing the deficit of enlisted aviation ratings in the fleet. Unfortunately, the quality of their training left much to be desired.

Problems with standardization, curricula, budgeting, physical maintenance of the schools, and instructor training forced BuAer and BuPers to collaborate on a new administrative structure that would take primary responsibility for the education of the technical aviation ratings. NATTC was established on September 11, 1942. The command was assigned responsibility for all aspects of technical aviation training. BuPers and BuAer worked alongside NATTC to ensure that quotas, budgets, and material needs were met as World War II intensified. NATTC changed the face of naval aviation technical training from a disjointed, unstandardized, antiquated program into a modern, progressive-thinking administrative organization. Educating future naval aircraft technicians also involved the Navy accepting a culture change within its institution. White women and Black men soon had a role to play in the naval air war and its sustainment. Segregation, official and unofficial, was on the way out, and the era of a more diverse U.S. Navy was on the way in.

Chapter 5 explores the transition of aviation maintenance into a specialized labor force aboard the aircraft carrier. Prior to World War II, aircraft maintenance was relatively simple when confined to naval facilities that were located on land and usually in the vicinity of a major naval air station. Maintenance was routinely limited to land-based work spaces completed by a few skilled technicians that were considered experts on all parts of airplanes. It was even common practice for pilots to work on their own airplanes along with a small crew of enlisted technicians. In effect, aircraft maintenance in the peacetime Navy was a highly personalized operation that attracted little attention from anyone outside of the pilots and technicians themselves.

The final chapter examines and analyzes the available data sets of aircraft availability during the war and suggests a connection with the availability of technicians and supplies. Procurement policies with respect to spare parts and life expectancies of carrier-based aircraft had a profound impact on the Navy's progress in the latter half of the war. An analysis of yearly budgets and the fluctuating cost of aircraft and spare parts also reflected the changing nature of aviation maintenance policy in the latter half of the war.

In 1943 a midyear survey was given to carrier aviation officers. In it, supply and spare parts were identified as the greatest detriments to the fleet. Supply and logistics played a critical role in the World War II carrier warfare. The effectiveness of a fast carrier task force depended on the availability of its aircraft. The number of "mission capable" aircraft directly reflected the supply system, as well as the technicians' ability to do their jobs effectively. Ultimately, revisions in naval aircraft maintenance policy and procedures met the challenges of supply and repair. As the aircraft industry's rates of production soared, the Navy no longer had to rely solely on the technician to "keep 'em flying."[17] The vast number of airplanes being delivered on a monthly basis by 1944 changed the nature of aircraft maintenance at sea and undoubtedly shortened the duration of war.

By 1944, the striking power of the U.S. Navy carrier task forces in the Pacific Ocean was unequaled by any other nation. At no other time in modern naval warfare had the world ever experienced such matériel strength and firepower. But machines, manufacturing, and money alone do not win wars. This book demonstrates the importance of considering all elements of the military institution, not just those that correspond to operational or battle history, when studying naval war in the age of the aircraft carrier.

Drastic institutional changes accompanied an increase in naval maintenance personnel from less than 10,000 to nearly 250,000 over just four years. The complete restructuring of U.S. naval aviation's technical educational system, in conjunction with developing a highly skilled, specialized labor force on board the aircraft carrier was essential to winning the Pacific war. *Sustaining the Carrier War* is the story of that transformation, one that changed the nature of naval war forever.

Even in the modern era of technologically advanced warfare, people still matter.

Chapter 1

Progress and Shortcomings

In the 1920s the battleship was considered the preeminent weapon of naval warfare. U.S. Navy carrier aviation was a novel concept that many considered to be nothing more than a future auxiliary force in support of the battleship fleet. Twenty years later, these roles would be reversed, with the main burden of fighting assumed by carriers. This change in status came as a result of advances in aircraft performance, improvements in carrier design, increases in carrier numbers, and the development of new operational practices in response to war experience. However, the spectacular success of the American carrier forces in the war against Japan was not just a matter of combat with planes, pilots, and platforms, but it also required an enormous body of skilled technicians to service and maintain the state of the art airframes, complex engines, electrical, hydraulic, and ordnance systems under the harsh conditions of war at sea. The practicability of the carrier formations that were the cutting edge of the U.S. Navy's strike capability rested upon the labor of enlisted aircraft technicians. While those in charge of BuAer had recognized the importance of aircraft mechanics during the interwar period, they failed to anticipate the level of effort that the colossal expansion of naval aviation beginning in 1940 would necessitate. A growth in skilled service personnel like never before would be required. The following three years would thus prove to be an uncomfortable, and even difficult period of playing catch-up with regards to aviation technical training and labor supply for the Navy.

Any discussion of U.S. naval aviation in the 1920s and 1930s must consider the influence of the British Royal Navy (RN) in World War I. During this period, the RN possessed the most advanced naval air arm in the world. U.S. Navy forces operated closely with the British and were influenced by their aircraft carrier operations.[1] The RN had invented the aircraft carrier and operated aircraft from ships extensively throughout World War I. British carrier aircraft were utilized mostly in a scouting or reconnaissance role rather than air strikes with bombs or torpedoes. In 1916, plans were drafted for the British aircraft carrier *Hermes*, which was the first purpose-built aircraft carrier.[2] The British converted an ocean liner, battleship, and three battle cruisers into carriers during the 1920s.

After 1930, the RN added no new aircraft carriers until commissioning the *Ark Royal* in 1938. None of the six operable British carriers at that time carried more than forty-eight aircraft.[3] The United States would not challenge the RN's number of aircraft carriers at sea until the end of the interwar period. However, what the U.S. Navy carrier fleet substituted lethality and strike capability for its lack of quantity. The larger American carriers built after the Washington Naval Conference maximized the number of airplanes on board, never dropping below seventy-two. This held true until the Navy began building smaller escort and light carriers on the eve of World War II, which typically deployed with an average of thirty airplanes.

After World War I, the U.S. Navy's interest in carrier aviation briefly waned as seaplanes (aka "flying boats") and land-based scouting operations took precedence over the development of carrier tactics and procedures. A year after the war ended, the Navy decided to convert the *Jupiter*, a coal collier, into its first aircraft carrier, the USS *Langley* (CV 1). The *Langley* began its conversion in 1920 and was commissioned as a fighting warship in 1922. Initially the *Langley* did not embark any aircraft squadrons for extended periods but was only used for training pilots, testing carrier equipment such as catapults and arresting gear, and developing tactics through fleet battle experiments.[4] While the *Langley* provided a test platform for new technology, the Navy was simultaneously developing plans for two more aircraft carriers.

The *Langley* did not embark her first permanent squadron, Fighting Squadron Two (VF-2) and its twelve VE-7S bi-wing fighters until 1924. With its relatively small hangar space, it was initially designed to only operate a dozen aircraft at one time. The *Langley* was smaller and slower than all other subsequent U.S. aircraft carriers.[5] Her flight deck was only 534 feet in length, nearly 350 feet shorter than that of the final design of the *Lexington* (CV 2) and the *Saratoga* (CV 3), then under construction. Yet even with all of its shortcomings, the *Langley* served its purpose at a time when the U.S. Navy's experience in aircraft carrier operations was minimal at best.

In 1925, Capt. Joseph M. "Bull" Reeves, commander, Aircraft Squadron Battle Fleet, designated the *Langley* as his flagship. Development of carrier tactics continued in the fleet with the *Langley*'s aircraft and pilots. Reeves, an officer who always sought to improve upon the status quo, sought suggestions from his pilots on how to conduct air operations more efficiently.[6] After discussions with aircrew, Reeves initiated keeping all aircraft on the flight deck rather than in the hanger for the duration of at-sea maneuvers. Until this point, aircraft had been moved up and down via elevator after every launch/landing cycle, making for a tedious and lengthy operation that was burdensome on the flight deck crews responsible for conducting aircraft movement. Reeves' new method required maneuvering each plane to the bow of the ship, forward of the landing zone and protected by a crash barrier after landing. Once all aircraft were on board, they were repositioned to the stern of the ship in preparation for the next launch cycle. Reeves' procedure reduced the landing interval between planes to just a few seconds. For the rest of the interwar years, and much of World War II, U.S. carriers would continue to park airplanes on the flight deck for the majority of underway periods. Routine maintenance and servicing were conducted on the flight deck. The hangar was used for spare aircraft, parts, and repair only when absolutely necessary. Ultimately Reeves' ingenuity, albeit admittedly more dangerous than the previous procedure of stowing planes in the hangar after landing, would allow many more aircraft to embark in U.S. carriers.[7]

After promotion to rear admiral, Reeves' continued to push the limits of aircraft complement. In 1928, he decided to have the *Langley*'s flight deck enlarged in order to operate more aircraft. Upon doing so, he eventually found room for another thirty airplanes, raising the *Langley*'s new aircraft complement to forty-two. The ship's commanding officer (CO), Cdr. John Henry Towers, future chief of the Bureau of Aeronautics (BuAer), did not support the drastic increase in airplanes on his deck. He argued that it was unsafe to clutter the deck with so many airplanes. But Reeves was the battle fleet commander, and had ultimate authority over the Navy's carriers in the Pacific. Reeves was changing the nature of carrier aviation, and as his nickname suggested, did not care whether Towers or anyone else liked it.[8] The decision to keep aircraft parked on the flight deck for long periods may have been a good one tactically, but as far as aircraft maintenance went, it was troublesome. Deck parking exposed the aircraft to one of the most austere environments on the earth—the open ocean.

+++

Corrosion, a common problem for any aircraft operating in a salt water environment, has plagued naval aviation since Eugene Ely's first shipboard landing in 1911. Acidic salt-laden ocean air and salt water chemically react with metal aircraft parts and accelerate corrosion many times faster than inland air or fresh water. Parking airplanes on the flight deck only made the situation worse due to constant exposure to ocean air and salt spray.

However, due to design, corrosion of the earliest carrier-based aircraft was a relatively minor problem. The Navy's first fighter aircraft, the Vought VE-7 Bluebird, was constructed mostly of noncorrosive materials such as wood and airplane fabric. Much of the forward fuselage, however, was covered in sheet metal to withstand the heat generated by the small 180 horsepower (hp) engine. The engine and flight instruments were constructed with metal alloys as well.[9]

The BuAer recognized the costly effects of corrosion to its airplanes, as did the U.S. Naval Aircraft Factory (NAF). The NAF had performed all of the overhauls and major maintenance on naval aircraft since 1917, even manufacturing some of its own aircraft directly in its Philadelphia plant. Most of the NAF-built aircraft were of the patrol type such as the PN-9, the Navy's first all-metal hull "flying boat." Engineers in the NAF spent years experimenting with various metal alloys in hopes of finding one that would resist corrosion and lighten the gross weight of airplanes. Navy aircraft could suffer critical damage from salt corrosion very quickly. Hidden corrosion under the nonmetallic skin of the airplane was of great concern to aircraft mechanics. It jeopardized the structural integrity of the airframe and weakened aircraft structural parts. Additionally, corroded metal engine parts could fail prematurely and endanger the lives of the aircrew as well.

The environmental hazards of naval aviation forced scientists, technicians, and aircraft manufacturers to seek alternative materials and coatings that would be both durable and corrosion resistant. Duralumin, one of the earliest aluminum alloys first used in naval aircraft, showed promise in its durability, but did not hold up well against corrosion. In 1927, a new aluminum alloy called alclad was introduced to the Navy by the aluminum manufacturer Alcoa. Alclad provided the corrosion resistance that the Navy desired. It soon became the standard in metal naval aircraft airframes.[10]

As more aircraft were flying to and from carriers in the late 1920s, BuAer stepped up its efforts to prevent corrosion. According to the BuAer manual of 1927, all metallic parts of airplanes were to be treated with a protective coating of rust inhibiting agent and then painted as an extra measure. This procedure would carry over into the supply divisions that packaged aircraft spare parts. It became a standard procedure to apply a coating of rust inhibitor to any spare parts containing metal before packaging or shipment. The Navy would continue to battle corrosion throughout the interwar period and beyond. The scientific advances that were made in the prevention of corrosion during this period would have lasting effects on the institution of naval aviation maintenance. Thanks to the aircraft maintenance personnel and procedures of 1920s, naval aviation has continually considered the effects of corrosion on the performance and durability of its aircraft.

The latter half of the 1920s saw increased aircraft procurement for the Navy in concert with ongoing construction of the *Lexington* and the *Saratoga*. In 1926 Congress authorized a gradual procurement program of a thousand additional airplanes for the Navy over a period of five years. In order to best determine the nature of how and what to spend the Navy's money and efforts on with regards to aviation over the following five years, a board was convened of progressive-minded supporters of naval aviation. Chaired by Adm. Montgomery Meigs Taylor, the board included some of naval aviation's biggest proponents including William Moffett, "Bull" Reeves, H. E. Yarnell, Theodore G. Ellyson, and Marc Mitscher. All were advocates of a strong aviation component within the Navy.[11] The Taylor Board suggested that building a greater number of smaller aircraft carriers at a rate of one per annum would be preferable to adding fewer carriers but of larger size like the 36,000-ton *Lexington*. This would permit the Navy to increase its carrier fleet, employ the additional aircraft, and still remain within the limits of the 1922 Washington Naval Treaty.[12] Plans for the Navy's fourth carrier, the *Ranger*, were already being drafted, but construction did not commence until after 1930. Congress did not approve the proposed carrier buildup due to declining peacetime military budgets and lingering demobilization efforts.[13] BuAer would have to make do with the three carriers it had until the middle of the 1930s.

The other problem with the Five-Year Program was that the plan for a thousand-plane air force made no provision for additional personnel or personnel support. Earlier, in 1924, the first chief of the BuAer, Rear Adm. William A. Moffett, testified before Congress that for every aircraft operating from U.S. aircraft carriers, an average of eight to ten enlisted aviation technicians were necessary for proper maintenance.[14] At that time, this meant another two to three thousand sailors would need to be assigned to the naval aviation community.[15] Even in naval aviation's earliest years, BuAer acknowledged the importance of the enlisted technician to the success of naval aviation, but manpower requirements were not always met. The operation of the Navy's technical service schools suffered in the latter half of the 1920s and formal technical training of new recruits was limited due to lack of funding. Many of BuAer's assembly and repair (A&R) facilities, such as the Naval Aircraft Factory served as informal training venues. Existing technical schools, if not completely shut down, were "skeletonized," leaving a lack of experienced instructors, and therefore trained technicians, throughout the fleet.[16]

Moffett had estimated that in order to properly operate and maintain 1,000 airplanes, 3,136 rated aviation technicians plus 9,503 general service rated sailors (for a total of 12,639 personnel) would be required by 1930.[17] Even with the limited funding for personnel programs, Admiral Moffett, a persuasive and appreciated arbiter between the government and the Navy, acquired what BuAer needed in order to survive its aviation labor demands during the leaner years. Remarkably, Moffett nearly reached his goal of twelve thousand men in 1928, even when the Navy as a whole, had reduced its overall strength by two thousand during the same period.[18] Unfortunately, progress would stall following Moffett's untimely death in 1933 in the crash of the airship USS *Akron* off the New Jersey coast.

✛✛✛

Labor demands on board the carrier in the early interwar period varied with size of the ship and complement of aircraft. While the *Langley* was originally designed with twelve embarked aircraft in mind, it was routinely deploying with more than forty by the end of the decade. The *Lexington* and the *Saratoga* were each commissioned with the capability of operating seventy-two airplanes, but complements could vary from fifty to eighty.[19] The *Langley* required an operational personnel complement of just under five hundred (officers and enlisted).[20] The *Lexington* was built to deploy with more than seventy aircraft and required a crew of 2,800 sailors including aviation personnel. As the United States continued construction of aircraft carriers in the 1930s, the labor requirements of naval aviation grew significantly. The *Ranger* (CV 4) was commissioned in 1934 with an expected complement of 76 aircraft and 2,200 sailors. Eventually, every carrier that would be built under the "CV" designation throughout the Pacific war would sail with no fewer than 2,000 personnel, including between 600 and 700 enlisted aviation personnel. The escort carriers (CVE) and light carriers (CVL)—the bulk of which would be built after World War II began—required a much smaller labor footprint as their aircraft complement remained near thirty. Their labor requirement was only a few hundred greater than that of the *Langley*.[21]

As in the *Langley* design, the hangar bays inside aircraft carriers were originally intended as a storage location for spare airplanes, providing an onboard replacement to the strike force when necessary. In stowing the replacements below, the flight deck was less cluttered with parked aircraft when conducting flight operations. The protected environment of the hangar was also beneficial to preserving the material condition of the airframes. But the inefficiency of the aircraft elevators on board made getting quick replacements to the flight deck a problem. Aircrew and maintenance personnel preferred to use the hangar deck only for critical aircraft maintenance and repair that could not be performed on deck, as well as storage of spare planes and spare parts.[22] Storing the majority of its aircraft on deck increased the pace at which aircraft carriers could affect launch and recovery cycles, but the procedure could be costly to the airframes. More airframes on deck would require more technicians to service and properly maintain them.

By June 1934 both the *Lexington* and the *Saratoga* were operating with eighty airplanes on board. The squadrons assigned were a mix of fighters, scouts, and torpedo bombers. When embarked on the carrier, the squadrons made up what was termed the "Carrier Air Group" (CAG). During the interwar years, squadrons were designed as completely autonomous units. Even though squadrons were often assigned to a single ship for many years, flight operations at sea were considered temporary, and thus all maintenance personnel were assigned to the squadron vice the ship. An average enlisted complement of a squadron before the war was 120 sailors, which included technicians and nonaviation ratings such as yeomen, cooks, bakers, and pharmacist's mates.[23] Officer numbers varied anywhere from twenty to fifty depending on the number of airplanes per squadron and whether they were single-seat or two-seat designs.

The size of squadrons and air groups increased over the interwar and war years. Much of this expansion should be attributed to the ingenuity of the Navy's engineering leadership. During the early 1930s, the Bureau of Construction and Repair (BUCON) and BuAer began experimenting with a procedure called "tricing" in order to free up limited space in the hangar. This procedure permitted completely assembled spare or damaged aircraft to be "hung" in the overhead with a system of pulleys and wires. In the *Lexington*-class carriers, it allowed an additional seventeen aircraft to be stowed on board. The tall height of the hangar spaces provided enough clearance underneath to park another airplane, allowing aviation technicians to conduct maintenance as necessary.[24] It was not an easy procedure, but to the ship's air department, it was well worth the trouble. One officer recollected, "It [tricing gear] made a difference. We could put 17 more airplanes on the ship. If you could trice up 17 of them, it was well worth taking a lot of inconvenience for."[25] Ultimately, more planes on board meant more technicians needed to be available to maintain them, but institutional change from the "way it had always been done" was difficult for the Navy's bureaucracy to embrace. Therefore, the Navy would soon find itself shorthanded on the skilled labor necessary to properly support the growing fleet of carriers.

The final five years before the war afforded the United States an opportunity to add another five carriers to its order of battle. The 14,500-ton *Ranger* had not exhausted the Washington Naval Treaty's total allowance for U.S. carrier tonnage, and thus construction began on the *Yorktown* (CV 5) and the *Enterprise* (CV 6) in 1934. Each were designed to carry at least ninety aircraft. Commissioned in 1937 their tonnage was less than that of the *Lexington*, weighing only approximately 20,000 tons. The personnel complement was 2,200 total, with approximately 700 assigned to aviation duties. Construction of a third vessel, the *Wasp* (CV 7), began in 1936 and was completed in 1940. It was a smaller version of the *Yorktown* class, designed to only carry 76 aircraft. Its enlisted aviation personnel complement was about fifty less than that of the larger *Yorktown*.[26] The lapse of the Washington accords in 1937 allowed work to begin on the *Hornet* (CV 8), a third unit of the *Yorktown* class, which was commissioned in December 1940. By the outbreak of war in December 1941 these four warships—plus one smaller escort carrier, the *Long Island* (CVE 1)—had added a capability of deploying another 360 aircraft to the almost 250 already operating from the *Lexington*, *Saratoga*, and *Ranger*, for a grand total of slightly more than 600.[27]

✦✦✦

The six hundred aircraft that were operating from U.S. carriers in 1941 and beyond were technological marvels compared to the VE-7S bi-wing fighters that were landing on the deck of the *Langley* in 1924. The most significant advances were in their performance capabilities such as engine design, horsepower, and airspeed.[28] Due to the extreme operating environments of most naval aircraft, BuAer favored air-cooled radial engines over liquid cooled. Compared to liquid-cooled engines, they weighed considerably less, had better reliability, and were less vulnerable to gunfire.[29] Air-cooled engines were also less prone to radiator and coolant line breakage that could result from seaplane water landings in heavy seas and high impact carrier landings.

Progress was not only made in engine power and performance in other areas as well. Increased reliability and reduction of maintenance costs in aircraft engines took priority in much of BuAer's research and development. The Navy's Bureau of Supplies and Accounts assisted with implementing a new cost accounting system at the overhaul shops (A&R facilities). This new accounting system reduced the number of man hours required for airplane and engine overhaul. The chief of BuAer at the time, Rear Adm. Ernest J. King, boasted that it allowed his bureau to release a hundred enlisted technicians from the overhaul units to serve the fleet on ships instead. Modifications to the *Lexington* and the *Saratoga* were also made to accommodate bomb and air-launched torpedo stowage and handling. Corrosion resistant steels and alloys, new enamels, and primers were constantly under development. Improving engine preservative compounds was also noted in the list of BuAer's accomplishments during the interwar period.[30]

The gross weight, wingspan, and overall length of naval aircraft also increased. As aircraft design evolved with each new model, the Navy had to consider how to operate its new aircraft from carriers that were designed years earlier. This included how and where to park, land, and launch the airplanes. In addition, BuAer and its aircraft technicians had to learn the maintenance procedures for each new engine and aircraft systems.

Carrier fighter aircraft such as the Vought F3B-1 (1928) had an engine rating of 450 horsepower. Its maximum speed was 136 knots and it weighed 2,950 pounds. The wingspan was 33 feet and overall length was slightly less than 25 feet. The Boeing F4B-4 (1930) increased horsepower to 550 and its airspeed to 147 knots. Gross weight increased by 200 pounds. But in a sign of things to come, it also added bomb racks under the wings so it could carry a 116-pound bomb under each wing.

As newer aircraft entered the fleet, engine ratings increased with every new model. Grumman's FF-2, a modified version of the original FF-1, was delivered to the fleet in 1933. Its engine was rated at 700 horsepower and overall weight increased to 4,826 pounds. Airspeed of the FF-2 increased to 179 knots. Grumman then delivered the F3F in 1935. Its engine horsepower was 950 and maximum speed was 207 knots.[31] The Navy's first monoplane fighter, the Brewster F2A Buffalo, entered service at the very end of the interwar period; it had 1,200 horsepower and a maximum speed of 258 knots and was delivered in 1939. Its gross weight was a very heavy 6,538 pounds, but the wingspan and overall length were only a couple of feet longer than the earlier F3B-1.

At the risk of operating outside of the chronological boundaries of this chapter, it is necessary to look past the interwar period briefly in order to fully comprehend the scope of advancements in carrier aircraft engineering. Grumman's F4F Wildcat was the Navy's standard fighter at the outbreak of U.S.–Japanese hostilities in 1941. It was by far the most widely used, capable, and reliable fighter of the first years of the war. Its characteristics were similar to that of the Buffalo, but it was slightly longer and 1,400 pounds heavier.[32] Yet once war was declared, the aircraft industry made another jump in fighter aircraft technology. The Wildcat's successor, the Grumman F6F Hellcat (1943) was 33 feet long, had a wingspan of 42 feet (with wings folded, only 16 feet), and a maximum sustained engine rating of 2,000 horsepower. Top speed was 323 knots. The heaviest version of the Hellcat was nearly 14,000 pounds, more than twice that of the Buffalo. Vought's F4U Corsair had similar dimensions, weighed just over 12,000 pounds, and was powered by the same Pratt & Whitney R-2800 engine as the Hellcat, rated at 2,000 horsepower.[33] Over the course of the war, the Wildcat, Hellcat, and Corsair constituted the vast majority of the Navy's carrier-based fighters. The technological advancements that naval aircraft went through in roughly fifteen years were remarkable. Figure 1.1 illustrates the degree at which horsepower alone increased from naval aviation's earliest carrier fighters on board the *Langley* through those in service at the end of World War II.[34]

Consider a young sailor enlisting in 1930 and learning the technical skills to become a carrier aircraft technician on the F4B-4 biplane fighter. Within a decade of service, he could be responsible for maintaining an all-metal monoplane F4F Wildcat with an engine three times as powerful as what he apprenticed on. The learning curve was steep for the aircraft technician throughout the 1930s. Why the desire for better technical

Figure 1.1. Navy Fighter Engine Horsepower

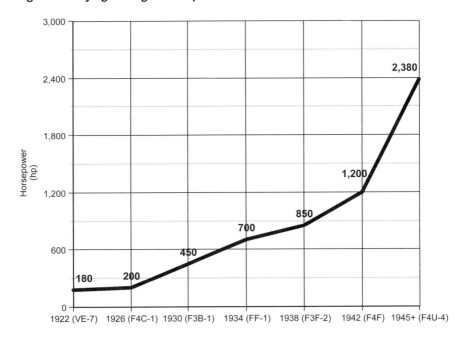

training or more proficient aircraft technicians did not have equal visibility as did the need for pilots remains unclear. One plausible explanation is that the Navy's small number of aircraft and aircraft carriers did not seriously warrant more technicians than were already available. The low inventory of aircraft on both land and sea had been properly maintained thus far, and no serious contradictions to that fact existed before the period of naval expansion that was to come after 1939.

Based on the size of its aircraft carrier fleet throughout the interwar years, BuAer had managed to maintain its small inventory of carrier-based aircraft with little difficulty. Not until the prospect of war became clear did BuAer begin to seriously consider expanding its capacity for training technicians and reconsidering carrier aircraft maintenance procedures. Change on an institutional level was necessary to counter the rising Japanese threat.

Acquiring more pilots and aircrew had traditionally drawn the most attention from lawmakers and Navy leadership. Acquiring and training more enlisted technicians was not a regular point of contention. One would be hard pressed to find anything more than a cursory note in the "recommendations" section of the chief of BuAer's Annual Report to the Secretary of the Navy prior to 1939 that simply said, "Provide required increases in naval personnel to support the expansion program."[35]

While a peacetime Navy was able to get by on two to three thousand designated aviation technicians during the last few years of the 1930s, it was only a matter of time before the threat of war forced the United States to radically change the complement and size of its aircraft and aircraft carrier force. The strength of naval aviation received a much-needed boost when President Franklin D. Roosevelt signed the Naval Expansion Act of 1938. With a stroke of the pen, the Navy was authorized to increase its air arm from 1,900 to a contingent of 3,000 aircraft. This required a corresponding increase in aviation personnel, especially rated technicians. Even though the cadre of experienced aviation technicians serving in the fleet in 1938 was insufficient to meet the needs of a 3,000-plane navy, the incoming chief of BuAer, Rear Adm. John H. Towers, planned to gradually bolster his personnel numbers over a matter of years rather than months. In his eyes, and almost everyone else's at that time, another 1,100 aircraft would take years to acquire based on manufacturing practices of the 1930s. Little did Towers know that after December 7, 1941, he would be proven wrong on all accounts.

Chapter 2

Expansion, Turf Wars, and Estimates

Historians of U.S. naval aviation in World War II have failed to recognize that skilled labor, or the maintenance of naval aircraft, played as critical of a role in the war as did the pilots and airplanes. Comparing only the technological, matériel, and tactical factors of the Japanese and American naval air forces fails to appreciate the behemoth task that the Bureau of Aeronautics (BuAer) and the Bureau of Navigation (BuNav) faced in filling the carriers and their squadrons with skilled aircraft mechanics and technicians.[1] Even with the surge of voluntary enlistments after Pearl Harbor, the Navy still had difficulty fulfilling its manpower requirements. When a naval war with Japan became a reality, the Navy was caught short in both matériel and trained manpower. There were only a few carriers to deploy, a limited number of carrier-based aircraft in service, and just a few thousand aviation technicians trained and ready to deploy.

These problems should not have come as a surprise. Just two years earlier, in 1939, the Navy found itself scrambling to answer the question, exactly how many maintenance personnel would it need to successfully support a protracted naval war? An equally important second part to that question was from which pools of manpower was the skilled labor to be drawn. How these tasks would be managed was complicated; the fact that the Department of the Navy was not even sure which of its administrative bureaus was best suited to accomplish it made for an even more problematic situation. And leaving much of this business unfinished until after war is declared also brought with it serious difficulties.

Before World War II, the BuAer was responsible for the procurement of naval aviators and enlisted personnel. By law BuNav, later renamed the Bureau of Personnel (BuPers), had ultimate authority with regards to selection and placement of both officer and enlisted personnel throughout the Navy, but in matters of aviation personnel, the Navy usually followed the suggestions of BuAer. Specifically, it was BuAer that made recommendations to BuNav "for the distribution in the various ratings of the enlisted personnel required by aeronautic activities," and "on all matters pertaining to aeronautic training."[2] This had been the standard practice since Congress authorized the establishment of BuAer on July 12, 1921. However, with the establishment of the Deputy Chief of Naval Operations for Air in August 1943, BuAer relinquished most of its responsibility for training, procuring, and assigning aviation personnel to the fleet. Surrendering control of enlisted rating distribution and associated training was not the most desired outcome, but based on the enormous expansion of planes and aviation personnel, it was necessary. No matter who was in charge, the issue of determining how many technicians were required to keep the Navy's aircraft operating had provoked intense discussion at the highest levels since the earliest days of BuAer. Funding was often based on personnel requirements. Providing a reasonable number to those authorizing appropriations had been part of BuAer's role in naval policy over the preceding two decades.

In December 1924, Rear Adm. William Moffett, chief of BuAer, and members of his staff testified before Congress in hearings for the Naval Appropriations Bill of 1926. The additional requirements in personnel in relation to the introduction of carrier aviation were at the forefront of the discussion. At the time there was both a shortage of officers and enlisted men in the Navy. Naval aviation was very young, but Moffett and his team had done their homework. When asked by Sen. Frederick Hale of Maine how many additional enlisted men would be required for naval aviation as more aircraft carriers were added to the fleet, Cdr. Laurence T. DuBose (one of Moffett's staff officers), consulted with his boss and answered, "You would need eight to ten men to the plane."[3] This number only increased later with advances in technology. According to *The Technicians' War*, the ratio of men to airplanes in 1945 varied between ten and twenty to one, depending on the model and the level of maintenance required.[4]

By the mid-1930s—a decade after Moffett had argued that more aircraft mechanics would be required to service aircraft—the Navy had accepted the aircraft carrier as being a significant component of the fleet's striking power.[5] In 1936, the United States had three operational carriers, the *Langley*, *Lexington*, and *Saratoga*, plus the *Ranger* was under construction. In addition, the *Yorktown* and the *Enterprise* had just been authorized for construction by Congress under the statutes of the Vinson-Trammel Act of 1934. By 1940, the Navy's procurement goal for large fleet aircraft carriers was a total of eighteen, excluding the smaller cruiser-conversion light carrier and the even smaller escort carriers that were being contemplated.

By the mid-1930s, the Navy had standardized aircraft inventory on board aircraft carriers. Large carriers such as the *Yorktown* (CV 5) and the *Enterprise* (CV 6) embarked four squadrons: one fighter, one dive-bomber, one scout-bomber, and one torpedo-bomber. Each squadron was authorized eighteen aircraft for a total of seventy-two airplanes per carrier.[6] Smaller "escort" and "light" aircraft carriers (CVE and CVL) were two to three years away from entering service, as was the enormous *Essex* class carrier that would have a complement of ninety aircraft to begin. In the summer of 1941, the Navy's inventory of aircraft, both carrier and land-based reached four thousand. That number would double in less than a year. As impressive as that number was, simply having planes parked on ships or at airfields did nothing for the country's defense without personnel to fly and maintain them.

The entire January 1942 issue of *Flying and Popular Aviation* was dedicated to U.S. naval aviation.[7] The U.S. Navy officers writing the articles were adamant that machines were not enough to meet the Japanese threat that was rising in the West or Hitler's push toward the Atlantic in the east. The expansion of the Navy's team of skilled aircraft technicians would have to match that of the growth in numbers of pilots and aircraft in keeping the fleet combat ready.[8]

Aircraft maintenance before World War II involved a plethora of tasks. Broadly speaking, it included servicing of airplanes, their engines, and component parts. On board ships and at naval air stations, technicians did not attempt to perform serious repair work or overhaul such as complete disassembly and reassembly of aircraft engines. Fleet technicians' or maintainers' daily routines encompassed regular inspections of aircraft structures and their component parts to ensure that the airplane was safe to fly. Major overhaul was not a regular occurrence at sea. Typically, aircraft overhauls occurred only when the damage was irreparable on board the ship, or the aircraft had reached a predetermined number of flight hours, which rendered the parts and airplane unsafe until complete overhaul was accomplished. Overhaul and major repair work was normally completed at facilities ashore, such as the Naval Aircraft Factory.[9] The quality of work done at the shore-based facilities by technicians directly affected the performance of aircraft at sea.

One of the primary tasks for an aircraft mechanic on board a carrier was to "find and correct defects before they can cause serious trouble."[10] Aviation units operating on carriers had to be self-sustaining, capable of making various small jobs such as propeller changes and minor repairs as needed. Most of all, their highest priority was to ensure preventive maintenance such as engine oil changes and corrosion control was completed regularly. If a plane suffered major mechanical trouble at sea and was no longer flyable, it had a ripple effect. A plane that could not fly reduced the combat operating capability of the squadron and became an obstacle in everyday operations. The logistics of making room in the hangar bay for an airplane that could not fly interrupted the daily flight operations of the entire ship. Storage and parking space was limited on board ships. There was little room for "hangar queens." Effective preventive maintenance and battle-damage repair by squadron mechanics was thus essential to sustain operational efficiency.[11]

These backstage actors had to be qualified to maintain essential and highly complex mechanical systems at all times, which included engines, airframes, hydraulics, armament, ordnance, communications, and electronics during deployment. Work that had been previously done at shore facilities now had to be completed on the ship. Before the United States entered World War II, squadron technicians were initially trained at naval trade schools and received follow-on, more advanced training during shortened tours of duty at the shore-based overhaul facilities, such as the Naval Aircraft Factory in Philadelphia.[12] Many of the enlisted technicians were trained in multiple facets of repair and overhaul. This made them more like jacks-of-all-trades than sailors identified by their specialty rating.[13] Learning the skill set needed to work on naval aircraft was acquired through multiple tours of duty inside advanced engineering facilities where naval aircraft underwent overhaul.

Assembly and repair shops were the mainstay of the Navy's aircraft overhaul program throughout the interwar years. The Navy's methodology of using them as advanced technical training schools was suitable for aviation maintenance at that time. The Naval Aircraft Factory had been one of the more proven feeder systems of technical maintenance for the fleet throughout the early interwar years. Producing a surplus of trained labor in aircraft systems was the hallmark of the Naval Aircraft Factory.[14] However, as the production of aircraft and spare parts went into overdrive on the eve of the war, it was evident that the lengthy process of training an aircraft mechanic on the job had become a liability. This method of technical training would be unable to keep pace with the fast-paced demands of naval aircraft operations once the United States entered the war.

✦✦✦

Prior to 1939, a relatively small unit within the BuAer was able to manage the supply of ratings and fleet aviation personnel. This department was designated the Flight Division; in 1939 the name was changed to the Naval Personnel Section of the Administrative Division, and remained so until it was officially renamed the Personnel Division in 1945.[15] According to the 1940 *Bureau of Aeronautics Manual*, it was the responsibility of the Personnel Division to determine the requisite number of ratings and their distribution throughout the fleet.[16] The Personnel Division was tasked with the "preparation of recommendations for the distribution in the various ratings of enlisted personnel required for aeronautic activities." Additionally, it was responsible for "maintenance of commissioned and enlisted complement charts of all aircraft operating units, aircraft carrier and tenders, and aeronautic shore establishments."[17]

The BuAer Personnel Division did not operate in a vacuum. Coordination with the Maintenance and Plans Division helped determine future requirements as new technology came on line. It was the Maintenance and Plans Division that made "recommendations to the Chief of the Bureau as to numbers of new aircraft of each type" and "for the distribution and organization of available aircraft and the assignment of aircraft squadrons and detachments."[18] The Personnel Division was the primary source for ratings numbers and personnel distribution, but each report given to the chief of the bureau considered the views of other administrative units. Within the BuAer Personnel Division, there was both a Reserve and Regular Navy Section. Each managed the distribution of its own personnel throughout the fleet. The responsibilities of the Reserve component of the Personnel Division were outlined in a memo to Capt. George D. Murray, director of the Personnel Division, dated August 18, 1939: "The section makes recommendations to BuNav in regard to enlisted men required, and the distribution of stationkeepers, numbers and rates of men, and officer complement requirements in Naval Reserve organization squadrons. Squadron organizations, as shown on copies of personnel reports, are scrutinized for proper balance of rates."[19] According to the official history, the section that managed the Regular Navy personnel was responsible for the same aspects of the active-duty enlisted force. "Correspondence files on personnel matters indicate comparable participation on the part of the Personnel Division in matters affecting regular navy personnel of the aeronautic organization."[20] Ultimately, BuNav had to agree on the personnel requests made by BuAer's Personnel Division. However, since the Moffett era, BuNav routinely defaulted to BuAer's requests when issuing orders to aviation-rated personnel.

On September 9, 1939, a week after war had broken out in Europe, President Roosevelt ordered the Navy to raise its inventory of enlisted men from 110,000 to 145,000. Less than a year later, on June 14, 1940, FDR ordered an expansion of naval aircraft numbers from 3,000 to 4,500 planes. The following day he increased the goal to 10,000. Four days later the president boosted the requirement to 15,000 aircraft.[21] The impending rise in the level of administrative workload that accompanied such a buildup was too much for BuAer. Captain Murray recognized the potential for an administrative disaster within the Personnel Division. Having recently served on the Aviation Personnel Board of 1939 (commonly referred to as the Horne Board) as Rear Adm. Frederick J. Horne's senior ranking member, Murray was keenly aware of the requirements associated with an expanded naval aviation arm.

The primary focus of the 1939 Horne Board was solving the problem of meeting the need for pilots associated with an increase to a three-thousand-aircraft navy. Yet, there was some minimal discussion regarding procurement of enough skilled enlisted technicians to meet the increased demand. Much of the dialogue focused on injecting the Naval Reserve component with trained technicians to meet the demand anticipated in the event of war. The board's discourse was influenced by the expectation of additional large increases in aircraft force levels over the coming six years.[22]

By June 1940 a 3,000-airplane force was no more than a memory. President Roosevelt's requirement to increase the inventory of airplanes to 15,000 disrupted all the planning Murray and Horne had done a year earlier. Murray quickly pointed out in a memo to BuAer chief, Rear Adm. John H. Towers and his assistant chief, Capt. Marc A. Mitscher, that his division staff size was the same as it had been in 1935 and would never survive the massive increase in workload with the upcoming expansion. At that time, the Personnel Division consisted of eight officers and seven stenographers (clerks) who managed an inventory of 800 aviators and 12,500 enlisted personnel. By September 1940, his staffing had only increased to 14 officers and 14 stenographers, but they were handling 2,150 aviators and an enlisted detail that would reach 38,000 by October 1940. He respectfully informed his bosses that the Personnel Division would soon be unable to keep up with its assigned administrative duties.[23]

Captain Murray suggested two possible courses of action: BuAer could transfer its entire Personnel Division to BuNav, or BuNav could surrender its role in the administration of aviation personnel completely. The latter option would involve BuAer assuming office staff from BuNav workspaces. The former would include posting a senior BuAer officer in BuNav as a permanent liaison.[24] Murray did not express a preference for one course over the other, but his anticipation of future personnel administrative requirements was justified. Murray recognized the obvious administrative implications of a massive increase in naval aircraft for both the BuNav and BuAer, and sought to avoid the chaos that was bound to accompany a rapid surge of personnel and matériel. Yet, neither Towers nor Mitscher showed any desire to expand or reorganize the BuAer.

Archived documents record that both Mitscher and Towers answered Murray's memo with penciled-in comments in the margin. Mitscher recommended to "stand pat" and make no changes to procedures for fear of having to revamp the BuAer manual and possible laws governing the actions of either bureau. Towers amplified Mitscher's comments, stating he preferred to keep the arrangement as-is. He did not support "relinquishing all control" to BuNav nor did he want to cut BuNav out of the loop completely. Towers felt that the present agreement between himself and BuNav chief Rear Admiral Nimitz was satisfactory. In the marginal notes, Towers instructed Murray to "build up your organization as needs indicate."[25] On paper, Towers did not indicate that his organization, as it currently stood, needed any restructuring. But later, changes within the administration of personnel would prove that he was either too proud or too complacent to admit that the way that BuAer handled administrative operations in 1940 was insufficient to meet the impending demands of the aviation expansion program.

Ultimately, increases in planes and personnel requirements forced the Personnel Division to restructure. On December 28, 1940, Mitscher issued a statement to all bureau personnel that the division would be reorganized beginning January 2, 1941, "in order to meet the needs of the expanded flight training program and to coordinate the planning and personnel requirements for the increased Aeronautical Organization."[26]

A planning and training section was established within the Personnel Division that supervised training activities along with managing enlisted allowances. Officer and enlisted detailing each had its own section. In addition, by July 1941 the Chief of Naval Operations (CNO), Adm. Harold Stark, was well aware of the increased manning and training requirements. He made a formal request to Towers to take any and all necessary action to assure that the training of officers and enlisted, flight and technical, was coordinated. The BuAer was to make the appropriate adjustments necessary to ensure the "effective coordination of all phases of aviation training and the expeditious accomplishment of the planned expansion of naval personnel."[27]

Towers, having learned a thing or two about what it meant to play the politics of naval bureaucracy from his time as Moffett's chief assistant, could not have missed the signs that Nimitz was next in line for a promotion and a major fleet assignment. There had been previous struggles between the two bureau chiefs over personnel issues, primarily regarding pilots. When the Navy was authorized to increase their aviator corps to three thousand Regular naval aviators and a minimum of six thousand in the Naval Reserve, the relationship between Nimitz and Towers was placed under greater strain. Nimitz was evidently reluctant to lose more officers to flying duty when he was under pressure to continue filling surface and submarine officer billets. In 1939, there was only a limited national emergency based on events in Europe and Americans were not flocking to the recruiting stations just yet. Towers, in a shift from his younger days, was becoming more of a bureaucrat as he settled into his position as BuAer chief. He had learned from one of the best, Adm. William Moffett, and was seeking approval for more naval air stations and more schools. The tension between Towers and Nimitz could have resulted from intraservice rivalry between aviators and non-aviators, but it might also have simply been a personality clash. One of Nimitz's aides recalled that "he just didn't care much for Admiral Towers," and his methods of doing business.[28] The feuding between the two admirals would continue for the better part of the war, but neither would permit it to get out of hand and jeopardize the Navy's mission although at times, it came uncomfortably close to doing so.

In one instance during August 1940, Towers had asked Nimitz to permit a select number of recent graduates of the Aviation Metalsmith School to stay for a follow-on assignment as instructors. Nimitz refused the request. His task as chief of BuNav was to get trained technicians on to the ships and squadrons at sea. Holding back even a few sailors for instructor duty could have detrimental effects on fleet readiness.[29]

A few months later, in November 1940, Adm. James O. Richardson, commander in chief of the U.S. fleet (CINCUS) made it known to the bureaus that the Pacific Fleet was still lacking technical ratings among its aviation units. These units needed maintenance personnel, but neither BuNav nor BuAer could fill the present shortfall with the system operating as it was.[30] The Navy's technical training program, still under the cognizance of Towers was insufficient to meet the demands of the Navy's massive increase in airplanes, ships, and squadrons.

Unfortunately, Admiral Horne's reports spent little time on concerns over the shortage of aviation technical ratings in the fleet. The majority of Horne's suggestions were focused on pilot training and officer problems, which was the original reason for appointing the board. Even more interesting is the fact that much of what Horne released as his official report looked very similar to the inputs that Towers had sent him in memo format on September 27, 1939. The answers that Horne provided regarding which ratings were required, advancement in rank, and rotation of duty stations all followed BuAer's suggestions and were facilitated by Murray and other aviation officers interviewed by the board.[31] When Towers responded to Horne's inquiries, the president had only authorized an increase of the Navy's enlisted by 35,000 and an aircraft increase to 3,000 planes. Even this strained the existing administrative apparatus of BuAer. Nevertheless, Towers believed the bureau could handle it.[32]

He strongly advised that much of the technical training be handled within the overhaul facilities themselves. He also indicated that those trained in facilities within the continental United States would be best suited to take their expertise to repair facilities outside of the border, such as Midway Island.[33] There was no mention of a possible increase in numbers, nor any recommendation as to from where BuAer would acquire more sailors other than from the general pool of enlisted personnel already authorized by Congress. Even after the expansion was authorized, as recommended in the second Horne Board Report of November 25, 1940, there was little discussion of where and how the Navy would procure, train, and distribute technical aviation ratings throughout the fleet.[34] Congressional authorization of enlisted strength within the Navy was insufficient to satisfy the enlisted personnel requirements of BuAer, but unfortunately Horne either did not recognize this or, more likely, regarded this to be a general personnel problem that had to be addressed by the Navy as a whole. His first report in January 1940 claimed that the required enlisted aviation ratings could be drawn out of the general labor pool of the Navy: "The situation [enlisted men of the Navy] can be met, and there can be made available sufficient enlisted men of the Regular Navy to meet the demands of the aeronautic organization."[35]

The findings of the Horne Board did not identify the problem of procuring a sufficient number of aircraft technicians as a numbers issue, but rather as a training concern.[36] The report reflected Towers' suggestion that the present authorized aviation technical ratings be continued, but also recommended that specific entries should be made in the service records of any enlisted men who held special aviation experience. Designations such as aircraft-engine overhaul expert, propeller overhaul specialist, aircraft instruments repair technician, aviation welder, bomb-sight mechanic, aircraft painter, radioman qualified in aircraft, and automatic-pilot technician were all included in the list of twenty-two specific qualifications.[37] While not at the forefront of either BuAer or the Horne Board's concerns, it was evident that those already trained in the skilled labor of aircraft maintenance were a resource that should not be overlooked.

The latter part of Horne's report made significant mention of Naval Reserve enlisted personnel filling the future needs of naval aviation. It also discussed the potential of filling the ranks with ex-servicemen who held aviation ratings or those currently holding civilian occupations in the commercial aircraft industry. The intent was to recruit individuals to the Naval Reserve who could quickly qualify as an aviation technician. The board also believed that a large number of trained aviation technicians would be available for reserve duty in the coming years due to the rapid expansion of aviation in the commercial sector over the last decade. However, this would not solve the immediate problem of filling the ranks with technical expertise. The board wisely suggested that in order to obtain a satisfactory number of qualified maintenance personnel in the Naval Reserve units, additional training facilities and schools, along with the appropriate funds for sustainment, should be made available immediately.[38]

By the beginning of 1941, the lack of experienced instructors at both the pilot and technical schools had also become obvious. Neither Nimitz's nor Towers' organizations were able to remedy this problem. However, what mattered most to the decision makers in Washington was sustaining efficiency with able bodied sailors to fly and maintain the swelling aircraft fleet. Admiral Stark made it clear to Nimitz and Towers that withdrawing experienced sailors from the fleet units to serve as instructors was unacceptable. Stark informed Nimitz directly via confidential memo that any more reductions of aviation petty officers assigned to tactical aviation units would be looked upon unfavorably.[39] The CNO did not want his tactical units losing experienced maintenance personnel to the training commands under BuAer's charge.

Nimitz was aware of the tug-of-war between the needs of the aviation and Regular Navy, but filling the personnel quotas of sea-duty aviation units under the CNO's cognizance took priority over shore-based aviation facilities delegated to BuAer's control. By March 1, 1941, aviation commands at sea were 100 percent manned, yet shore-based facilities were only staffed at 65 percent. This meant that BuAer had to make do with just 9,115 manned billets of the nearly 13,660 requested, a labor shortage of 4,545 personnel.[40] Stress on the overhaul and repair facilities had grown since the aircraft expansion had been authorized in June 1940. On April 3, 1941, Nimitz requested that the commanding officers of Naval Reserve air bases (NRAB) within the continental United States train as many aviation machinist's mates and aviation metalsmiths assigned to their commands as possible in aircraft and aircraft engine overhaul procedures to mitigate the shortage in mechanics. He did not call for the base commanders to affect negatively day-to-day operations or recall Reservists from fleet assignments, but the technicians who were to be trained in overhaul work should come from within the NRAB's present complement of enlisted men.[41] The dilemma of getting experienced technicians to the fleet and overhaul shore facilities was adding to the predicament of training enough aircraft technicians for fleet squadrons. The pressure of making trained aviation technicians readily available was becoming a common thorn in the sides of both bureau chiefs.

Even after Horne's report was submitted and supposedly provided answers as to how the Navy would meet the personnel needs of an enormous air arm, the problem of determining the appropriate number of billets and where to assign those billets still was not solved. Instead, most of the creative talent was put to work solving the question of how many pilots would be needed as the number of aircraft increased and where the pool of cadets would come from. BuAer was focused on aircraft and pilots because no one had any experience in procuring, training, and distributing the vast number of technical aviation ratings such a large fleet of aircraft required. BuNav was well versed in detailing sailors to the few ships and the squadrons that were in existence during the interwar years, however neither bureau comprehended the massive effort it would take to maintain the thousands of airplanes that would be operating from the flights of aircraft carriers in a few short years.[42]

As chief of BuAer, Towers knew enough to not alienate BuNav. By law, the two bureaus were forced to work together on aviation personnel distribution and a feud between the bureaus would only exacerbate the shortage in technical ratings. Not wanting to burn any bridges, but desiring complete control over aviation personnel issues, Towers voiced his opinion in a letter to the Secretary of the Navy, ensuring it went through both Nimitz and Stark beforehand: "The functions of procurement and distribution of aviation personnel can be handled satisfactorily under the present system [BuNav and BuAer coordination]. On the other hand, it is strongly felt that the marked improvement in training of pilots and technical aviation ratings could be effective through the centralization of all functions pertaining to these matters under one Bureau. For reasons above, it is believed that the Bureau of Aeronautics should be designated and the Cognizant [sic] Bureau."[43]

It only took the Secretary of the Navy, Frank Knox, three days to grant Towers' request. On October 6, 1941, he approved a reorganization of BuAer that included reducing the number of major divisions to five, "Personnel and Training" among them. By November, Personnel and Training was split into two separate divisions, each under the auspices of a separate director. Even in the new system, however, BuNav still maintained a segment of control in manning the aviation community. Although BuAer was given oversight over all aviation training, controlling the ebb and flow of personnel within naval aviation was still a joint effort between Towers' and Nimitz's bureaus.[44]

+++

In 1940 the United States simply did not have the active-duty manpower to fill the ranks of naval aviation with qualified technicians. However, the

Naval Reserve forces did have a significant number of trained personnel—a fact that the Horne Board had specifically pointed out. Ultimately, it was BuNav which made the call for an involuntary mobilization of Reservists in July 1940. Nimitz directed the commandants of each naval district to ensure any fleet Reservists with the following ratings were brought back to active duty: radioman (qualified in aircraft), aviation machinist's mate, aviation metalsmith, aviation carpenter's mate, and aviation ordnanceman. The two other Naval Reserve components in existence at that time, the Organized Reserve and the Volunteer Reserve, were not subject to the compulsory mobilization.[45] In the summer of 1940, it still appeared that both Nimitz and Towers believed that the limited mobilization of fleet reserve technical ratings would suffice.

In June 1940—when President Roosevelt ordered the increase of naval aircraft to 15,000—Knox, Towers, and Nimitz must have realized the dire straits that they were about to be in. On October 5, 1940, Knox sent a dispatch to district commandants that read, "Call retired enlisted men who may be usefully employed . . . no volunteer reserves will be sent to active duty for less than one year."[46] Towers followed Knox's lead two weeks later and recommended that BuNav retain the squadron personnel of the Organized Reserve "in a skeleton status at their home Naval Reserve Aviation Base and . . . enlisted personnel be made available for infiltration into the aviation component of the Fleet and Shore establishment."[47] Towers' recommendation was endorsed by Admiral Stark, CNO. Then on October 17, Towers formally recommended that BuNav mobilize the Organized Reserve at the earliest date possible. Towers firmly believed that the only way to solve the problem of mustering enough trained aircraft technicians was through mobilization of veteran technicians of the interwar years.[48] Unfortunately, rapid advances in technology would complicate matters even more, making Towers' plan insufficient to alleviate the shortage of maintenance personnel.

Nimitz quickly complied with Towers' recommendation to mobilize the Organized Reserve by ordering aviation squadrons to do so the following week. Nimitz's plan structured the mobilization of squadrons in thirds with November 7, 1940; December 1, 1940; and January 1, 1941 as the intervals for district commandants to reach their milestones. The Navy was trying to alleviate some of the strain on the commercial aviation industry by activating the Reserve units in thirds. BuNav directed that any Organized Reservists employed in the airline industry were to be mobilized in the November or January rounds. This gave the men an opportunity to submit their resignation from the Naval Reserves, accept a discharge, or request a transfer to voluntary classification as active duty. Every effort was made to minimize the impact on the commercial airline industry since commercial airlines were considered vital to national defense.[49]

Aircraft technicians who were employed as civilian aircraft mechanics at naval air stations and naval aircraft repair facilities created another quandary for the Navy. A year earlier, BuNav had assured the district commandants responsible for such facilities that those employees were considered "key" men, and that they would not be mobilized until sufficient replacements were hired and trained. However, as word of the aircraft buildup to 15,000 came down, Nimitz relented and warned the commandants in August, that this policy would not most likely be negated based on current events. He directed them to ensure that all naval activities under their jurisdiction took appropriate steps to "train replacements for the Fleet Reservists still employed in a civilian capacity."[50]

The Navy also set up a specific board to review those who were on the Organized Reserve list, where they were employed, and what their jobs entailed. Admirals Nimitz and Towers were concerned about damaging the operations of aircraft manufacturers and airlines and other industries that were considered critical to defense. After reviewing each individual's employment records, the board decided which Organized Reservists would be activated. By November 1940 the situation had become critical. Secretary of the Navy Knox released a message that authorized BuNav to order members of the Volunteer Reserve back to active duty, with or without their consent.[51] Finally, the tide had turned on the relative banal service requirements of the Naval Reserve forces. But the question remained, would it be enough to alleviate the shortage of trained aircraft maintenance personnel in the fleet?

✦✦✦

Murray's concerns over managing the personnel distribution of fleet aviators and technicians were valid in 1939. Despite the fact that there was a national emergency with Europe on the brink of war, BuAer and BuNav saw little need to deviate from the status quo regarding distribution of technical aviation ratings throughout the fleet. The situation was similar for fleet carrier aircraft, if not the same models that were flying throughout the late 1930s. Recalling reservists provided temporary relief from the problem, but by 1942, much of the relief had been exhausted. As convenient as it may be to try and fault Towers or Nimitz for not adjusting to the future needs, the Navy was still flying Grumman's F3F (1938) biplane fighter when the second Horne Board Report was published. Only a limited number of the Brewster F2A Buffalo monoplane fighters were launching from carrier decks at that time. Both aircraft were products of mid-1930s engineering, delivering little in the way of tactical or technological advancements. Grumman was in the process of delivering a more modern, technologically advanced monoplane fighter. Yet, it was not until December 1940 that the Navy took delivery of its first Grumman F4F Wildcat. Only 179 additional were delivered to the fleet throughout the following year of the war. Production did not reach peak level until 1942.[52]

Navy fighter squadrons had been operating on aircraft carriers for over a decade. There did not appear to be much concern over the numbers of trained technicians in prewar planning other than what Captain Murray had expressed. Obviously, actions taken by Towers to remedy the situation fell short of expectations. In an unsigned memorandum to Towers in May 1942, most likely from someone in the Office of the Assistant Secretary of the Navy for Air, the Bureau's ability to handle personnel planning is highly criticized. The memo, which is based on an interview with H. C. Emery, of the Office of the Assistant Secretary of the Navy for Air, stated: "The Planning Division [of BuAer], though it has comprehensively, thoroughly and creditably fulfilled its functions in regard to material planning, exercises little or no control of the Personnel, Training, and Flight Divisions. It has apparently never occurred to anybody that planning of this nature is equally important with material planning. . . . If Naval Aviation is to meet its wartime responsibilities properly, this obvious deficiency should be corrected immediately."[53]

The primary focus of the Navy was on matériel and technology during the prewar period, rather than on the skilled labor requirements necessary to employ such weapons. Neither Towers nor Nimitz had made any significant changes in response to the massive requirements for skilled labor among the enlisted ranks in naval aviation squadrons.

It would be incorrect to say that the war caught BuAer by surprise, since plans were in place by 1939 to meet the requirements of a three-thousand-plane navy, thanks to George Murray.[54] Estimates of how many enlisted personnel were needed to support naval aviation were constantly updated by Towers and his staff through yearly budget estimates and annual reports. In his response to the Horne Board's questions in September 1937, most likely via Murray's input, Towers put forth a six-year estimate on how many enlisted personnel would be required to support a three-thousand-plane Navy. These numbers did not reflect the specific number of technical aviation ratings such as aviation ordnancemen or aviation machinist's mates, but rather a general number of both technicians, supply, and administrative personnel to support the aviation fleet. Yeomen, supply clerks, and boatswain's mates worked alongside aircraft mechanics and radiomen on board aircraft carriers and naval air stations. It was not an exact science, but the BuAer Personnel Division did its best to predict the requisite numbers of sailors based on numbers of aircraft available to the fleet. From the following table, it is apparent that Towers even understood the gradual increase in manpower required each year as the number of fleet aircraft increased to three thousand.[55]

Table 2.1. BuAer Enlisted Aviation Personnel Estimate, 1937 [1]

YEAR	ENLISTED PERSONNEL IN AVIATION SERVICE REQUIREMENT
1940	20,164
1941	24,021
1942	27,978
1943	29,518
1944	32,133
1945	33,110

[1] Chief BuAer to Senior Member Aviation Personnel Board, "Personnel in the Naval Aeronautical Organization, recommendations concerning." RG 72, Stack 470, Row 63, Box 189, NARA II.

Following President Roosevelt's authorization for a 15,000-plane navy, BuAer drastically increased its requirement to a total projected force of 120,533 enlisted aviation personnel.[56] The new aircraft were scheduled to enter service on a gradual basis, over a multiyear timeline culminating in 1945. This number did not include enlisted pilots and was a combination of both aviation ratings and general ratings required to support flight operations around the globe as were the previous estimates of 1937. The following table represents the actual numbers of enlisted personnel serving in support of naval aviation activities just before the United States entered the war. The numbers reflect both Regular Navy personnel and Naval Reserve personnel recalled for active duty.

Table 2.2. Aviation Enlisted Personnel on Active Duty [1]

DATE	ENLISTED PERSONNEL IN AVIATION SERVICE
July 1, 1940	22,503
September 1, 1941	48,267
October 1, 1941	50,634
November 1, 1941	56,402
December 1, 1941	59,353

[1] Chief BuAer, "Personnel in the Naval Aeronautical Organization."

Considering the 15,000-plane program was not law until the middle of June 1940, Towers' estimate in 1937 was on target to what the Navy should have to support a 3,000-plane force, keeping with the ten to one ratio that was suggested by Moffett a decade earlier. Even with an estimated requirement of 120,000 enlisted personnel, an undertaking of this magnitude in naval aviation was unprecedented in United States history. Would it be enough?

In mid-summer 1940, Rear Admiral Horne was tasked with providing an update to his personnel requirement recommendations of a year earlier. Once the Vinson-Walsh Act was signed into law on July 19, 1940, Horne's team went back to work. His second submission came on November 25, 1940, and his end goal for the total number of enlisted men in the naval air arm totaled 119,092. Furthermore, he recommended that 47,960 enlisted men should be serving in support of naval aviation by the end of fiscal year 1941.[57] However, of the approximately 48,000 enlisted men that were supporting naval aviation on September 1, 1941, only 11,000 were qualified aviation ratings.[58] Was that enough for a navy that would soon be at war?

The difference between skilled and unskilled labor of the Navy's air arm continued to gain the attention of decision makers. During the interwar years, the peacetime navy did not focus on the amount of skilled labor versus unskilled labor that a war required. The Secretary of the Navy's Annual Report of 1945 provides a statistical record of the war, including the actual number of officers and enlisted on duty that was divided into six-month intervals.[59] Unfortunately, it is not further divided by rating other than flying and nonflying, but it does specify that its data represents only aviation personnel, rather than including those personnel supporting aviation activities. The numbers are significantly smaller in this report compared to the Horne Board estimates and the monthly status reports generated by BuAer for the War Department and Congress. For example, the BuAer monthly summary report lists 22,503 enlisted as the "Total Number in Service" on July 1, 1940, but the statistical record states that only 5,924 enlisted (who were not pilots) were part of "Aviation Personnel."[60] The reason for the discrepancy comes down to specific ratings. Horne did not specify in his report how many of each rating was required. If the Navy met Horne's estimated numbers on paper, then it would have appeared as if everything was working as planned. In addition, Towers did not want to give up control of aviation matters. Towers had told George Murray in December 1940 that the personnel operations of the bureau were sufficient to handle the increased requirements. But as the United States' entry into the war slowly became reality, the question of how BuAer would determine exactly how much skilled labor would be needed to effectively fight a major air war was still unanswered.

The CNO, Admiral Stark, understood the requirements necessary to meet the 15,000-plane order. If the expansion program were to be successful, a trifecta consisting of thousands of planes, hundreds of pilots, and tens of thousands of ground personnel would have to come together at once. Recruitment alone would not solve the problem. Very few new recruits entered the Navy previously qualified as aviation technicians. Stark understood that merely throwing more personnel at the problem would not equate to building a naval aviation arm strong enough to fight wars in both the Atlantic and the Pacific. "The future success of our active air operations at sea depends in no small measure on the thoroughness of the preliminary training given on shore." Stark went on to say that new aviation training schools needed to be established, and "every effort is being made to maintain a very high standard in our training institutions." Stark's comments were published in the "U.S. Naval Aviation" issue of *Flying and Popular Aviation* that appeared on newsstands in January 1942. It can be inferred that these article contributions were written before Pearl Harbor—probably in the fall of 1941, based on the information and tone of the articles—as well as the advertisements in the magazine. No mention of being "at war" was found in any of the articles. Most advertisements referenced the "preparation" for national defense, and so on. Hence "the recruiting of large numbers of men for Naval aviation duty" might have seemed daunting before the emotional response and rush to the recruiting stations by the American public after December 7, 1941.[61] As Stark indicated, the key to success was not just bringing Americans to the recruiting centers, but the nature of their training and schooling after boot camp as well. For naval aviation, vocational training and technical education of its enlisted labor force mattered as much, if not more, than simply filling the ranks with bodies.

Chapter 3

Establishing the Trade Schools

Naval aviation technical training prior to 1940 was a conglomeration of small independent maintenance schools that operated through an apprentice-style, on-the-job training. Trainees were given ample amounts of time to study on their own outside of classroom instruction. The Navy was accepting of shortcomings in ship and squadron personnel due to nonstandard syllabi and lengthened the "time to train" depending on an individual's talent, large or small.[1] Not until war was imminent, and FDR had authorized a buildup of naval aircraft, did Bureau of Aeronautics (BuAer) and Bureau of Navigation (BuNav) change gears to ensure a more structured and disciplined, and therefore effective, training system for aircraft technicians for the Navy. Once the training of maintenance personnel became a priority, both the quality and quantity of training increased exponentially. What was considered an afterthought during the interwar years, soon became a critical need that required cutting-edge engineers and industry giants to partner with the Navy to remedy the problem. It also demanded vast amounts of funding to establish a training program sufficient to produce the number of properly trained technicians necessary to support the fleet's burgeoning aviation units. Solving the Navy's aircraft technician training dilemma did not occur overnight, but by early 1943 the Navy had figured out a way forward.

Throughout the 1930s, there had been little standardization of aviation maintenance curricula for student aircraft technicians. Most of the Navy's enlisted technicians learned their trade by apprenticing with a veteran mechanic. These young, untrained "strikers" as they were called, worked alongside veterans who had earned their ratings through hard work and hands-on experience. The training usually occurred at local naval air stations or the nearest assembly and repair (A&R) facilities. Since World War I, BuAer had relied on a regular rotation of sailors in and out of the A&R facilities for most of the Navy's aircraft technician training. In 1938, A&R facilities in San Diego, Norfolk, and Philadelphia handled the majority of the fleet's overhauls, with a limited number of smaller facilities located elsewhere. The Navy also relied on instruction from the Army Air Service schools to train many of their technicians simply because the Army already had the infrastructure in place. Another challenging factor was that the Navy's technical training program more closely resembled that of commercial trade schools than formal training centers. The caliber of each school and its graduates depended more on the ingenuity and motivation of its officer in charge and veteran personnel, than on the curriculum or training material itself.[2]

Until the spring of 1940 only nine formal trade schools designed to teach aircraft maintenance were in existence.[3] The Naval Training Center (NTC) in Norfolk, Virginia, housed one basic and one advanced trade school for aviation machinist's mates (AMM), plus advanced schools for aviation ordnancemen (AO) and aviation metalsmiths (AM). Aviation machinist's mates and metalsmiths also had schools in Pensacola and San Diego. Additionally, there was a small school for aircraft instruments located at the Naval Aircraft Factory in Philadelphia.[4] The 1939 Horne Board estimated that by 1942, assuming a 3,000-plane Navy, there should be 556 naval aircraft technicians under training in aviation maintenance schools at any given time.[5]

Everything changed when FDR authorized more aircraft with the expansion program, eventually settling on 15,000 in June 1940, five times the number authorized just two years earlier. The Navy realized that the number of trained aircraft technicians currently serving, plus those undergoing training, was wholly insufficient to support an aviation fleet of such magnitude. The old system of utilizing A&R shops to complement the limited number of trade schools, could only provide 15 percent of stated technical labor requirements. BuAer recognized the shortcomings of the existing arrangements, and sought funding to establish an aviation technical training school in Jacksonville, Florida. Construction was projected to be completed in just six months, opening its doors to three thousand new students in January 1941. Prospective AMMs, AMs, ARMs, and AOs would learn their respective trades at Naval Air Station (NAS) Jacksonville and report to the fleet as qualified technicians upon graduation.[6]

As far back as 1938, naval aviation had recognized there was a problem with the imbalance of logistical support capacity in relation to the projected force expansion. Based on findings from a board convened to study the U.S. defense capability and infrastructure, chaired by Adm. Arthur J. Hepburn, the Navy lacked shore establishments along the Eastern Seaboard that could carry out required maintenance and operational tasks. Hepburn's 1938 report was informally titled "A Guide for Expansion of Peacetime Shore Establishments." However, it was no secret that the increased threat of war was front and center in his thought process. Much emphasis was placed on establishing operational bases in the Pacific, but there was deliberate mention of Jacksonville being developed into and operational training facility for aircraft maintenance.[7] In 1940 the decision of how to manage the assignment of personnel for aviation duties including technical, or "vocational," training was first placed into the capable hands of a few experienced aviation officers within BuAer, most notably Lt. Cdr. Austin W. Wheelock.

Lieutenant Commander Wheelock reported to BuAer on May 7 and was immediately assigned to the Personnel Division. A 1925 graduate of the Naval Academy, his previous assignments included flying patrol aircraft in with VP-4 (stationed at Pearl Harbor), torpedo bombers with VT-1B from the USS *Lexington* (CV 2), and scouting seaplanes in VS-5B from the light cruiser USS *Marblehead* (CL 12). He also served on various staff tours including the headquarters of Aircraft Battle Force.[8] Wheelock was an experienced pilot who understood the needs of fleet maintenance and the technical skills required of technicians to keep the Navy's air force aloft.

The initial mission for Wheelock's section was to establish a training system for officer and enlisted airmen under the cognizance of BuNav. The thought process was since BuNav managed personnel entry and detailing throughout the fleet, Nimitz's staff should have cognizance over the training, while officers from BuAer served as key liaisons and advisers.[9] This plan was part of George Murray's 1939 short-lived remedy which he proposed to Towers and Mitscher due to the sharp increase in new aviation personnel. As discussed in the last chapter, this plan did not survive for long.

With the buildup of naval air forces came the increase in size of the aviation training program. Shortly after Wheelock had settled into his billet within the Personnel Division, BuAer requested that the commanding officer of NAS Norfolk establish a school that could house four hundred AMM students. They also requested a similar facility addition for NAS San Diego, but larger so that it could house eight hundred AMM students. It was assumed, as was the custom during the interwar years, that adequate instruction could be accomplished through the A&R shops located within the naval air stations. Problems arose however, when A&R shop personnel could not keep up with the demands of both training new technicians and simultaneously completing their routine overhaul work. Thus, the quality of the Navy's new aviation labor force deteriorated.[10]

Steps were taken to provide the students with facilities and instructors that were separate from the A&R shops. Existing schools were expanded as much as possible and the number of trained graduates began to increase. By the end of 1940, BuAer was on pace to graduate approximately nine thousand technicians every four months. Rear Admiral Towers was quite comfortable with these numbers and the overall status of his training programs throughout the following spring. When testifying on the status of BuAer's training programs before Congress on July 22, 1941, he stated, "Subject to obtaining the requisite number of planes for advanced [pilot] training, I can report the Navy's aviation training program is shipshape and under way ahead of schedule for both pilots, flight crews and maintenance personnel."[11] Towers' response to Congress was either inflated, ignorant, or simply erroneous. The fixes that had been put in place over the previous fifteen months since Wheelock had reported to BuAer were only improvised expedients for a systemic problem facing BuAer and BuNav.[12]

In September 1941, the Assistant Secretary of the Navy for Air, Artemus Gates, appointed a board to analyze the current efforts to train both officer and enlisted personnel in pilot and technical matters. It was chaired by Cdr. G. F. Bogan. Based on interviews and historical data, the Bogan Board determined that the size of the aviation training program had grown so large, that aviation officers concluded that the program would be better placed under BuAer cognizance. The request was thus submitted up the chain of command with the following explanation:

> The scope of aviation training, both ground and flight, has become so great that its operations under existing conditions is slow, cumbersome, and difficult in administrative control. It is strongly recommended that responsibility for this training be made that of the Chief of the Bureau of Aeronautics, and that the administration thereof be under the Bureau. In this connection, the formation of a training division within the bureau, solely for training, has been considered. Consideration has also been given to the assignment of an officer of suitable rank, who, together with his staff, should function as Director of Training.[13]

Towers recognized that here was an opportunity to break free from oversight by Nimitz and BuNav. He strongly supported the Bogan Board's recommendation that the control of all facets of aviation training be placed under BuAer's purview. On October 3, 1941, Towers responded to the Bogan Report. In his memo to the Secretary of the Navy he said, "Our present training effort can be speeded up appreciatively through administrative action within the Department."[14] Towers understood the original 1920 Navy charter, which placed responsibility of all personnel training programs under the cognizance of BuNav. However, he was aware of the "duplication of effort" and the resultant time lag in accomplishing associated tasks and did not support the status quo. He recommended that BuAer be responsible for planning and executing all aspects of aviation training, to include pilots and technicians.[15]

Towers backed his opinion with the following facts: BuAer already had a framework to administer all stages of training; the majority of training schools were geographically located on naval air stations that depended on BuAer for material support; the training of aeronautical personnel was specialized and could only be administered by aeronautically trained personnel. This last proposal was comparable to the Bureau of Medicine's training program, which for similar reasons operated independently of BuNav. The shift in supervisory authority would promote faster and better-informed corrective measures to training programs than would be the case if BuAer only operated in an advisory role.[16]

Naturally, Nimitz objected to completely handing over the administration of aviation personnel and training to Towers. His objections were based on precedent and the current status of aviation training. He countered Towers' reasons by claiming that excellent cooperation had always existed between BuNav and BuAer and that there was no duplication of effort. Only a small staff of BuNav officers was present to administer the program in accordance with BuAer wishes and coordinate incompatible direction from the Office of the CNO. Nimitz did not interpret the Bogan Report to say that BuNav should completely give up its functions with respect to aviation. He concluded his argument by suggesting that separating control of aviation personnel from the Department of the Navy's personnel Bureau was contrary to the principles of the bureaucracy's design. Instead, Nimitz recommended that offices and staff of BuAer's Training Section and the Training Division of BuNav be located together so that they might function more as a single unit and increase the pace at which they achieved their goals. Nimitz's response was forwarded to the Secretary of Navy on October 13, 1941, just ten days after Towers had made his wishes public.[17]

Approximately two weeks later, Navy leadership met with hopes of reaching an agreement to send up to the Secretary of the Navy for approval. Admiral Stark and the Assistant Secretary of the Navy for Air, Artemus Gates, both sided with Nimitz. Everyone except for Towers was against the change. They agreed upon colocating personnel for each bureau and suggested a new billet be established to oversee the entire process. Admiral Stark suggested that the new billet be one of a senior-ranking officer who would have equal allegiance to the offices of

CNO, BuAer, and BuNav. His primary job would be to administer the training program. The senior officer would assume the title of director of aviation training. In addition to reporting to Towers at BuAer, he would also report to Nimitz at BuNav, as well as the CNO, on all matters of aviation training. His primary duty would be director of aviation training at BuAer, with additional duties named as assistant for aviation training in both the Office of Chief of Naval Operations, and the Bureau of Navigation. The Secretary of the Navy formally approved the measure on November 21, 1941, and Capt. Arthur W. Radford was appointed the first director of aviation training.[18]

Radford quickly implemented changes within the administration of BuAer's training program. One of the first changes he made was to place Lieutenant Commander Wheelock in charge of all technical training. This put the onus of managing both officer and enlisted training on Wheelock's shoulders. He was in charge of all basic aviation rating training taking place in the existing trade schools, in specialized and advanced enlisted training centers, and in radar training schools. He was responsible for officer and pilot ground school training as well. However, radar and ground school training for pilots were soon separated from the Technical Training Section and given their own sections under the Aviation Training Division.[19] In narrowing the focus of Wheelock's section on training the technicians, the expansion of the Navy's aviation labor force began to show progress. However, the Navy's trade schools were geographically dispersed throughout the country and operated with little BuAer oversight. Unsupervised and unstandardized training would prove to be insufficient to meet the demands of the fleet.[20]

+++

A year earlier, it had been decided that NAS Jacksonville, Florida, would be the site for the Navy's newest school for aviation technical training. Initial planning for the massive trade school had begun during the summer of 1940 and the school's doors were forecast to open in January 1941. Unfortunately, the Navy still needed to train technicians, so San Diego, Pensacola, and Norfolk had to increase their output of graduates threefold until Jacksonville was operational. For example, NAS San Diego had a regular capacity of 500 AMM at one time, but under duress 1,500 graduates passed through its doors in 1940. NAS Pensacola normally accommodated 160 AMM and 280 AM at one time. But by January 2, 1941, 480 AMMs and 840 AMs had completed the curriculum and joined the fleet. NAS Norfolk saw a similar push for new AMM graduates and tripled its output from 400 to 1,200 trained sailors. By January 1941, the Training Section under Wheelock had overhauled the existing schools and curricula to graduate 5,520 aviation technicians (ARM, AMM, AM, and AO) in just six months, when the normal capacity was 1840.[21] Yet again, it was only a temporary fix for a more serious problem.

NAS Jacksonville was officially commissioned as a base for what the Navy first called "trade schools" on October 15, 1940. Recently retired Cdr. Junius L. Cotton was ordered back to active duty on August 10, 1940, in order to serve as the trade school's first officer in charge (OIC). The first trade school classes at NAS Jacksonville did not convene until March 2, 1941. The trade school facilities were built to house 3,000 students at a time, consisting of programs for certification as aviation metalsmith, aviation machinist's mate, aviation ordnanceman, and aviation radioman (ARM) ratings. Courses were designed to take an average of four months from start to finish. The BuAer Training Section estimated 43,000 enlisted aviation technicians would complete their respective training courses between 1941 and 1944.[22] The first classes for prospective AMs and AMMs began in March 1941. The following month, ARMs and AO candidates began their respective courses.

The aviation schools in Jacksonville were initially designated as Class A schools. This denoted that they were structured to "give basic training designed to equip men to carry out the duties of a third class petty officer."[23] Sailors were sent to A schools immediately following basic training or "boot camp." It was the first step in qualifying in "rate" rather than remaining an "undesignated" seaman. In order to advance in rank, new sailors had to "make rate." The schools covered a broad range of various phases of technical aviation. The Navy also had Class B schools, which were designed to deliver more advanced training suitable for more senior petty officer ratings. There were also Class C schools for specialized skill sets, but they did not fulfill full requirements for advancement in rate.[24]

Cotton made his initial inspection of the school's facilities, as it was undergoing construction immediately after his recall to active duty.

Before he arrived in Jacksonville, he studied the trade schools in Norfolk in order to understand how they operated and what materials were required. Cotton used this information to determine whether or not what was being built and the material provided by BuAer was sufficient to handle such a massive student load. To his credit, he did not think it was satisfactory. He reported his findings to the prospective commanding officer of NAS Jacksonville, Capt. Charles P. Mason, specifically noting that the list of material the BuAer had prepared for the Metalsmith School and the Machinist's Mate School was entirely "inadequate in many items."[25]

Cotton elaborated on the details of his initial assessment in Norfolk, which he believed needed to be considered during construction and curriculum development in Jacksonville. Problems like proper ventilation in the auditorium or how much to slope the deck in the auditorium so all students could have an unobstructed view of their instructor and media were first on his list of grievances. Other issues were identified, including where to place the movie curtain so it would not be damaged when converting the theater to a dance hall, and where to locate the scullery within the cafeteria system. As trivial as they might have appeared, Cotton felt they were valid concerns.[26]

His report also outlined his personnel requirements for the administration of the school. He asked BuAer for a total of 290 men, including officers, to meet the staff and faculty requirements. Cotton was concerned about the availability of officers assigned to the school because of competing requirements. When asking for an experienced officer to run each of the four trade schools on base, he admitted to Mason, "Officers are as scarce as hens' teeth."[27]

The initial plans for the trade schools called for an instructor cadre of 15 officers and 190 petty officers. The expectation was to house 1,850 students in the Aviation Machinist's Mates School, 400 in the Aviation Metalsmith School, 200 in the Aviation Ordnance School, and 150 in the Aviation Radioman School. According to a local newspaper article published on the commissioning day for NAS Jacksonville, opening an official trade school was a first for the Navy and for the country. Its graduates would only be assigned to units that were part of naval aviation, something the Navy had not done before. The article concluded, "In this respect, the Trade School at Jacksonville is unique, for there is no other school in the country where so many specialties will be taught and where the men are being trained exclusively for aviation duty."[28]

Even before classes began, there were concerns about the quality of instruction in the schools. Initial staffing and maintaining a cadre of experienced instructors was paramount for the trade schools' success. The first instructors were rated petty officers selected from operational and existing training units. They were technicians by trade, but not trained in educational theory and practice. They were skilled aircraft technicians, but not necessarily skilled educators. As was the case across the fleet, veteran aviation technicians from 1940 to 1941 had been taught under the old system of on-the-job training. The schools they had attended were of a broad, general nature pieced together over the interwar years. The new naval aviation arm in this period of expansion was designed to operate specialized aircraft systems and required technicians who were specifically trained on such systems. A basic understanding of aeronautics, physics, and engineering theory was necessary for technicians to maintain modern aircraft engines, aerodynamic structures, and communications systems. The newly appointed instructors were weak in their ability to transmit such knowledge as their teaching experience to this point had been of a practical nature.[29]

✦✦✦

During the previous two years, the aircraft manufacturing industry had adopted the practice of mass production lines and embraced sophisticated technology. Grumman, Martin, Pratt & Whitney, and other aviation companies were beginning to resemble the auto industry of the 1920s. Recognizing there was a lack of knowledge of these new systems en route to the fleet, some manufacturers supplied training equipment and factory technicians to the trade schools directly to assist the new instructors. The manufacturers provided additional opportunities for training at the factories for select petty officer instructors and maintenance officers. These augmentations were not unique to Jacksonville, but were in practice at other naval trade schools across the country.[30]

The need for technical instructors was no small issue for the Navy or the government. The United States Office of Education was enlisted to supplement teaching staff at military training schools. Together with the

National Defense Training Program and the Florida State Department of Education, BuAer recruited experienced tradesmen from civilian jobs to work as civilian instructors at the Jacksonville Trade School and eventually others. It was a good idea in theory, although these individuals faced the same problems as the active-duty Navy instructors—most of their experience was practical, not relevant to classroom instruction. Additionally, few of the civilian instructors had any experience with naval aircraft and weapons.[31]

In 1941 a civilian teacher program was set up through a joint Army-Navy program operating out of Chanute Field in Rantoul, Illinois. It was based on BuAer's design for technical training at NAS Jacksonville. At this site a joint board sifted through numerous applications for technical aviation instructors at the naval trade schools and U.S. Army Air Corps technical schools. While successful at first, grumblings began when the pay gap between civilian teachers and military instructors widened; civilians were paid a higher salary than the enlisted instructors for the same duties. Also, many of the civilians hired ended up being less effective at teaching than expected. Although the program fulfilled a critical gap in training at first, as time went on, the reality that civilian and military roles were not interchangeable became apparent. Still, the civilian teaching corps carried a greater share of classroom instruction until the program was ultimately ended in June 1942.[32] While many individuals left the school houses after this, some stayed on and enlisted in the Navy to continue their work. Others transferred to civil service, keeping their roles as aviation maintenance technician instructors.[33]

Another source of instructors was found among the ranks of newly graduated trade school students. These men had a working knowledge of the course material, but lacked the operational experience with much of the equipment. They were also handicapped by having little expertise in the area of theory.[34] As had been the case in other trade schools during the previous year, getting BuNav to approve retaining freshly trained technicians in the schools instead of detailing them to the fleet was almost impossible.[35] BuAer's Training Section had a serious dilemma on its hands, and Nimitz's staff did not help matters.

Another obvious concern was the availability and quality of training equipment for the technicians. Due to the unrelenting requirements of the fleet, there was a limited supply of operationally representative aircraft and aircraft parts for students' instruction. What material they did have was usually obsolete or salvaged from crashes and mishaps. In one particular case, a chief petty officer reported traveling to Norfolk to inspect a crashed PBY aircraft for the possibility of salvaging parts. He found nothing valuable from the damaged airplane, but instead located two other working, albeit very worn out, models which he arranged to be transferred to Jacksonville where they served as teaching aids. The process to procure up-to-date aircraft systems for technical training purposes was without formal direction until 1943. The wartime fleet was the priority for aircraft and aircraft parts. Until a surplus was reached, the trade schools had to beg, borrow, and steal what they needed. When the Jacksonville Trade School established its own Material Department on December 17, 1942, the procurement process for teaching aids was formalized and became more successful than its earlier version had been.[36]

Curriculum development was also a concern during the initial planning stages of the Trades School. In March 1941 Lt. Cdr. Daniel J. Brimm Jr., USNR, was called to active duty for the sole purpose of developing instructional materials for the various BuAer technical trade schools.[37] He was an aviation engineer with a vast amount of experience in civil aviation during the interwar years. Brimm was well versed in aviation maintenance as well as flying. He was a former test pilot, but had made his mark in the aviation technical world. He was a licensed airplane engine mechanic and an airplane engine instructor at the New York City School of Aviation Trades. Additionally, Brimm had been the manager at Marine Flying Service and chief engineer at the Ireland Aircraft Company. Most relative to his assignment within BuAer, he was a published technical author with three authoritative works on aviation to his name: *Airplane and Engine Maintenance for the Airplane Mechanic* (1936); *Seaplanes Maneuvering, Maintaining, Operating* (1937); and *Aircraft Engine Maintenance* (1939).[38] His experience and knowledge in the field made him an excellent candidate to supervise curriculum development desperately needed in BuAer's technical training.

In the fall of 1941 Brimm was sent to Jacksonville to observe the progress of the trade school and comment on curriculum implementation. What he observed was not impressive. His first observation was that the schools were short on instructional material and instructors. In one instance, Brimm observed only one aircraft available for hands-on training for nearly a thousand students. He reported that classes of two hundred students at a time would spend hours sitting in a hangar with nothing to do because of the shortage of technical models to work on. Often students spent their class time playing cards or other games.[39] Brimm's observations were described in a powerful memorandum that his coworker, Wheelock, sent to Radford on December 1, 1941. In this paper, Wheelock mentioned many problems in the trade schools. These were shortcomings in quality and number of instructors, lack of technical training equipment, and problems with standardization across sites. Additional challenges included updating instruction to most current methods, efforts to consolidate trade schools, factory training, and officer training.[40]

Brimm's observations were corroborated by Columbia University's dean of engineering, Joseph W. Barker, who was also serving as special assistant to the Assistant Secretary of the Navy for Air. Barker's formal title was chief of the Division of Training Liaison Coordination for the Secretary of the Navy. Barker toured other trade school and A&R facilities in Jacksonville and Pensacola from May 8 to May 16, 1941. His observations confirmed Brimm's, repeating the earlier charges that there was little standardization in instruction and methodology across geographically separate training centers. By early summer 1941, Brimm and others in the Training Section were working feverishly to remedy the inadequacies of the existing program before it began to damage the fleet's combat effectiveness.[41] A generation of poorly trained naval aircraft technicians would undoubtedly have long-lasting ill effects on the Navy's ability to fight an air war. It was up to Brimm and Wheelock to prevent such a disaster.

Finding qualified sailors to attend the trades schools was a serious challenge. Recruits had to show a general aptitude in their intended fields of future study, have an interest or previous experience in the field, and had to have "high degrees of petty officer potentiality" according to historical accounts. The minimum required scores in the General Classification Test (GCT) varied depending on rate.[42] For AMM the score was sixty-two and for the AO community it was seventy. Little mention is made in official documents regarding different score requirements between ratings. However, one can infer that the Navy wanted to ensure those technicians whose jobs required the most unforgiving tasks, such as weapons handling, were some of the brightest in the hangar. BuAer also recognized that the intellectual requirements of an aviation technician were greater than what general service ratings needed. Thus, they set limits on what scores were acceptable and what scores would get you reassigned to general shipboard rating schools. Taking it one step further, the ordnance community required a personal interview with interested recruits that focused on their interest in the ordnance program.[43] BuAer did not want to give up the investment it was making in each one of these sailors once a sailor graduated from a trade school. Therefore, graduates were assigned an aviation rating commensurate with their field of study, which ensured they would only be assigned to aviation activities for the remainder of the war.[44]

The Jacksonville Trade School was instrumental in developing a model for recruitment and rating selection. In a 1943 version of the "U.S. Navy Interviewer's Classification Guide" the Bureau of Personnel (formally BuNav) stated that the minimum GCT score for AO and AMM was a fifty-two for both ratings.[45] The GCT was revised by the Navy around the same time, but it is debatable if the lower score reflected intricacies of an updated test, or more likely, a lowering of standards in order to meet the labor demand of naval aviation.

Nevertheless, the complexity of modern aircraft and their weapons system required a higher degree of aptitude in its technicians. A comparison of other minimum GCT scores for nonaviation ratings such as machinist's mates (MM) or gunner's mate (GM) shows a fifty and forty-five respectively. This does not imply that aircraft technicians were the brightest of all the Navy's ratings, however. The radio technician (RT) rating had a minimum of sixty and quartermaster (QM) was fifty-five. Another difference in classification standards was in what the Navy listed as part of the "personal" qualifications for selection to aviation rates. AMM and AO both listed "calmness under stress" as a qualifier. MM and GM had no such requirement. In all fairness however, there were some nonaviation ratings that had comparable if not more stringent criteria. The minimum GCT score for fire controlman (FC) was sixty and also made "calmness under stress" a prerequisite.[46] Candidates for aviation ratings were not necessarily the most scholastically astute of all enlisted men and women, but they were among the top of the available labor pool.

The capacity of Jacksonville to deliver technicians to the fleet fluctuated both before and during the war. After the attack on Pearl Harbor, the demand for graduates increased greatly over the next few years, reaching its peak during the summer of 1943. At times, Allied technicians from Great Britain, France, Brazil, Cuba, and even three students from Uruguay were trained at Jacksonville. Table 3.1 breaks down the numbers of enlisted Navy and Marine Corps students per month from March 1941 through December 1943.

The rapid influx of students by mid-1942 through mid-1943 coincides with aircraft manufacturers' increased production. Grumman signed a contract with the Navy to build and deliver 675 F4F (-3 and -4 models) Wildcat carrier fighter aircraft beginning in August 1942 and continuing through March 1943. Earlier contracts on the F4F assured a delivery of 819 airplanes between December 1940 and March 1943.[47] Wheelock and his staff must have foreseen the tidal wave of technician requirements that was on the horizon and therefore, responded with the uptick in technical students under training that coincided with the manufacturing output of Navy fighters.

The high number of students also parallels the shipbuilding industry's production of aircraft carriers. Looking at the contract data for the *Essex*-class aircraft carriers, the first keel was laid down on April 28, 1941. Construction on two more began that same December. Four *Essex*-class aircraft carriers were commissioned before January 1944: the *Essex* (CV 9), *Yorktown* (CV 10), *Intrepid* (CV 11), and *Hornet* (CV 12). In 1943 designs were adjusted for an increase in aircraft complement from the original 82 aircraft per ship to 90. By August 1944 the number had been raised to 96, and to 103 in June 1945.[48] The original *Hornet* (CV 8) maintained a complement of 72 aircraft and 601 enlisted personnel assigned to aviation department. It is worth noting that the number of personnel decreased with the new *Essex* class. The CV 9 only made space for 537 enlisted aviation ratings in the original plans drawn up in 1940.[49] There is no obvious explanation for this. One can only infer that perhaps there

Table 3.1. Summary of Enlisted Personnel by Month[1]

DATE	NAVY STUDENTS	MARINE CORPS
Mar. 31, 1941	1,424	189
Apr. 30, 1941	2,097	264
June 30, 1941	2,727	301
July 31, 1941	2,495	320
Aug. 31, 1941	2,683	350
Sept. 30, 1941	2,647	267
Oct. 31, 1941	2,577	451
Nov. 30, 1941	2,576	447
Dec. 31, 1941	2,591	489
Jan. 31, 1942	2,991	336
Feb. 28, 1942	2,741	285
Mar. 31, 1942	2,898	1,260
May 1, 1942	3,271	2,099
June 1, 1942	3,164	2,416
July 1, 1942	3,286	3,107
Aug. 1, 1942	4,439	3,548
Sept. 1, 1942	4,324	3,429
Oct. 1, 1942	4,705	3,632
Nov. 1, 1942	5,298	4,037
Dec. 1, 1942	5,501	3,577
Jan. 1, 1943	5,582	3,363
Feb. 1, 1943	5,633	3,691
Mar. 1, 1943	5,663	3,691
Apr. 1, 1943	5,687	3,538
May 1, 1943	5,434	3,848
June 1, 1943	5,275	4,161
July 1, 1943	5,089	3,942
Aug. 1, 1943	4,835	3,838
Sept. 1, 1943	4,406	3,838
Oct. 1, 1943	4,215	3,063
Nov. 1, 1943	3,975	2,771
Dec. 1, 1943	3,207	2,541

[1] "History of Naval Air Technical Training Center Jacksonville, Florida," 45–47.

was an expectation that the newer airframes and ships would require less maintenance. The other possibility could be that the Navy realized there was an insufficient number of trained aviation personnel to fully outfit all of the aircraft carriers that would be required to deploy a portion of FDR's 15,000-plane program. Nearly a hundred smaller, unplanned "light" or "escort" carriers were built during the war. The Navy had to maintain its armada of aircraft and supply the labor needs on the smaller carriers. Perhaps the decreased numbers per ship was a strategic decision to spread their technicians sparingly to make up the difference. Nevertheless, the demand on the trade school command was high. After analyzing the capacities of the Navy's operating trade schools, Brimm sent a memo to BuAer director of training, Captain Radford, on November 29, 1941, that illustrated the actual and desired output. Brimm's recommendations are depicted in Table 3.2.

The greatest increases in student matriculations were planned at Navy Pier Chicago and NAS Jacksonville. These two locations would become the backbone of aviation technical training for the Navy in the first year of the war. Even with the planned increase, the Navy was still short on technicians due to its inadequate aviation training program during the interwar period. The Navy needed trained technicians and was funneling fresh boot camp graduates to Jacksonville as quickly as they could, but there were only so many available seats in each classroom. It would take a creative mind willing to embrace institutional change for there to be any measurable impact.

In December 1941 the new OIC of NAS Jacksonville Trade Schools, Lt. Cdr. Ronald D. Higgins, proposed a plan to modify the daily operations of the schools in order to graduate more students without having to utilize a commensurately larger number of instructors. This was in response to the recent expansion to accommodate nearly 4,500 students at one time since the Marine Corps had made a request to begin sending its own student aircraft technicians to the schools for training.[50] Higgins' plan involved staggering classes, so two groups of students instead of one could cover the same amount of material each day, expanding the output of the trade schools.

On March 2, 1942, the NAS Jacksonville Service Schools transitioned from one shift per day to two.[51] This was the only way the school could

Table 3.2. Current and Planned Capacity of Trade Schools as of November 29, 1941 [1]

SCHOOL	CAPACITY, NOVEMBER 1941	PLANNED/FUTURE CAPACITY
NAS Jacksonville	AMM: 2080 AM: 400 ARM: 300 AO: 200 Total: 2,980	4,372
NAS Pensacola	AMM: 176 AM: 280 Total: 456	456
NAS San Diego	AMM: 500 ARM: 360 AO: 200 Total: 2,060	1,060
NAS Alameda	AMM: 448 AM: 152 ARM: 200 Total: 800	1,600
NAS Seattle	AMM: 448 AM: 152 ARM: 200 Total: 800	1,400
Navy Pier Chicago	AMM: 700 AM: 300	6,000
NAS Norfolk	AMM: 600 Total: 600	600
NTS Norfolk	AMM: 75 AM: 25 AO: 24 Total: 124	124
Detroit (Dearborn)	AMM: 628 AM: 272 Total: 900	0 (Students transferred to Chicago when Navy Pier school became fully operational)

[1] Memo from Lieutenant Commander Brimm to Captain Radford, November 29, 1941, as referenced in Bureau of Aeronautics, "Aviation Personnel and Training," 1959, 322.

manage to keep up with the incoming waves of students. The early shift began their day at 0430, with breakfast at 0450. First period classes began 0550 and ended at 0650. Second period went until 0750, third until 0850, and every hour so forth until the academic day officially ended at 1850. Lunch and supper were squeezed in at 1005 and 1530, respectively. Official lights out, or taps, was at 2030 each day. The late shift was held to an identical schedule, except their day began at 0630 with reveille and taps was at 2230.[52] The two-shift policy was successful and soon became the norm within other naval aviation technical schools. The schools also transitioned from a five-day work week to a six-day work week in September 1942 which significantly cut down the training time in all rates. At the Aviation Machinist's Mate School, training time was reduced from twenty-six weeks to twenty-one as a result of the six-day week.[53]

The Aviation Machinist's Mate School at Jacksonville was the largest of all four schools. Its enrollment routinely represented one-half to two-thirds of all students on the base. When the school first opened in 1941, sailors were graduated without a rating. BuNav quickly recognized the problem with this because new graduates were leaving the school and then being reassigned to jobs that did not apply anything they had learned over their sixteen-week course of instruction. BuNav made a change in late 1941 that stipulated 25 percent of each graduating class would be rated as AMMs. By June 1942 the bar was lowered to rate "all who were satisfactory," presumably to get rated aviation technicians to the fleet. In May 1943 the number was restricted to 50 percent, and finally in November 1943, returned to 25 percent. By this time, the Navy had reached an excess of petty officers in the fleet, and it was desired that only those who possessed the most technical acumen and leadership should start their first operational tour as a petty officer. Students who did not graduate with grades satisfactory enough to warrant their immediate promotion to petty officer third class were given ample opportunities to do so once they reported to their next assignment.[54]

The twenty-one-week course of instruction for an aspiring aviation machinist's mate was broken down into four phases. The "Basic" phase lasted two weeks and included blueprint reading, mathematics, basic ordnance, and hand tools. The airplane phase took seven weeks and covered the following topics: fabric, instruments, hydraulics and landing gear, controls, structures, and emergency equipment. The eight-week "Engine" phase was the longest. It taught overhaul, lubrication, accessories, ignition, propellers, and troubleshooting. The last four weeks of school was the "Operational" phase, which covered aircraft recognition and squadron operations.⁵⁵ The training did not always employ the most experienced instructors, nor did it have the most up-to-date models for hands-on learning, but after Brimm made his changes to the curricula, it was certainly thorough. Upon graduation most technicians were sent to the carrier navy, but some made their way to shore-based commands such as patrol squadrons, A&R facilities, or carrier aircraft service units (CASU).⁵⁶

In addition to the problems of standardization, instructor availability, and training, it did not take long for BuAer to realize NAS Jacksonville's facilities would fall short, mostly because of the high numbers of students required to meet the needs of the fleet. The Navy needed to expand beyond NAS Jacksonville for the majority of its aviation technical training. Fortunately, there were a number of smaller technical training facilities already in existence before the war began. During the summer of 1941, another school for AMMs was established in Chicago. The Chicago Vocational School, located at 87th Street and Anthony Avenue, Chicago was initially a civilian technical school, but partnered with the Navy to provide much needed technical training to AMM rates that could not be billeted in Jacksonville. While the training itself might have been sufficient, the logistics of getting students from their barracks to the classroom every day was not. Housing for the students was situated at the Naval Armory. The armory was located eighty-seven blocks away from the vocational school and it housed other sailors attending various other schools throughout the city. The situation was less than ideal and the Navy had to make a change.⁵⁷

In the fall of 1941, commandant of the of the Ninth Naval District, Rear Adm. Henry V. Butler, recommended a service school be built at Navy Pier in downtown Chicago. Butler was responsible for all naval activities in the greater Chicago area.⁵⁸ His plans included housing and classroom facilities for six thousand students, initially for AMMs and AMs.⁵⁹ BuAer and the Navy agreed with his proposal and acquired

Navy Pier from the City of Chicago. Classes began almost immediately in December 1941, relieving some of the pressure on Jacksonville.[60]

Chicago was not the only city with a naval technical school that was struggling to keep up with the student demand. Norfolk, Pensacola, and San Diego were all expanded to handle more students. Additional technical training schools were also set up in Alameda, California; Seattle, Washington; Dearborn, Michigan; and Great Lakes Naval Station north of Chicago. Henry Ford hosted a naval training school (NTS) in Dearborn on the grounds of the Ford Motor Company plant. Barracks and messing quarters were built next to the River Rouge Plant in Dearborn. Ford entered into agreement with the Navy to provide instructors and a specialized curriculum for aviation machinists' mates on aircraft engines. The Ford Motor Company was subcontracted at the time to produce the Pratt & Whitney R-2800 series engine, which was a common engine in the Navy's carrier fighters and medium bombers. The Grumman F4F Wildcat operated with the Pratt & Whitney R-1800 and the newer F6F Hellcat was being built with the R-2800. Initially, Dearborn seemed like a perfect location for technicians to receive specialized engine training. However, it was soon discovered that Ford's curriculum did not correspond to the Navy's for AMMs.[61]

The four-month course was specific to the R-2800, thus it lacked training in other general duties of the AMM rating such as aircraft characteristics, hydraulics, fabric, and basic ordnance. The Navy did not operate like a mass production plant. Aircraft technicians were required to be a part of any and all evolutions on ship or shore, not limited to one part or system of the vehicle like automobile manufacturer labor. For this reason, graduates of Dearborn often failed the follow-on examinations required of AMMs once they checked out of Ford's school and reported back to their parent training command. Dearborn graduates were extremely knowledgeable in the operation and repair of the R-2800 engine but little else. It was for this reason that BuAer eventually abandoned the school as a program for AMMs, but the Navy retained Ford's services and facilities for more general fleet technician education on different types of gas and diesel engines, electrical systems, and a variety of other systems. Dearborn was capable of housing nine hundred students at any given time during the war until its closure in May 1946.[62]

After Pearl Harbor, some of the schools where enlisted aviation technicians were learning their trade were closed or thinned out to make room for increased pilot and general aviation training. NAS Pensacola transitioned to a primary flight training center and the technical schools it once hosted were disbanded completely as pilots and navigators filled the former enlisted barracks and mess halls in for flight training. In 1942, BuNav had formally changed it title to the Bureau of Naval Personnel (BuPers) to better reflect its mission. By that spring, BuAer and BuPers had a relatively concise list of service schools that were doing their best to satisfy the requirement of the aviation Navy. Until World War II, the U.S. Navy had never really concerned itself with standardized courses of instruction for its aviation technicians. Following a period of trial and error at the end the interwar years, BuAer and BuPers finally settled on a uniform length of study in each of the aviation ratings by 1942.[63] The standard time frame from start to finish for "A" schools was either four or six months. To put this into perspective, the average length of the basic aircraft mechanic course given by the Army Technical Training Command in 1942 was eighteen weeks. Between 1938 and 1942 the Army also expanded the number of its technical aviation courses from three to twenty-two.[64]

The Navy's length of schooling was consistent across the board due to the overarching efforts to standardize the curriculum. The Navy finally had a refined technical training program for its technicians that operational commanders could use to project the arrival of their next wave of freshly trained maintainers. Table 3.3 depicts the schools and length of instruction in April 1942.

In 1942 the technology of naval aircraft was advancing far beyond anything technicians had seen during the interwar years. The Navy sought to compartmentalize its labor force to keep up with the changes. Some aviation ratings tended to have a bigger workload than others. For example, an AMM was required to know the intricacies of almost every moving part on an airframe, including engines, propellers, and hydraulics. The aviation radio technician (ART) was an expert with the radio—its operation, electronics, antenna, and so forth.[65] All ratings were important to the success of naval aviation, but not all ratings were as critical to the safety of the aircrew as others were.

Table 3.3. Length of Curriculum by School and Rating[1]

RATING	SCHOOL LOCATION	LENGTH OF COURSE
Aviation Machinist's Mate	NAS Norfolk NAS Seattle NAS Jacksonville NAS Alameda	6 months
Aviation Machinist's Mate	NTS Great Lakes NTS Dearborn	4 months
Aviation Metalsmith	NAS Jacksonville NAS Seattle NTS Navy Pier NAS Alameda	6 months
Aviation Radioman	NAS Jacksonville NAS San Diego NAS Seattle NAS Alameda	4 months
Aviation Ordnanceman	NAS Jacksonville NAS San Diego NAS Seattle	4 months

[1] T. B. Haley, "Historical Report of the Technical Training Section through December 1943," 6.

Certain ratings required a longer period of schooling because of the volume of material and critical nature of their work. If an engine was repaired incorrectly, a second chance after failure in flight was unlikely. The AMM and AM schools took an average of two months longer than other aviation ratings. Additionally, these two ratings made up the majority of the Navy's enlisted aviation technician force, therefore it was imperative that the trade schools find a way to graduate more technicians in less time.[66] These technicians were responsible for maintaining naval aircraft from its nose to its tail. While an airplane could safely takeoff and land with an inoperable radio or a faulty bomb rack, one cannot say the same thing about a malfunctioning engine or major delaminating surfaces on the skin of an airplane.[67] Ratings that focused on aircraft systems that were "safety-of-flight" systems tended to be in greater demand and required a longer term of instruction. Even with a standardized curricula and predictable matriculation of newly qualified technicians, the Navy was still not meeting the needs of the fleet. Wheelock suggested to Towers that more extreme measures were required in support of technical training in the face of the wartime crisis.[68]

On April 16, 1942, Towers submitted a recommendation to the CNO and the Secretary of the Navy for the establishment of two new Class A schools to supplement the schools currently in existence. His plan called for the Bureau of Yards and Docks to construct two large training centers away from coastal naval air stations that could handle ten thousand students each. Memphis, Tennessee, and Norman, Oklahoma, were chosen as the sites for the new training centers.

The Secretary of the Navy approved Tower's recommendation on April 24, 1942. The initial funding for the project, an amount of $25,000,000, was approved by Congress in the National Defense Act of 1942. Coordination with local and state governments began immediately, and by late July, the Navy had already established a temporary headquarters space in a downtown Memphis office building.[69] The NTC Norman, Oklahoma, was commissioned on September 20, 1942. NTC Memphis was commissioned three days later on September 23. Both facilities were designed as aviation maintenance centers, thus designating their curriculum for AMM, AM, ARM, and AO ratings only. A month prior, the CNO had requested that BuPers transfer all staff, students, instructors, and equipment from the Aviation Machinist's Mate School at Norfolk and the Aviation Ordnanceman's School in San Diego to NTC Memphis by October 1 and October 15 respectively. The Aviation Machinist's Mate Schools in Alameda, Seattle, and San Diego; the Aviation Metalsmith's Schools in Alameda and Seattle; and the Aviation Ordnanceman's School in Seattle were all ordered to do the same beginning in September 1942. These transfers were based on BuPers approval of earlier recommendations by Wheelock's Technical Training Section that the Navy should consolidate its major aviation technical training centers into four geographic locations: Jacksonville, Chicago, Memphis, and Norman.[70]

Even with the ability to have 37,237 aviation technicians undergoing training at any given time, the Navy was still unable to meet the requirements of the fleet.[71] At the end of the fiscal year, within a week of the Navy's two newest technical training centers openings, Wheelock's section recommended that Memphis, Norman, and Jacksonville increase their student load capacity. Memphis and Norman expanded their facilities from 10,000 to 15,000 students, and Jacksonville increased its capacity by 800. BuAer and BuPers were doing their best to manage the ever-increasing workload of getting quality aircraft technicians out to the fleet in 1942.[72] However, no matter how hard they tried, and how many revisions they made to original plans, the numbers still fell short.

There was one other system in place at the start of the war that provided the specialized education necessary for naval aviation personnel on aircraft systems. A small program was put into place in 1941 that sent select petty officers to aircraft or aircraft parts factories for limited, streamlined training. This was based on an agreement between BuAer and BuPers that BuAer would recommend a few key personnel on an irregular basis to study with factory engineers and artisans for a short period of time. Essentially, it was temporary assigned duty to a factory for a few days to a few weeks of training. This training varied from engines, to aircraft weapons systems, servicing equipment, aircraft structures, and aircraft instruments. There were no regular courses or a standard curriculum for each system. But nonetheless, after the brief period of hands-on instruction, sailors returned to their commands with a better knowledge of the latest equipment on the flight deck.[73]

The factory training program continued to grow throughout 1941 and into the following year. BuAer was pleased with the results and began to explore options to incorporate it on a larger and more routine scale. In one instance, BuAer's Personnel Division coordinated with Pratt and Whitney to develop a consistent program of twenty technicians per month, all housed at the factory at no cost to the Navy. Often the manufacturers themselves reached out to BuAer or BuPers and offered their services at little or no charge. This program was relatively successful and grew throughout its inception and into the spring of 1942. Ultimately, BuAer's Technical Training Section under Wheelock made the pitch to have naval barracks built at certain factories. Wheelock anticipated future growth of the program and requested Towers' approval. Towers did not support such a "permanent" agreement with factories and thus rejected

Wheelock's plan. He did, however, establish a policy that encouraged the continued use of the factory training programs. Towers had a few stipulations, including that the maximum student load from the Navy be limited to fifty men per month, and the length of training period should not exceed one month.[74] Factory training was a valued program, but not a robust one.

Additional factory training arrangements were made with wartime manufacturers. The decision to formally enter into contract with a manufacturer was not an easy one. In April 1942 Towers recommended that BuPers contract with the Curtis-Wright Corporation to provide a more in-depth education into the nuances of the newly developed SO3C Seamew observation seaplane. Towers proposed that Curtiss conduct training for four men per squadron and BuAer manage the training through its colocated naval aircraft inspectors. He expected that BuPers would fund it. BuPers did not agree on the basis that entering into subsequent contracts with companies already in production contracts with the Navy was legally inadvisable. However, since most factory training was relatively small and usually was furnished without charge to the Navy, a formal contract was not really necessary. Therefore, the BuAer Technical Training Section chose to manage the training and small contracts (if any) with the few companies that were in production for BuAer. Goodyear Tire and Rubber Company, Lockheed Aircraft Corporation, and the Douglas Aircraft Corporation were some of the more prominent companies that provided training pro bono.[75]

As the number of small contracts grew, BuAer sent a request to the Navy paymaster general suggesting that the training costs be absorbed into the production contracts. The paymaster general agreed, and notified current and future manufacturers that the expense of training key squadron personnel was to be considered tied directly to the delivery of new equipment and any cost therein should be included in the total cost of the aircraft or associated equipment.[76] These contractual actions afforded BuAer more opportunities to acquire specialized training for its technicians. By September 1942, thirty factories were providing instruction to naval personnel in conjunction with production contracts. Regular quotas were setup with large aircraft manufacturers such as Grumman, Douglass, Vought-Sikorsky, and Curtiss-Wright. Soon these companies began to develop syllabi that were sent to BuAer for recommendations and comment. This way the Navy had some input into the methods in which its aviation technicians were trained.[77]

As the technology of aircraft systems matured, the number of small training courses grew. The administration of such programs began to weigh heavily on not only Wheelock's staff in the Technical Training Section, but on Captain Radford's Training Division as a whole. The aviation technical training program was growing into a colossal, multifaceted activity that was becoming more difficult to manage each day. The training of aviation technicians needed its own command and dedicated staff. Captain Radford's Training Division had more than it could handle managing the in-air, on-ground, and technical training of an entire navy. A forthcoming major change in the administration of such duties was about to permanently revise the role of BuAer in the Navy.[78]

Chapter 4

Paradigm Shift

As the Navy's operational activity intensified throughout 1942, the demands of the war compelled the Navy's bureaus to deliver unprecedented output. The Bureau of Naval Personnel was heavily engaged in procuring men to outfit ships, aircraft, and submarines. The Bureau of Ordnance was trying to acquire the requisite number of weapons to outfit every ship and airplane with state-of-the-art armament. The Bureau of Yards and Docks was struggling to build up enough infrastructure overseas and within the United States to support the ever-growing fleet. The Bureau of Ships was heavily engaged in design and ship construction. Bureau of Aeronautics was still trying to manage all facets of the aviation training programs, in addition to the procurement and maintenance of new aircraft. In particular, the Aviation Training Division of BuAer was overburdened with having to solve numerous and difficult problems related to technician and pilot training. BuAer found the growing number of personnel and complexity of the instruction programs overwhelming. In response to this situation, Towers responded with a change in BuAer's administrative structure.[1]

Until September 1942 all aviation training activities (pilot and technician) were managed under BuAer authority, but supervision of the physical facilities or bases themselves was overseen by the Commandant of each particular Naval District. For example, the 9th Naval District included Chicago, and its commandant had direct control of all naval facilities within its geographical boundary. As the trade schools tried to accomplish the herculean task of training so many technicians, the necessary expansion of instruction facilities required increases in funding. In order to secure additional fiscal resources, the trade schools had to go outside the BuAer chain of command and seek approval of the district commandant. This process ultimately became unworkable simply because commandants had many other responsibilities and fiscal demands to meet. In addition, the commandants themselves were not aviators and had little familiarity with the complicated and extensive requirements of aviation training and maintenance, which meant that essential needs of a naval air force did not receive priority.[2]

In December 1940, Congressman Melvin J. Maas of Minnesota and Capt. Marc A. Mitscher spent two weeks touring the Navy's shore aviation training facilities as a subcommittee of the Naval Affairs Committee. Maas reported back to the chairman, Congressman Carl Vinson of Georgia, that the majority of the enlisted barracks and facilities were unsatisfactory. Both Maas and Mitscher believed that the procedure of requiring "administration of personnel and assignment and general policy" to be cleared through nonaviator district commandants was the main reason for such poor conditions. They recommended administrative duties be placed under the cognizance of BuAer instead of the commandants.[3]

Little was done, however, to remedy this situation over the following year. As a result, BuAer's Technical Training Division was eventually overwhelmed with the demands of numerous schools spread out over multiple locations. Wheelock observed in late 1941 into early 1942 what Maas and Mitscher had noticed a year earlier—the inadequacies of assigning management of aviation operations at the training sites to the district commandants. He noted, in particular, that the allocation of appropriate funding for the trade schools was in competition with the other training and shore-based activities, which were not necessarily aviation related. Wheelock suggested that in order for the technical training to run more efficiently, a separate command should be established. An autonomous command could operate the technical schools independently from the district commandants, thus relieving them from the administrative headache of managing both the naval base facilities and technical aviation schools. Wheelock's plan would also centralize the command authority of the technical trade schools. Wheelock believed that a single unified authority could better manage the technical education across the geographical and bureaucratic jurisdictions than asking the various commandants to respond to BuAer and BuPers' training requirements.

On September 11, 1942, the Secretary of the Navy issued a letter establishing the Naval Air Technical Training Command (NATTC) as its own authority, directly under the Secretary of the Navy. NATTC did not fall under the jurisdiction of BuAer or BuPers, but was chartered to work in conjunction with the two bureaus. By November, BuAer transferred all but four personnel from the Training Division of its Technical Training Section to NATTC. Wheelock, recently promoted to full commander, remained behind with three others to function in a liaison capacity between BuAer and NATTC. At this time, the BuAer Technical Training staff had developed into a robust group of professionals developing training films, curricula, and technical manuals. But, the task of disseminating these materials throughout the various trade schools was a significant administrative burden for BuAer. Thus, transferring this responsibility along with the outgoing Training Section made the most sense.

Wheelock's Training Division had become well versed in negotiating the bureaucratic maze of the Navy Department. A significant part of their job had been to formulate accurate estimates that would ensure that the proper amount of funding for aviation technical training was requested in the annual BuAer budget. To his credit, Wheelock had become accustomed to the consistent fiscal requirements that accompanied facility maintenance and daily operations at the trade schools, as well as the significant costs of providing training materials such as books, films, and aircraft models.[4] This administrative skill set was extremely valuable, and would undoubtedly serve the newly formed technical training command.

With the establishment of NATTC, Wheelock was made the primary liaison between BuAer and the NATTC. This was a good decision for Wheelock's fiscal sense and administrative expertise made him an invaluable asset to both commands. His role as liaison limited the burden on the NATTC staff in terms of budget requests and estimates. Wheelock immediately folded the financial needs of NATTC into BuAer's supplemental budget requests beginning Fiscal Year (FY) 1944, since inputs for FY 1943 had already been submitted by the time NATTC was established. Wheelock's actions allowed the NATTC staff to focus their efforts more on the immediate task of training and to avoid the distraction of budget estimates and matériel procurement.[5]

The Secretary of the Navy's letter, establishing the NATTC as a separate command, specifically stated that "within each naval district, all activities specifically and exclusively assigned to an Air Functional Training Command shall be excluded from the jurisdiction of the Commandant of the District."[6] The Chief of the Naval Aviation Technical Training Center (CNATTC) reported directly to the Vice Chief of Naval Operations (VCNO), not the chiefs of BuAer or BuPers.[7] This allowed NATTC to make its own decisions and run its own affairs on the bases where the trade schools were housed. As shown in Table 4.1, the enlisted technical schools were located throughout the country, spread out over ten states. The logistical challenge of trying to communicate individually with each district commandant was an unnecessary burden for BuAer's Training Division. Consolidating administrative control under a single central authority helped to ease that burden.

Fortunately, the schools were already established and NATTC only became responsible for taking over where BuAer had left off. However, in doing so, NATTC had to accept full responsibility of all technical training. This included more than just the enlisted schools. Officer technical training also fell under NATTC's responsibility, which in itself was no small logistical task either. Note in Table 4.2, that officer schools were also dispersed throughout the country.

Whether training was conducted at public universities, private colleges, manufacturers' plants, commercial airline schools, or Civil Aviation Administration (CAA) schools, it all fell under the responsibility of NATTC. The administrative burden placed upon the newly established command was colossal, and it would take someone with exceptional management ability and substantial aviation experience, to lead the Navy's aviation technical community through uncharted waters.

✦✦✦

Table 4.1. Enlisted Technical Schools as of September 1942[1]

ENLISTED SCHOOLS	LOCATION	LOCATION	LOCATION	LOCATION	LOCATION	LOCATION
Naval Training School (Aviation Maintenance)	Jacksonville, FL	Navy Pier, Chicago, IL	87th and Anthony St., Chicago, IL	Memphis, TN	Norman, OK	Dearborn, MI
Naval Training School (Advanced Aviation Maintenance)	87th and Anthony St., Chicago, IL					
Parachute Material School	Lakehurst, NJ	San Diego, CA	Corpus Christi, TX			
Bombsight Maintenance School	Dahlgren, VA	San Diego, CA	Jacksonville, FL	Norden Factory, New York, NY		
Aerographers' School	Lakehurst, NJ					
Photographers' School	Pensacola, FL					
Instrument Schools	87th and Anthony St., Chicago	Sperry Gyroscope Company, Brooklyn, NY	Sperry Gyroscope Company, El Segundo, CA			
Link Trainer Schools	Pensacola, FL	Naval Reserve Aviation Base, Atlanta, GA				
Aviation Radar School	Ward Island, TX					

[1] Haley, "Historical Report of the Technical Training Section through December 1943," 16–17.

Table 4.2. Officer Technical Schools, September 1942[1]

OFFICER SCHOOLS	LOCATION
Indoctrination	NAS Quonset Pt., RI
Indoctrination & Photography	NAS Pensacola, FL
Teacher's Training Center	Chicago, IL
Air Combat Intelligence School	NAS Quonset Pt., RI
Air Operations School	NAS San Diego, CA; NAS Norfolk, VA
Fighter Direction School	Naval Base Norfolk, VA
Gunnery Officers' School	NAS Jacksonville, FL
Engineering Officer's School	Pratt & Whitney Company, East Hartford, CT

[1] Haley, 17.

Rear Adm. Albert Cushing Read was chosen as NATTC's first chief. Read and Towers had a relationship that dated back to two decades. Read was the famed commander of seaplane NC-4 in 1919 that completed the first transatlantic crossing by air. Towers had been the overall commander of the operation, which consisted of four total aircraft, but Read's plane was the only one to complete the flight by air. Read's career was fairly ordinary throughout the interwar years, but his long-standing relationship with Towers most likely had some influence on his selection as the first chief of NATTC.[8]

Administratively, the greatest impact that NATTC's creation had was on the financial arrangement between the Department of the Navy, BuAer, and BuPers. Prior to January 1, 1943, all funding for the operation and maintenance of aviation training schools had been funneled through the district commandants. After 1942, BuAer and BuPers no longer had to compete with the naval districts for funding. Now Read, from his headquarters in Chicago, could appropriate his monthly and yearly funds when and where it was needed most. NATTC funding was allocated from both BuAer and BuPers budgets, based on the requisite monthly estimates.[9]

In order to differentiate which funds came from which budget, the Secretary of the Navy's instruction provided that any technical training activities that were geographically located on a naval air station were to be funded by BuAer funds, designated from the congressional appropriation "Aviation Navy." All other funding for technical aviation training activities not specifically located on a naval air station were provided in the "Instruction Navy" designation within the BuPers budget. This new method of administering finances for training purposes was a centralized partnership between the two bureaus. It placed the budgetary structure of NATTC on a well-defined and stable administrative footing. Training budgets had been a part of the Navy since its inception. It was not until 1943 however, that the problem of distinguishing between technical aviation naval training and technical surface naval training became a concern. The potential for misadventure was enormous when two different bureaucratic entities were responsible for various aspects of a single form of training. Yet thanks to Wheelock and others who appreciated the importance of understanding *who pays, how much, and why*, the Navy took an innovative step in the right direction when it came to aviation technical training in World War II.[10]

Once NATTC had full cognizance of the technical training program, changes followed. One of Read's first actions was to eliminate the civilian Teacher Training Program which had already had its funding cut back by Congress in 1942. The program, a partnership with the U.S. Department of Education that trained civilians to be instructors at the aviation technical schools, was a financial burden on the Navy. It had also caused a rift between civilian and active duty instructors over pay rates; civilians were paid more than their enlisted equals. Read wasted no time in formally requesting the program's discontinuation. As the approving authority, BuPers had to agree and make the formal decision to terminate the program. By January 1, 1943, the facilities in Chicago that housed the program were emptied of civilian instructors and were opened up to additional classes for advanced technical training.[11]

The period that followed NATTC's installment as an individual command brought with it changes in the structure of the technical training program for the aviation navy. Within six months of operating as an independent command, NATTC reorganized the numerous schools into four different groups based on who made decisions with regards to training matters. Group I centers were designated a separate command with its commanding officer directly under the chief of NATTC. Group

II centers were also a separate command, but were located within the physical limits of a larger naval establishment, what could be considered a "tenant command."

Tenant commands were essentially a command within a command. It was usually a smaller unit that had its own administrative structure to include a commanding officer, responsible to another senior officer located in another geographic location. For example, Group II commanding officers had to follow the local regulations and orders that the naval base commander had promulgated, but in terms of technical training, graduation rates, or specific training issues, they would report directly to Admiral Read, chief of NATTC.

Group III schools were not considered "commands," but as their title suggests, they were viewed as schools. These schools were located on a base or other establishment that did not possess any other NATTC facilities. The military commander of such an establishment had authority over military matters while CNATTC had charge over all training matters. An officer in charge (OIC) was in place locally as CNATTC's direct administrative representative at each Group III school. Similar to Group III, Group IV schools were small, specialized training schools or factories located at other-than-Navy facilities, such as U.S. Army bases. CNATTC still had oversight of all training matters through an OIC.[12]

The change in schooling was a major accomplishment. By 1944, NATTC had consolidated most of the technical training schools for enlisted personnel—primarily Group I and II activities—into six geographic locations. Class A schools were designed to give basic training to sailors in the first round of schooling and prepare them to carry out the duties of a petty officer third class. Class B schools consisted of more advanced training and were designed to prepare technicians for higher petty officer rankings. Class C schools only trained technicians on unique subjects or skills, omitting the full requirements for advancement like the other schools taught. "C1" denoted that the school was located at a Naval establishment, whereas "C2" signified that the school was part of a manufacturing plant facility.[13] Class P schools provided follow-on training at the basic or preparatory level. Figures 4.1 and 4.2 illustrate each separate category of activity and which schools were characterized under its classification.

Figure 4.1. Group I NATTC Activities [1]

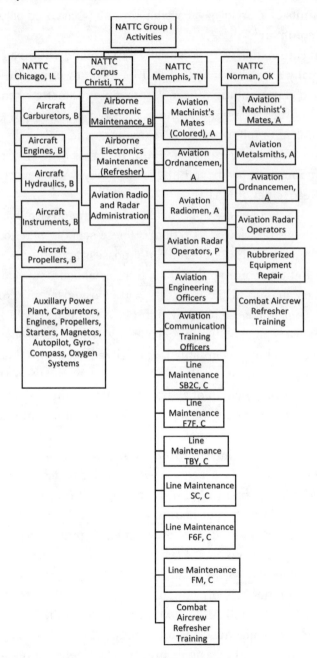

[1] "Organizational Chart of Naval Air Technical Training Command," December 15, 1944, WWII Aviation Training, Box 68, NHHC.

Figure 4.2. Group II NATTC Activities [1]

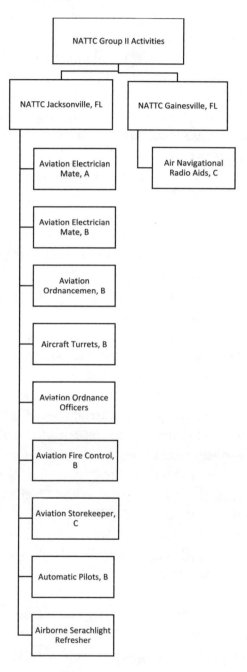

[1] "Organizational Chart of Naval Air Technical Training Command."

Group III NATTC activities consisted of schools that were focused more on supporting aircraft flight operations than on aircraft maintenance. Schools for aerographers, parachute riggers, control tower operators, and photographers were included in Group III. There were a few other technical schools lumped in with the others such as a segregated Class A Aviation Metalsmith School at Great Lakes Naval Training Center designated for African American sailors only, and a Turbo-Supercharger Regulator Course at the Naval Air Station in Minneapolis, Minnesota. Slightly fewer than twenty Group III schools were operating in 1944. They were generally either Class A or C1 in design, if they were designated at all.[14]

NATTC Group IV activities varied in location and subject. Figure 4.4 is a depiction of Group IV activities that were in existence by the end of 1944. At this point, NATTC operations were well-established and consistent with BuAer's previous emphasis that both commercial and public facilities be utilized to provide specialized training for aviation technicians. Prior to World War II, there were more than one hundred of these specialized manufacturer schools in existence. After NATTC was established in 1942, the number of these schools decreased as the Navy-operated schools became the mainstay of technical education. However, it was still routine throughout the war that technicians with the potential to be billeted into a teaching role either at a technical school or in the fleet would be sent to these manufacturer-operated schools.

Training the enlisted technician was the primary factor when it came to figuring out training requirements. However, in order for the maintenance divisions to run smoothly, the officers in charge had to be well versed in aircraft maintenance as well. Aviation Engineering Officers' School operated as a subset of the AMM school at NATTC Memphis. Most of the schools' graduates were assigned billets with aviation repair facilities such as CASUs.

Students were trained in general overall knowledge of combat aircraft such as the F4F, F6F, TBM, and SB2C. The course length was twelve weeks. Every week a new group of 25 officers began their course of study. The average enrollment at one time was about 120 officers. Students were given four hours of practical, hands-on shop work and three hours of lecture each day. Also included in their routine was three hours of physical

Figure 4.3. Group III NATTC Activities [1]

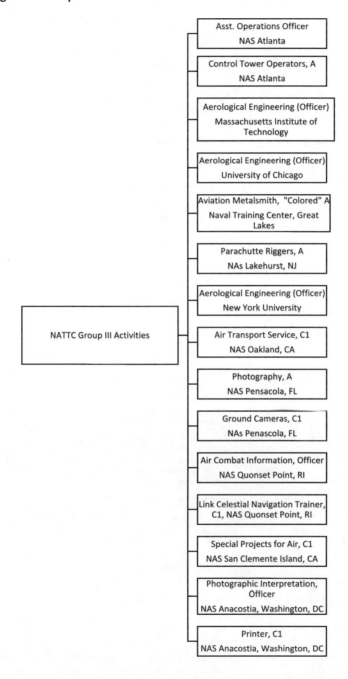

[1] "Organizational Chart of Naval Air Technical Training Command."

Figure 4.4. NATTC Group IV Activities as of December 15, 1944 [1]

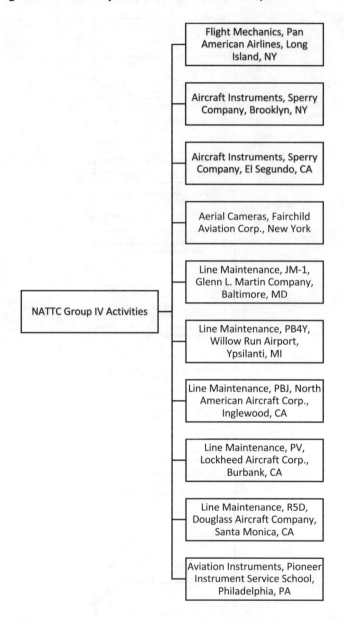

[1] "Organizational Chart of Naval Air Technical Training Command." All aircraft listed were flown by the U.S. Army Air Forces under a different designation: JM-1 was also known as a B-26, a PB4Y was designated a B-24 in the AAF, the PBJ was a B-25, and an R5D corresponded to a C-54. Thus, it can be assumed that manufacturer training schools supported the Army technicians as well. For a complete list of aircraft that were flown by both the Army and Navy, see DCNO (Air) World War II Administrative History, Volume 22, "Aviation Personnel, 1939–1945," Appendix A.

fitness per week and three hours of familiarization in radio, ordnance, gunnery, and enemy recognition. Classes were in session six days a week.

The officers were given no special treatment while at the school. They dressed in dungarees and coveralls just like their enlisted counterparts and were taught by enlisted instructors. Entrance to the school was awarded to both veteran officers from the fleet and new officers on their first service assignment. Some were prior maintenance officers and some were even pilots who had been assigned to nonflying billets.

Throughout the period of instruction, each week constituted a new phase: structures, metal work, electrical, hydraulics, engine familiarization, propellers and instruments, fuel and oil systems, accessories, ignition, trouble shooting, engine changes, and squadron operations. A student received hands-on training in everything from tire changes to engine changes. At the end of the course, in order to graduate, the officer even had to qualify as a "taxi pilot" so he has a working knowledge of how to maneuver the airplane around the tarmac or flight deck as did the plane captains and other enlisted technicians.[15]

✦✦✦

BuAer Training Section's reformation of technical training schools under Wheelock, and ultimately NATTC, was successful. But what good were school houses without curricula? The experience and knowledge in authoring technical aviation instruction books that Lt. Cdr. Daniel J. Brimm brought with him was just what BuAer needed to remedy the problem. Prior to 1941, there were only three small booklets supplying all the technical knowledge an aspiring aviation machinist's mate was expected to know before joining the fleet forces.[16] There was also the *Bureau of Aeronautics Manual* published every year that contained a few sections on maintenance. The 1940 edition contained the many technical chapters with general instructions on routine upkeep, repair, and inspections. However, it was not specific to any one aircraft.

The older material was written in such a way to suit a broad audience without getting too far into the details of maintenance procedures that varied between aircraft type. For example, in the nineteen-page "Propellers" section located within the "Miscellaneous Equipment" chapter, there is one page on repairs, one on corrosion, one on pitch settings, and two pages on balancing. Other subsections include hubs, service settings, inspection, and a few paragraphs on how to substitute a different model propeller when the original manufactured equipment was not available. The section ends with a paragraph stating that manufacturer manuals were the primary source of information, "The Bureau intends that the service make full use of information and instructions contained in propeller manufacturers' manuals . . . and that the instructions contained therein relative to inspections, operation, and maintenance of propellers be observed in all cases."[17] Other chapters within the manual discuss maintenance and operating instructions of power plants (engines), general operating maintenance, aircraft instruments, radios, electrical equipment, repair and overhaul, aircraft markings, and storage. The 1940 manual also contains a nine-page discussion on supply, stores, and transfer of parts along with a general description of BuAer publications and standard reporting and record keeping procedures.[18]

As Brimm settled into his job at BuAer, four new texts were quickly published for naval aviation technicians, two for aviation metalsmiths and two for aviation ordnancemen. The seven text books BuAer now had on hand from which to train its three primary enlisted aviation ratings was an improvement, but still insufficient to properly train the swelling numbers of young, inexperienced sailors en route to the trade schools. Brimm and others took note of this. More data was compiled and additional staff were brought on to assist in the development of new texts throughout 1942. Eventually, a combined officer-enlisted staff of forty was fully engaged in producing new training curricula for naval aviation technicians. By mid-1943, the textual material consisted of 14,850 pages, equating to forty-three new training manuals. NATTC had assumed responsibility for accumulating this material once the new command was established ten months prior. Most of the BuAer staff who began working on this project were placed in the NATTC organization at that time and more were added as the command matured.[19]

When the final drafts of the texts were submitted to BuAer for review and approval, it was apparent that the task was much greater than BuAer could handle with its current staff. Thus, BuPers was brought alongside for assistance. As designed, BuPers had ultimate authority over all naval training courses and material, but had delegated the aviation side of that to BuAer since the 1920s. BuPers already had billets for a director of standards and curriculum and an OIC of the Training Courses subunit, therefore the bureau had experience and the capacity to manage this task. Nimitz had moved on from BuPers to run the war in the Pacific and Rear Adm. John S. McCain replaced Towers. More than likely, the prior tension between the two bureaus had transferred to the Pacific Fleet Command Headquarters in Pearl Harbor, Hawaii where Nimitz was fleet commander. Towers was given a third star and assigned as commander, Pacific Fleet Air Forces (COMAIRPAC) under Nimitz. BuPers agreed to BuAer's request, but requested that NATTC be intimately involved in the process as a technical advisory or consultant role.[20]

The subject material and intent of these forty-three manuals deviated radically from what the Navy had been producing. In the past, enlisted textbooks were published for the sailor trying to "make rate," that is, advance in rank to petty officer or higher. The older text focused on more general concepts and theories, similar to the setup of the Bureau of Aeronautics Manual. Brimm and the others moved away from this to a format that more closely resembled a subject manual for a particular part of an airplane system. The shift from rating books to single subject manuals allowed for easier revisions, a far more comprehensive discussion of the main topic, and created a more specialized labor force better suited to the newer technology emerging in naval aviation.[21] For example, the 1945 edition of *Aircraft Metal Work* contained eight chapters: "Metal Processes," "Forming Aluminum," "Riveting," "Fasteners," "Structural Repairs," "Tanks," "Tubing," and "Plastics."[22] Another example of how detailed the training manuals had become was the *Aircraft Propellers* textbook. Its chapters consisted of: "Background for Propellers," "Two-Position Controllable-Pitch Propeller," "Constant-Speed Propeller," "Hydromatic Quick-Feathering Propeller," "Electric Propeller," and "Troubleshooting."[23] The drastic differences between what was available for study in 1940 and just five years later is indicative of the fundamental changes in the Navy's overall philosophy of technical education and training.

In short, those pursuing their aviation ratings no longer had merely a single text from which to learn. The new design allowed for multiple shorter manuals that sailors could study in relationship with each other, but also independently, if focusing on a specific system. The books were also much smaller in physical size so that they could be carried around in one's hip pocket for quick reference on the job or during leisure time. The type was easy to read and the material was written for the technician, not the engineering scholar. Drawings, diagrams, and pictures were a mainstay throughout the manuals. Paragraphs were no longer numbered, but given titles. Standard grammar rules were applied throughout. When emphasis was needed, uppercase was substituted instead of italics. Illustrations with commentary were heavily used. The reader was addressed directly in the second person singular, making studying a more relatable experience. Historical and patriotic anecdotes were woven throughout in hopes of generating a sense of pride about one's chosen rating and justifying the challenging study undertaken. Naval aviation rating manuals adopted a more popular tone in 1943, abandoning the academic texts that had been prevalent in technical studies until then.[24]

Until the very end of the war, about a year after the Fast Carriers had begun to make their impact on the outcome, most, if not all, technical textbooks were designated "restricted" in their distribution category. Of course, the Navy did not want its manuals and teaching material to fall into enemy hands. However, when the threat of espionage within the naval aviation maintenance program became a minimal threat, and a shorter "time to train" factor weighed more heavily on leadership decision-making, NATTC removed the "restricted" status from all of the aviation training course textbooks.

Once the texts became unclassified, recruits and sailors in the pipeline to attend technical schools were given access to their academic material before the first day of classes. Any sailors assigned to schools, or simply wanted to learn more about aircraft systems, could buy their respective textbooks directly from the government. As of June 1945, BuAer was actively advertising in *Naval Aviation News* that "books can be bought by a Navy technician who sends a small sum to Superintendent of Documents, Government Printing Office, Washington, D.C." Further, "ship's stores are even starting to stock them," and "now the technical trainee can buy the entire library."[25] Considering the amount of material technicians were responsible for, it made sense for NATTC to provide the resources for sailors to increase their knowledge base on their own.

The formula of waiting until showing up at A, B, or C schools to become familiar with their prospective systems was dated and made little sense when the technology to print and distribute ahead of their arrival was available. An incoming student with a working knowledge of the subject to be taught will usually progress through the syllabus faster than one who has none.

Naval warfare communities other than aviation began to take notice of the new aviation rating subject manuals. Slowly, the rating manuals for nonaviation specialties began to adopt the style of what NATTC had done with its training manuals. In January 1944, BuPers recommended a complete overhaul of course material for established nonaviation rates. The OIC of the Standards and Curriculum Section within BuPers would have cognizance over the project. The old way of doing things was not easily overcome, as the various grades within certain rates such as machinist's mate had increased from four to twenty. The cost and workload of creating a separate subject manual for each grade was unrealistic in BuPers' mind. A compromise was reached in June between the progressives and old guard within the BuPers Training Unit. Rather than reproduce exhaustive amounts of repetitive material in the broader fields like machinist's mates, BuPers produced a series of five general manuals: *Basic Machines, Basic Electricity, Mathematics, Use of Tools,* and *Use of Blueprints*. These texts were based on similar volumes prepared for the aviation ratings. But in order to avoid the massive numbers of smaller separate manuals like that of the aviation community, the five texts aimed to provide a broader background of the subject matter, suitable for all rates. The popular, less academic tone of the verbiage suited young sailors looking to promote to petty officer.[26] Thanks to Brimm, Wheelock, and the staff of NATTC, the textual material of the entire naval technical training program was designed to reach even the least educated new recruit. This, in itself, was a revolution in technical education that translated into new methods of civilian technical training after World War II.

✦✦✦

While NATTC was administering the classroom-side of naval aviation technical training, Wheelock's Technical Training Section in BuAer was overseeing the remarkable expansion of duties required of the aviation machinist's mate and aviation ordnanceman ratings. The technological advances in aircraft led to increasingly complex maintenance. AMMs were required to work on much more than just engines. Hydraulics, instruments, carburetors, and other accessories all fell into their area of responsibility. AOs were charged with maintaining bombsights, bomb racks, delivery mechanisms, turrets, along with guns and the ordnance itself. Wheelock's section identified the problem that such specialized tasks were being farmed out to technicians with the most acumen in those subject areas on a regular basis, thus keeping them from maintaining proficiency in other areas of the rating. For example, if a particular sailor had an uncanny ability for fixing carburetors, that became his primary job. By default, he or she became a specialist within the rate, but suffered when it came time to compete for promotion against other nonspecialized AMMs, because the broad range of questions on the advancement exams favored those with general experience over specialists. Conversely, if a certain sailor had been sent to specialized training at a Group III or IV center, and was not utilized in such a way to keep those skills proficient, the specialized training was often forgotten and wasted.[27]

BuAer's Technical Training Section identified these problems and suggested a remedy on July 17, 1943. Wheelock's team acknowledged the need for such specialists in the naval aviation organization and proposed identifying or earmarking such specialists, so they were assigned to squadron or ship duties that coincided with their designated skill set. The Technical Training Section also recommended that the new ratings system recognize those with specialized training. New, specific ratings such as aviation hydraulicman, aviation bombsight mechanic, aviation instrumentman, and others were up for discussion. The proposal was accepted by the chief of BuAer and forwarded to BuPers for endorsement before going to the Secretary of the Navy for final approval. On September 27, 1943, BuPers forwarded a revised rating structure that they had developed with BuAer.[28] The revised ratings are detailed in Table 4.3.

The changes in rating classifications helped solve the problem of wasted training and improperly trained aviation technicians. The expansion of ratings permitted commanding officers, OICs, and supervisors to gain a better understanding of each technician's particular skill set. The tendency to underutilize a sailor with specialty training became less

Table 4.3. Sample SECNAV Approved Additional Ratings, September 28, 1943[1]

Aviation carburetor mechanic (AMMC)	Aviation flight engineer (AMMF)
Aviation hydraulic mechanic (AMMH)	Aviation turret mechanic (AOMT)
Aviation instrument mechanic (AMMI)	Aviation storekeeper (SKV)
Aviation propeller mechanic (AMMP)	Aircraft painter (PTRV)
Aviation bombsight mechanic (AOMB)	Aircraft torpedoman (TMV)

[1] Haley, 26. The proposed ratings were approved by SECNAV on September 28, 1943, but not officially adopted by BuPers into the personnel system until December 1943.

frequent once he was identified within the rating structure.[29] These rating changes signaled that the Navy was beginning to value the concept of specialization of labor within the aviation maintenance workforce.

In order to appreciate the drastic changes that the enlisted ranks of the aviation community underwent with regards to ratings over the course of the war, Table 4.4 lists all approved aviation ratings on December 7, 1941, and September 14, 1945.

In addition to the technical schooling, some naval aircraft technicians desired to see aerial combat firsthand, rather than just from the deck of the carrier. Those sailors who expressed an interest in flying as a naval aircrewman were given ample opportunities to earn the qualification in addition to their technical rating. Obtaining the qualification of aircrewman provided them an opportunity to fly as an aerial gunner, radioman, or both. During enlistment, if interested, a recruit would indicate so. The training pipeline was extensive, taking on average nine months from start to finish before a sailor was qualified to fly in the gunner's seat of a naval aircraft.

Beginning with boot camp, a typical enlisted technician desiring to serve as an aircrewman in addition to his technical rating attended an additional four to five months of gunnery and flight training. Upon achieving designation as an aviation technician rating (usually radioman, ordnanceman, or machinist's mate) from a trade school, the technician was transferred to air gunner's school at one of three locations: Yellow Water or Hollywood (both in Florida), or Purcell, Oklahoma. Here, aerial gunner's candidates were trained in the various aspects of what an

Table 4.4. SECNAV Approved Aviation Ratings, 1941 and 1945[1]

DECEMBER 7, 1941	SEPTEMBER 14, 1945
Aviation machinist's mate	Aviation machinist's mate
Aviation metalsmith	Aviation machinist's mate C (carburetor mechanic)
Aviation ordnanceman	Aviation machinist's mate F (flight mechanic)
Aerographer	Aviation machinist's mate H (hydraulic mechanic)
Photographer	Aviation machinist's mate I (instrument mechanic)
	Aviation machinist's mate P (propeller mechanic)
	Aviation machinist's mate T (gas turbines)
	Aviation electrician's mate
	Aviation radioman
	Aviation radio mechnician
	Aviation metalsmith
	Aviation ordnanceman
	Aviation fire controlman
	Aviation ordnanceman T (turret mechanic)
	Airship rigger
	Aerographer's mate
	Photographer's mate
	Torpedoman's mate V (aviation)
	Painter V (aviation)
	Storekeeper V (aviation)
	Aviation boatswain's mate AG (arresting gear)
	Aviation boatswain's mate CP (catapult)
	Aviation boatswain's mate GA (gasoline stowage)
	Aviation boatswain's mate PH (plane handling)

[1] Bureau of Naval Personnel, "Enlisted Personnel Distribution," in *United States Naval Administration in World War II* (Washington, DC: U.S. Government Printing Office, 1959), Appendix A and B.

aircrewman was required to do while flying in addition to attempting to shoot down enemy airplanes. Aircrew gunners were often required to handle communications while the pilots concentrated on flying. Students were instructed in semaphore signaling, and in-flight communications via telegraph. They also received a brief course of instruction in aircraft flight familiarization. Gunnery instruction was conducted separately.

Aircrew gunners were trained in basic marksmanship beginning with shotgun firing at clay pigeons and progressing to .50 caliber. Learning to fire from turrets, bucket seats, and swivel mounts was also part of the training. Successfully hitting rapidly moving targets from multiple angles and distances was also an integral part of the training. Another challenge was range estimation opposing aircraft. Using the naked eye to estimate the range of the enemy aircraft is a learned skill just as repairing engines and operating radios was. Students were taught how to estimate the distance between themselves and the enemy by positioning themselves in the path of oncoming aircraft and practicing sighting and simulating firing at the optimal distance. They were taught the complete mechanics of the aerial weapons used in combat, which included completely disassembling and reassembling .50-, .30-, and .20-caliber weapons. The entire course of gunnery instruction was completed in an average of eight weeks, after which they were assigned to an operational squadron for approximately another two months where they learned how to integrate themselves into the crew. While attached to a squadron, students flew in identical models of airplanes that they would fly in combat. Understanding the aircraft systems, how gunnery felt in the air, its idiosyncrasies, and capabilities all occurred at this stage of training. Pilots and the aircrewmen learned how to work together in the safer, less stressful environment, before testing their compatibility while fighting a Japanese Zero.

At the end of the training, pilots and aircrewmen were fully integrated as a combat team. In recognition of their new skill set, Aircrewmen were awarded a set of silver wings to wear on their chest, a promotion to third class petty officer in their rating, and began drawing 50 percent of what pilots received in extra flight pay. There is no doubt that winning the air war was due to the fast carriers, their aircraft, and their pilots. But as this monograph has argued, the role of the technician was not something relegated to the carrier deck or shore station repair. Technicians who qualified as aircrewman were on the front lines of the air war, engaging enemy aircraft with weapons and airplanes that they were responsible for maintaining on a daily basis.[30]

✦✦✦

BuAer and NATTC also took the lead in establishing opportunities for women in the Navy. The aviation side of Women Accepted for Volunteer Emergency Service (WAVES) was especially successful in supplementing the Navy's technical aviation labor requirements. The WAVES Program was authorized on July 30, 1942. When the first director of the WAVES program, Lt. Cdr. Mildred McAfee, reported to the chief of BuAer in September to discuss the role of WAVES in BuAer, Towers—ever the proponent of having women in active military service—bellowed, "Where have you been all this time? We've been clamoring for these WAVES and nobody's ever listened to us." BuAer had requested 20,326 WAVES at the outset of the program. This was twice the number BuPers had requested and the largest amount of any Navy bureau. BuAer's plans for utilizing WAVES eventually encompassed over 12,000 officers and 75,000 enlisted women. Initially, WAVES' duties involved clerical and administrative work, but soon the demands for skilled aviation technicians overcame reluctance to abrogate the established boundaries of gendered discrimination in work roles.[31]

Even so, gender did have its limitations. In 1943 however, these limitations did not seem as outrageous as they would be soon. The Navy's official position on WAVES' job limitations was straightforward—she could hold any technical job that a man could, with two exceptions: she was restricted to a billet within the continental United States, she could not exercise any military authority over men.[32]

Enlisted WAVES who were selected for aviation ratings attended trade schools like any other sailor. Aviation metalsmiths and machinist's mates were sent to Norman or Memphis for Class A school. A five- to six-month period of schooling was the norm. While in school, they received the same instruction men did. AMs were taught how to weld, forge, and braze. Bending and joining pipes were taught alongside basic theories of flight. Machinist's mates learned how to operate all machining tools that were commonly used in A&R shops, how to overhaul an engine on various aircraft types, and assembly of aircraft and their parts such as wings and fuselage.[33]

In addition to aircraft maintenance-specific jobs, many aviation WAVES were assigned jobs as parachute riggers, aerographer's mates, control tower operators, and Link Trainer (flight simulator) operators. Incoming WAVES with prior flight experience were often director to Link Trainers or control tower operations. WAVES striking to become Link Trainer operators were given schooling at NAS Atlanta on all aspects of the $10,000 devices—maintenance, assembly, and radio aids to navigation were part of the course. Over the ten-week course, WAVES were also given schooling in flight characteristics of the simulators, the effects of weather on flying, and flight regulations. Those that were intended to serve as control tower operators were given instruction at NAS Atlanta as well, although only over an eight-week course of instruction. A WAVE striking to qualify as a control tower operator learned the nuances of voice procedures, operation of radio equipment, radio navigation, and interpretation of weather reports. Control tower courses were taught at various locations, Atlanta and Jacksonville being the two primary training schools.[34]

The parachute riggers and aerographers attended school at NAS Lakehurst, New Jersey. Aerographers WAVES learned meteorological principles and theory, forecasting, and how to take accurate weather observations. Mastering the intricacies and capabilities of the sewing machine to make repairs to inflatable flotation equipment and flight clothing were part of the initial skill set taught to WAVE parachute riggers. The male instructors were surprised by the number of incoming WAVES who had little or no experience with a sewing machine.[35]

Gladys Marsheck Echols of Dundalk, Maryland, was a member of the first class of enlisted WAVES to complete the course at the Aviation Machinist's Mate A School in Memphis, Tennessee, at the end of 1942. Echols was a member of the first class of WAVES to attend aviation technical training. She recalled being given an option to attend Yeoman School and learn the administrative trade that would place her in the office environment for the duration of the war or attend a technical school. She had stenography skills from her previous job working for a local lawyer, but grew up as the daughter of a filling station and auto repair shop owner in East Baltimore; she knew her way around a mechanic's shop and how to handle tools. According to Echols' recollection, this was the primary reason she was selected for aviation machinist's mate rating upon graduation from boot camp. The other reason was the fact that she was tired of all the typing she had done at her stenographer's job and wanted to do something different in the Navy than what she had done as a civilian.[36]

The Aviation Machinist's Mate A School for WAVES was six months from start to finish, the same length for the male students. She was one of 144 WAVES assigned to Naval Training Center Memphis, which was a relatively small, but a significant number considering women had never had such an opportunity before. Even in the midst of the other 14,000 male students undergoing A-school training at the time, Echols' memories of the training were positive. When asked about her experience she recounted,

> It was terrific! There were 144 women and 14,000 men. So there was no wanting for dates. But the school was very, very interesting. We learned mechanical drawing. We learned how to sew the fabrics of airplane repair, the covering of the planes the pilots trained in. We learned all about carburetors and starters and timing and all kinds of mechanical things. We went into the shops with the men at the different bases, and some went on the flight lines to the planes going in the morning. When you were through, you would be the equivalent of a garage mechanic today.[37]

After graduating in June 1943, Echols was assigned to the fabric shop of an Assembly and Repair facility in Pasco, Washington. Here, she and other WAVES worked on aircraft fabric (or skin) to cover the airframes of Stearman airplanes used for primary pilot flight training. Her experience was one of gender-based integration, recalling that she and the other WAVES were routinely trained and placed into the same work spaces as their male counterparts.[38] However, traditional views of gender roles still governed behavior.

When she first showed up at the A&R facility in Pasco, the fully trained WAVES were assigned to the fabric shop because there was an expectation that they had more experience sewing than the male technicians, as the domestic stereotype of women was still alive in 1942.[39] But this was not a demotion or an assignment unworthy of their training received in Memphis. Sewing aircraft fabric was a routine job for AMMs and had been done by male technicians since naval aviation began. However, according to Echols, there were traces of old attitudes about gender roles that were evident while working in the A&R facility. Whenever one of the male sailors tore or split his trousers, he would place them in the "to do" pile for the WAVES to sew. Echols and the other women accepted this as part of the job and there were no bad feelings between the men and women in the shop. Echols specifically recalled that while at Pasco, the WAVES were treated with more respect there than any of her previous assignments. "We were accepted there better than any place we'd been, by the men. They were just great to us at Pasco."[40]

Eventually Echols and the other WAVES moved on to different jobs within their ratings, as well as being transferred to other bases throughout the country. Her next assignment was to NAS Olathe, Kansas, where she was placed into the A&R shop again. But here she began to work on the assembly and disassembly of aircraft engines as part of the overhaul process. She finished out her career with the rating of aviation machinist's mate second class (AMM2) stationed at NAS Bunker Hill, Indiana.[41] There she was assigned to the flight line as a mechanic whose daily duties included starting the airplanes in the morning and conducting postflight inspections and maintenance at the end of the day. As the war drew to a close, she was discharged in October 1945, a few days short of three years active duty.[42]

In June 1943, *Naval Aviation Newsletter* published a story on the makeup and experience of a typical WAVE. A sample size of one hundred enlisted WAVES were examined: 70 percent entered with office work experience, 15 percent joined from the professional sector, and another 15 percent had manual labor experience. Those coming from the "professional" sector with office work experience were most likely stenographers, clerks, or telephone operators. The other 15 percent performed manual labor such as radio assembly workers, mechanics, or waitresses. Various other jobs filled out the list such as beautician, cartoonist, pharmacist, and "child attendant."

Regarding physical characteristics, according to the survey, the average WAVE was 22 years old, 65 inches tall, and weighed 124 pounds. Hair color was predominantly brown (75 percent). Considering the range of their physical features, most weighed between 105 and 129 pounds and stood between 5 feet, 3 inches and 5 feet, 7 inches. Nearly all WAVES were White. During the War, the Navy commissioned only two Black WAVE officers, and no more than 70 enlisted were women of color.[43] There is no evidence that the selection process focused on physical appearance.

WAVES joined a service that was built on customs, traditions, and most importantly regulations. The Navy instituted specific regulations for WAVES, as their gender offered challenges to the norm. The following are some excerpts of what BuAer's *Naval Aviation News* magazine highlighted in its characterization of the WAVES program and the Navy regulations in 1943:

- "WAVES do not relieve Civil Service employees or fill Civil Service jobs. Each WAVE is assigned a billet to release a man for duty afloat." WAVES were not intended to replace other government jobs other than those held by male naval personnel.

- "WAVES are restricted to service within the continental limits of the United States."[44] Overseas duty or duty on board ship was not authorized for women in the Navy. Although late in the war, a limited number of WAVES were assigned to shore duty stations outside of the continental United States.

- "Salutes are always rendered to senior naval personnel regardless of sex." Saluting a female was probably a challenge for some men, but in order to maintain good discipline and order, withholding a salute due to gender was not accepted. Rank was rank, no matter male or female.

- "If a WAVE officer is addressed by name, it is preceded by Miss or Mrs. She may also be addressed by her rank, not as Sir. An enlisted WAVE is addressed by either her last name or her rating." I am not sure why anyone would call a female officer "sir," but apparently it was worth noting.

- "Enlisted WAVES mess with enlisted men, WAVE officers mess with male officers." Maintaining a separation between enlisted and officer eating areas had been part of naval customs and tradition since the age of sail. With the new addition of women to the ranks, naval leadership felt it was necessary to reaffirm such a practice.

- "Except when in training, a WAVE may marry within a branch of service. Women already married to Navy personnel may not enter the same service." This one seems odd considering the number of military-to-military marriages today with the Navy and other services, but the possibility of favoritism within the ranks should a spouse of a sailor or officer enter the naval service could be complicated to "good order and discipline."

- "Women offenders should not ordinarily be sentenced to the brig of a naval station. Restriction to the confines of the naval station should be substituted or, if the offense is of an aggravated nature, the woman should be discharged from the Service." A brig (jail) full of male offenders was not a place for a young woman to be incarcerated. There were no "female brigs" available at the time.

- "A WAVE may be disciplined at a Captain's mast only after consultation with the Women's Reserve representative, who should be present or represented at the Captain's mast by a member of the Women's Reserve." When a member of the naval service is accused or admits to wrongdoing, he or she is normally sent to unit commander for a hearing and "trial" that results in nonjudicial punishment such as restriction or forfeiture of pay. This regulation ensured WAVES were fairly represented, counseled, and protected in the mast proceedings.

- "WAVES will stand night watches, but provision should be made for their transportation through undesirable sections to and from the office." Perhaps a nod to chivalry, but common sense would deem this necessary in some locations where the safety of a young woman traveling alone at night would be a risk.

- "Officers and enlisted personnel of opposite sexes are permitted to attend social functions together." While the WAVES were indeed part of the U.S. Navy, they were also a bit separate. Similar to the Nurse Corps, male officers could date enlisted WAVES, and it was not considered fraternization. Hence the acceptance that WAVES were still considered a separate service within the Navy all together.[45]

American women not only served in the Navy as aircraft technicians, but also in the United States Marine Corps. On February 13, 1943, membership in the Corps was extended to women as it was to all men, but with the exception of combat assignments or overseas duty. By 1944, more than 12,000 women were serving as "Women's Reserve" (WR) in the USMC—most filling aircraft technician duties.

After a six-week boot camp at Camp Lejeune, a group of approximately 500 new female Marines were sent off to numerous specialty schools. Over half of each graduating class was sent to various technical trade schools associated with aviation. In September 1943, there were already 8,500 women serving in the Marine Corps WR. Approximately 2,000 of those were assigned to aviation duties, while 800 were actively enrolled in Navy trade schools alongside their male counterparts. It was expected that more than half of all women Marines would be involved in aviation jobs by the following year as more aircraft and pilots were assigned to the Marine Corps.[46]

Mixing in with male students at the various NATTC schools, the WR personnel were fully trained in aviation maintenance. The graduates of the mechanical schools were assigned to shore-based air stations. It was at these duty stations that the WRs performed "first and second echelon" maintenance on airplanes and aircraft engines. Minor repairs and adjustments to lubricating, ignition, carburetion, fuel injection, power plants, and replacement of structural parts were all expected daily jobs for the WRs. While much of our historical account of women in uniform during World War II has been viewed from the numerous clerical jobs that were held by women serving in the naval services, the skilled labor of the WAVES and WRs was critical to the success of the Navy on station in both the Pacific and Atlantic theaters. While the role of a WR in 1944 might have been a far cry from Lucy Brewer's alleged position on board the *Constitution* during the War of 1812, it proved that aircraft maintenance was as open to any gender then as it is today.[47]

The American Navy and Marine Corps were not the only forces to employ women in the skilled labor jobs of aircraft technicians to supplement positions due to males being sent to sea duty. The Royal Navy had a similar program called the Women's Royal Naval Service (members were called "Wrens"). The British utilized Wrens to fill aircraft technician jobs that were vacated by male technicians who were needed on air capable ships. The British simply did not have enough male sailors to fill all the ranks ashore and at sea, so the Admiralty began the task of training Wrens to work on its naval aircraft.

As was customary of the time, women were not viewed equitably with men in terms of labor capabilities. Thus, the Royal Navy decided that for every ten men assigned to aircraft maintenance ashore, there needed to be twelve women placed in those positions to do the same job. More simply put, the British believed that a women's work output was four fifth's that of a man. An inequitable formula at best, but it was the case in Great Britain in 1944. Initially, selected Wrens were trained in one of four broad aeronautical categories: airframes (A), engines (E), electrician (L), and ordnance (O). The letters were assigned to their ranks as designators similar to the enlisted ratings of American technicians. As the aircraft and systems became more specialized and advanced during the war, the training became more specialized and new "ratings" were issued, such as air mechanic (electrical), air mechanic (engines), air mechanic (airframes), air mechanic (ordnance), radio mechanic, and air maintenance helper. The fleet air arm of the Admiralty provided the technical training to the women just as it did for the men. Initial instruction was broad based and general in terms of aircraft operations and basic systems. As the weeks continued, the Wrens were placed into specific subgroups where the training became more specialized.

Much like their U.S. Navy and Marine counterparts, Wrens were expected to be able to complete any repair or routine maintenance necessary. The schools taught airframe mechanics, the basics of riveting, heat treatment, and line splicing. They were also instructed in fabric repair, cable splicing, hydraulics, pneumatics, and metal repairs. Engine mechanics learned the finer details of chipping, drilling, screw and bolt tapping, and using spanners. They were also given additional practice working directly on combustion engines, carburetors, and different aircraft engines. Electricians were schooled in soldering, simple circuitry, ignition and harness circuits, and electrical bomb and torpedo release mechanisms. The ordnance technicians were tutored briefly in general aviation armament and then moved on to highly specialized training on every weapon the British aircraft could employ. They practiced their craft on retired aircraft and inert bombs while in school. Similar to students in U.S. Navy trade schools, graduates were given orders to various shore commands where their skills were put to use in either pilot training bases or maintenance depots.

In a break from the status quo for women's military service jobs at the time, Wrens did get the opportunity to serve overseas from the outset, but the numbers were relatively small. After graduation, there was one option for Wrens to work with naval aircraft located outside of the British Isles. Some were assigned to the fleet air arm at Roosevelt Field, Long Island, New York. They were entrusted to inspecting newly delivered American airplanes enroute to Royal Navy forces before being loaded on the Atlantic convoys. They acted in a "quality assurance" role, ensuring the newly manufactured airplanes were safe for British pilots to fly upon delivery. In a show of solidarity, a number of American women of English or Scottish descent enrolled in the ranks of the Wrens for service in the British fleet air arm serving in the United States.[48]

The experience of women aircraft technicians varied from woman to woman, rating to rating, and service to service. Yet overall it was a telling example of the progressive thinking that John Towers and other naval aviation leaders embraced during World War II. Contrary to the well-known story of "Rosie the Riveter," where women worked on the production line of aircraft and shipbuilding companies, the U.S. Navy, U.S. Marine Corps, and Royal Navy all gave women the opportunity to contribute to the war effort in a uniformed capacity. Working on the flight line, A&R facilities, or in squadron maintenance spaces, female technicians applied their skills alongside their male counterparts. BuAer's willingness to lead the way in placing women into NATTC's schools and then into shore-based operational commands is a noteworthy chapter in the latter part of the first WAVE of feminism.

While women had a breakthrough experience serving in the active-duty Navy, the Black community continued to struggle with racist attitudes of some. Blacks gained more opportunities as the war continued, but there was still limited progress in many areas for the Black sailor. Black men were permitted to openly serve in the Navy, but frontline combat or technical jobs were limited. Much like the WAVES, Black men were often assigned to shore-based commands when they were working in the technical ratings.

In 1943 Wilbert Walker was a young Black man who had grown up in Baltimore during a period of extreme racial disparity. Segregation had been the norm for him. In 1942 he graduated with 306 other young Black men and women from Baltimore City's Frederick Douglass High School. Douglass, located at the corner of Calhoun and Baker Streets, was the alma mater of notable personalities as jazz musician Cab Calloway and Supreme Court justice Thurgood Marshall. Yet however notable one's high school diploma was, a seventeen-year-old Black male in Baltimore still faced the racist policies of segregation within the workplace, and skilled-labor jobs were rare for minorities. However, since the world was now at war, opportunities arose and Walker took full advantage.[49]

As the aircraft industry increased its production in support of the war, labor supply at local aircraft factories was at a premium. Walker, still seventeen, secured a job with the Glen L. Martin Aircraft Company in Baltimore just four months after graduation due to a manpower shortage. Martin was under contract with the U.S. Army Air Forces to build the B-26 medium bomber. The company would eventually deliver 5,266 units by the end of its production run in 1945. Walker was assigned to a division located in the Canton neighborhood of Baltimore City. The other Black employees he apprenticed with as a metalsmith typically worked the 1600–2400 shift, having every eighth day off. Often he was required to work a "double," which kept him on the job for sixteen hours straight. In Canton, his primary job was fabricating engine nacelles for the B-26 bomber. When completed, the nacelles were transferred ten miles northeast of Baltimore City to Martin's Middle River, Maryland, facility where final aircraft assembly took place.[50]

After a year on the job with Martin (and now eighteen years of age), Walker received his draft notice. Simultaneously, he also received a notice of enrollment at Morgan State College in Baltimore. The draft took precedence and Walker was glad to defend his country as a member of the armed forces. Upon reporting for duty, he was asked which service he desired to serve in. At this time, the Navy had recently rescinded its policy of assigning Blacks exclusively to the steward's branch, and an opportunity for a skilled rating was open. Walker told the officer of his experience at Martin, thinking he would be a perfect candidate for aviation metalsmith in the Navy. His request was approved immediately and Walker's papers were stamped "NAVY."

After progressing through boot camp, Walker was assigned to the aviation component of the Navy based on his civilian work experience at Martin along with a small group of Black sailors with an acumen for technical work. Little did Walker and his classmates know that they would soon be the first class of Black sailors to attend a Class A service school (the Aviation Metalsmith School) at NAS Whiting Field, less than an hour's drive inland from Pensacola, Florida.[51]

By 1944, the Navy established a completely separate aviation machinist's mate school at NATTC Memphis. But prior to NATTC officially taking over the schooling program and establishing its Group I and II activities in 1943, Black sailors like Walker were sent to the same schooling locations as Whites. They were not permitted to take the classes alongside White sailors and were often given separate class periods. Depending on the rating, some schools integrated better than others.

When Walker reported for duty at Whiting Field, he and his cohorts expected to be given the opportunity to take the petty officer third class test for the AM rating. When they requested to sit for the examination, the personnel officer told them that the rating was frozen, meaning the Navy was not taking any more technicians into that rating, thus they were not given a chance to achieve a rank of petty officer. This was extremely disappointing, but Walker and his fellow Black sailors did not give up.

Shortly thereafter, one of the maintenance chiefs made his way through the maintenance shops and announced an aviation machinist's mate school was beginning classes and looking for students. Unable to qualify in his original field, Walker chose a lateral transfer to machinist's mate, where he could at least work on airplanes rather than just routinely service and position the airplanes used for pilot training. Working on the flight line as part of the "line crew" was boring to Walker, and very hot during the summer days.

Since the school was not integrated with the White students, the so-called colored students were offered classes at night, rather than routine daytime hours. Nevertheless, Walker and the other Black sailors jumped on the opportunity to learn a new trade, and get back to what they had joined the Navy to do—maintain and repair airplanes. "If I couldn't get a rating as an Aviation Metalsmith I was going to learn to be an aviation machinist's mate."[52] The school lasted approximately four weeks and classes ran from 1800 until 2200 every day except Sunday. Few other duties were assigned to the students while they were in school. Twenty-five men signed up for the initial class open to Blacks. By the end of the course, only three—including Walker—graduated.

Afterward, thinking that AMM was his final destination with regard to his rating in the Navy, Walker opted to take the written test for advancement to petty officer third class in the aviation machinist's mate rating. After the exam, he had much more free time off duty since classes were over and the need to study for the test had come and gone. One evening Walker chose to go to the base movie theater at NAS Pensacola and take in a film. Arriving a few minutes after the movie had begun, he opted to sit in the only seats available, which were not in the customarily "colored personnel rows." At this time, September 1944, the U.S. Navy was officially integrated, and there were no official regulations that ordered Blacks to use separate entrances and exits or seating areas. However, it was the accepted norm at NAS Pensacola that Blacks were not to mix with Whites in off-duty venues.[53]

A few minutes into the movie, Walker was approached by a White sailor and reminded that he was not seated in the "colored row" and should promptly move his chair down to the front of the theater. Walker verbally resisted, and within a few minutes, the master-at-arms (MA) entered the theater. The MA reiterated the point that Walker could either move his seat or leave the theater. Walker, recognizing that due to his small physical stature he would most likely fail in a physical confrontation with the rather sizable and formidable MA, departed without further resistance. Unfortunately, however, the altercation was far from over. Walker was charged with disobeying naval regulations and taken to captain's mast the following day. Walker knew the charges would not hold up because there were no official rules on where Black men and women could sit at the movies. Segregation did not have a place in the Navy's training commands—or so he thought.[54]

Upon reporting to the base commander for mast, Walker was ready to fight the charge. Fortunately, the commanding officer agreed with him that sitting where he did was not against regulations, but then reiterated that not following an order is a violation. The captain said to him, "Walker, there is no regulation which requires you to sit anywhere in the movies, but if you get out of hand you'll be dealt with."[55] According to Walker's account, the CO was insinuating that Blacks were still not on equal terms with Whites, at the movies or anywhere else on his base. The CO said that he was dropping the charges, but that he would be referring the incident to the Honor Board for further review. Walker suffered no adverse effects from his resistance—at least not initially.[56]

So while on the one hand, the U.S. Navy officially recognized itself as an integrated institution in 1944, in reality segregation was alive and well in nineteen-year-old Wilbert Walker's world. The Honor Board was typically a group of senior sailors who handled issues within the barracks, often consisting of Black sailors themselves. Among the younger troops, they were known as "Uncle Toms," often reporting any and all questionable actions to the squadron or base CO. Walker was never contacted by the CO or Honor Board after the incident, but troubled times were just around the corner for him.[57]

Back at his assigned squadron, he began to feel ostracized for standing up to the White master-at-arms and stirring things up on account of his skin color. Having committed a few minor infractions (for which he was more or less hung out to dry by his squadron mates), Walker was called in to see the squadron's commanding officer. "Walker, you had been doing good work here, but now it looks like you're looking for trouble," said the officer without turning to face him. "Sir, I am not looking for trouble but it seems there are some persons in this squadron that would like to see me in trouble." "You think so, Walker?" "Yes sir, I do." And with that, the CO ended the conversation with, "Well if that's the way you feel, I'll transfer you. Report to Public Works in the morning."[58] Walker would never see the machinist's mate shop again.

Upon reporting for duty in the public works shop, Walker soon learned that the Navy had announced the rating promotional list based on the most recent exam cycle. Walker had passed the aviation machinist's mate petty officer exam soundly and expected to find his name on the list newly appointed AMM third class. When he was not on the list, he inquired of the personnel officer. Very quickly he was told that since he was assigned to Class A service school for the aviation metalsmith rating, he could not be promoted in any other rating. This flew in the face of what he was told when he had first checked in to the squadron at Whiting Field.[59]

Walker reached out to the base personnel officer and explained his predicament. "Walker, you went to class A service school for Aviation Metalsmith. You cannot be promoted in any other rating. Why didn't you take that exam?" Walker replied, "Sir, I was told that that rating was frozen by squadron personnel." "They told you that?" he exclaimed. "Yes, sir." Walker proceeded to tell the officer that he was assigned to public works and only chose to take the exam because he had no other option and just wanted to work on airplanes. The base personnel officer then asked him where he would like to work, to which Walker responded without hesitation, "The metalsmith shop, sir." He was transferred from public works to the metalsmith shop the following morning. Walker also mentioned that the three other Black sailors with whom he reported to A school faced the same predicament, and they were subsequently reassigned to the metalsmith shop with him.[60]

Walker and many other Black men faced racism and unofficial "rules" that challenged their civil rights throughout their time in the Navy. In another incident, Walker developed a splitting headache while at work one morning. He was given permission to leave work early and report to the medical clinic on the other side of the base. Instead of walking the one-mile trek, he chose to use the base shuttle bus. When boarding, he nonchalantly chose the front seat and was soon challenged. The driver, a middle-aged White woman, confronted Walker. "Sit on the back seat," she said. "No thank you, I'm comfortable here," Walker politely replied. The bus driver departed the stop, but instead of heading to the medical clinic, she drove straight to the transportation garage, parked the bus, and got out. "You got a passenger on the front seat and I ain't going to drive," she yelled to the obviously curious group of men standing outside the bus. Eventually another driver got on and took over the assigned route. Walker, with encouragement from the WAVES sitting behind him, never moved and was dropped off at the medical clinic.[61]

The next morning Walker was summoned to the transportation officer's office, along with the protesting female bus driver. When asked by the lieutenant why she would not drive, she argued that driving a bus with a Black man in the front seat was "against what I was brought up to believe in." The lieutenant quickly responded, "Now see here, I don't know what you believe about colored people, but the Navy is not going to tolerate your discriminating against anybody. Do you get this?" She persisted and said that she disagreed, therefore she preferred to be transferred. He obliged, and the next day she was driving a dump truck.[62] Walker continued to put forth his best effort in the metalsmith shop, and eventually earned another promotion to the rank of petty officer second class in the following summer and continued serving through the Korean War.[63]

The Navy made an effort not to tolerate discrimination against Blacks, but often it was unavoidable. Fortunately, some in positions of authority chose to follow the official policy of nondiscrimination and did their best to enforce it when necessary.

U.S. naval aviation technical training grew from a few part-time assembly and repair facilities that conducted technical instruction casually to a small number of men, to a training colossus that involved hundreds of instructors and hundreds of thousands of students. NATTC built upon the model BuAer had begun in 1939–40 with Murray and Wheelock's initiatives in personnel planning and technical training. In the mid-1930s there was no such thing as aviation Class A, B, or C schools. By January 1942 there were twelve Class A, six Class B, and ten Class C technical aviation schools operating throughout the country.[64] Shortly thereafter, each one of those schools was categorized into four categories of educational activities, amounting to over thirty total "class" schools. The impact of what NATTC had done in terms of the Navy's technical aviation training was tremendous. By the summer of 1945, NATTC had trained more than 300,000 aviation technicians among its sixty odd schools that were in existence at one point or another since

1942.[65] The notion that the training would naturally occur while operating in a routine, operational environment through hands-on, real-time experience had been forgotten. While most of Navy and congressional leadership were looking at the matériel face of the war in terms of aircraft and weapon technology, NATTC did not lose sight of the overall picture. What good was the latest technology if squadrons could not keep airplanes airborne? What difference would thousands of new pilots make with no airplanes to fly because they were inoperable? The NATTC technical graduates would soon become as important to the war effort in the Pacific as the Grumman fighters, torpedoes, and bombs they serviced.

Chapter 5

Specialization of Labor and Timing the Delivery

As the size of the U.S. Pacific Fleet's carrier force rapidly increased after 1942, maintenance of the high number of state-of-the-art carrier-based aircraft participating in combat operations compelled the U.S. Navy to transform its aviation technician labor force through specialization and division. Prior to the outbreak of hostilities, aircraft maintenance was a relatively simple affair, confined to naval facilities that were located on land and usually in the vicinity of a major Naval Air Station. Permanent, spacious structures provided ample work spaces for technicians. Fuel, lubricants, and spare parts were generally close at hand. It was common practice for pilots to work on their own airplanes along with a small crew of enlisted technicians from the squadron when it came to routine maintenance. For major repairs or comprehensive overhaul, aircraft were sent to dedicated assembly and repair facilities such as the Naval Aircraft Factory in Philadelphia.[1] Aircraft maintenance in a peacetime navy was largely an unhurried activity that drew little attention from anyone outside of the pilots and technicians themselves. During the 1930s, flight operations were relatively limited, as the Navy maintained no more than six aircraft carriers at one time engaged in undemanding deployments. Thus, the Navy did not have to face a myriad of challenges posed by having to support a large and actively engaged carrier force with a commensurately robust aircraft maintenance capability while engaged in a protracted war. Historical arguments that place technology, tactics, or matériel as the substantive keys to Allied victory are not necessarily wrong, but other things mattered a great deal as well. A critical examination of prewar and wartime naval aircraft maintenance herein confirms that until the Navy grew the size of its skilled labor force to match the size of its carrier fleet and supporting units at sea and ashore, the operational viability of the carrier force as the Navy's primary offensive instrument was open to considerable doubt.

As late as the latter half of the 1930s, U.S. Navy carrier aviation was a relatively novel concept. It had been a part of the Navy for only a decade and a half. Until 1935, aircraft maintenance aboard carriers did not make large demands on the Navy's resources. This was because the number of aircraft carriers in service was quite small compared to what it would become midway through World War II. The *Langley* had been consigned to mostly experimental or research and development operations by the middle of the decade. Thus, the U.S. fleet possessed only three battle-worthy carriers that only operated between 200 and 230 airplanes. The commissioning of five additional units between 1936 and 1941 added an additional capacity of 373 aircraft.[2] Although the number of aircraft operated by the Navy more than doubled, the total carrier aircraft complement at the start of World War II only came to approximately 600. Peacetime deployment schedules did not require squadrons to put aircraft to sea for long periods under stressful, combat conditions. However, once the United States entered the war, the proliferation of naval aircraft was staggering. Table 5.1 shows the strength of carrier-based aircraft based on aircraft carriers in commission over the course of the war. This table theoretically shows how many aircraft the United States could operate at any one time, separated by class of ship based on the number of aircraft carriers in service. The more planes that the Navy possessed, the more aircraft technicians it would need to support operations. Table 5.1 reveals an approximate doubling of total naval aircraft each year (except for 1945). What is interesting is the significant increase of carrier-based airplanes in 1943. Was the Navy intentional in withholding carrier aircraft from the fleet until it had the labor force in place to support flight operations? Another valid consideration was the number large of carriers under construction in 1942. Without the new *Essex*-class ships to fight from, what good would a bunch of new airplanes be? Fortunately, many Reservists were activated in 1941–42 and carried much of the early workload. By mid-1942 the number of trained aviation technicians was on a steady rise; inventories of aircraft and aircraft carriers soon followed.

Aboard carriers, personnel were split between those accountable for attending to the ship's operations and those accountable for the daily air operations. The Air Department was responsible for the administration and control of all aviation-related duties, as well as supporting the facilities for maintenance and operation of aircraft. Storage and upkeep of all accessories, work spaces, and even berthing for aviation personnel were also part of its responsibilities. Trained aircraft technicians performed the day-to-day maintenance on the airplanes. The Air Department as a whole, integrated with nonflying squadron personnel to perform jobs such as loading ordnance, directing plane movements, manning the crash, salvage, and firefighting crews, and fueling.[3] Once the group of squadrons—administratively known as an air group—embarked, the ship's company blended with squadron personnel to become a cohesive, unified unit. At its most basic level, the daily task of nonflying personnel was to ensure that airplanes launched per the daily flight schedule.

Table 5.1. Aircraft Strength per Aircraft Carrier Class[1]

	12/31/41	12/31/42	12/31/43	12/31/44	OCTOBER 1945
CV	570	330*	650	860	1,220
CVE	30	390	1,050	2,040	2,250
CVL	0	0	300	300	300
Total Carrier-Based	600	620	2,000	3,200	3,500
Total (Carrier-Based + Land-Based)	3,430	7,058	16,691	34,071	40,912

* Due to losses of the *Hornet*, *Lexington*, *Wasp*, and *Yorktown* in 1942.

[1] Norman Polmar, *Aircraft Carriers: A History of Carrier Aviation and Its Influence on World Events* (Dulles, VA: Potomac Books, 2006), 273.

Everyone worked to achieve this goal. Once an aircraft left the deck, it was the pilot's job to complete the mission. It was no secret that this was impossible to do without a properly maintained aircraft.

The larger carriers of the *Essex* class were originally designed before the Pacific war. In fact, the keels of the first three *Essex*-class aircraft carriers—*Essex* (CV 9), *Yorktown* (CV 10), and *Intrepid* (CV 11)—were laid before the attack on Pearl Harbor. These ships were designed with embarked air groups in mind, but the plans were based on carrier aircraft flying in 1939, not 1943 or 1944 when most of the *Essex*-class vessels would become operational. Therefore, the number of aircraft on board U.S. carriers fluctuated from original plans throughout the war, beginning with an average of 90 in 1943, then 96 in 1944, and finally 102 in 1945. Changes in aircraft design, especially the adoption of folding wings, flight deck modifications, and how many spare aircraft were carried on board were responsible for these changes.[4] The available pool of pilots also increased each year, which made larger-sized air groups possible. Table 5.2 shows the change in dissemination of type aircraft per air group from prewar through its end.

The increased number in fighters and decreased quantity of scout bombers coincided with the phasing out of the aging SBD Dauntless and the introduction of a newer, yet troublesome SB2C Helldiver. In addition, in the last years of the war, the Navy modified its F6F Hellcat fighters to carry bombs and function as a multi-role fighter-bomber airplane. This alleviated the need to carry as many SB2Cs as had been anticipated. Many of the Curtiss SB2Cs were therefore replaced with newer models

Table 5.2. Average *Essex*-Class CV Air Group Complement[1]

	1940[2]	1941–43	1944	1945
VF (Fighter)	27	36	54	73
VSB (Scout Bomber)	37	36	24	15
VTB (Torpedo Bomber)	18	18	18	15
Total	82	90	96	103

[1] Friedman, *USS Yorktown (CV-10)*, 20.
[2] 1940 figures are from original *Essex* design.

of Grumman's F6F, simplifying both maintenance and supply aboard the carriers, but ultimately increased the number of airplanes operating from the carriers.[5]

The technician-to-plane ratio in World War II changed very little since Commander Dubose suggested eight technicians to ten planes when testifying before Congress in 1924.[6] The *Essex* was originally designed to deploy with 537 aviation enlisted personnel and 84 aircraft.[7] This was a drop from 601 enlisted aviation personnel on the *Hornet* (CV 8), even though it carried only 72 aircraft.[8] Over the course of the war, aviation technicians in *Essex*-class carriers averaged between five to seven enlisted men per embarked aircraft. In 1945, the newer *Lexington* (CV 16) reported 765 enlisted in the air department with 102 airplanes, a ratio of 7.5 to 1.[9] By comparison, the U.S. Army Air Corps required eight enlisted technicians per fighter and sixteen per light bomber within their squadrons. The average size of an army fighter squadron was 25 airplanes, 41 officers (pilots), and 210 enlisted mechanics. A light bomber squadron of A-24 model airplanes consisted of 13 planes, 25 officers, and 211 enlisted men.[10] In terms of large unit size, if multiple Army squadrons were combined in a similar fashion to the makeup of a 102-plane naval air group (3 fighter squadrons, 2 light bomber squadrons), the total number of Army technicians would equal 1,052 men, three to four hundred more than the Navy had available. Even older carriers such as the *Hornet* had a smaller ratio, approximately eight technicians per aircraft, than the Army.[11]

On average, approximately one-third of the enlisted personnel on board aircraft carriers were there to support air operations. Managing a labor force of this size, while navigating the challenges of a relatively new work environment for most of the men, was a daunting prospect. Based on the experiences of an interwar-era carrier navy, the most efficient way to accomplish this task was through a division of labor.

Since the *Lexington*'s earliest days, aircraft carriers divided its personnel into two general categories: ship operations and aviation operations. Those who were assigned to ship's company were responsible for the traditional naval operations of the vessel, its integrated weaponry, navigation, daily operations, meals, etc. Their duties also involved maintenance of the flight deck, arresting gear and catapults, and physical condition of the hangar spaces. Men assigned to the air department were only responsible for the operation and maintenance of the aircraft including the associated support equipment and shops.

The air department was an independent unit within the ship, subdivided into five smaller units: flight deck division (V-1), engineering-maintenance division (V-2), combat information and control division (V-3), ordnance and servicing division (V-4), and the air group (V-5), which consisted of officer and enlisted aircrew (pilots, navigators, bombardiers, radio operators, and gunners). V-1, V-2, and V-4 personnel worked on the flight deck and in the hangar with the aircraft.[12] The enlisted men of the V-3 division did not take part in the maintenance of aircraft, as their jobs were associated primarily with flight operations, ship–aircraft communications, and radar. The V-3 was considered the "administrative division" of the air department because most of the paperwork required to operate a carrier air department was handled by the yeomen (YN), affectionately known as "paper shufflers," that were assigned to this division. They doubled as phone talkers during flight operations from the tower, or "pri-fly."[13] Neither was the V-5 division a part of the maintenance team per se, but on occasion would assist air department technicians as needed.

As the bulk of carriers were delivered to the fleet after 1943, the air department's organization varied slightly as each tried to utilize a structure that best suited their mission. For example, aboard the second USS *Lexington* (CV 16) to fight in the war (commissioned in February 1943), divisions within the air department were given different identifiers than some CVs. V-1, V-2, and V-3 were the same: deck, aircraft maintenance, and flight operations and radars. Yet on the *Lexington*, V-4 was responsible for messages, internal communications, and aerography or aviation meteorology. It was manned by YNs, aerographer's mates (AGs), and photographer's mates (PHs). The YNs were responsible for transmitting messages throughout the ship and operating the battle phones during general quarters. In essence, they became the messengers during combat in addition to their everyday duties associated with the administrative paperwork of the ship's air department. The AGs, or "wind guessers," kept tabs on weather and winds, made forecasts and observations for battle planning and aircrew flight planning. The PHs, or "shutterbugs," spotted and photographed targets and combat scenes for everyone from the pilots, to battle planners on the task force staffs, to the civilians at home paging through *Life* magazine. Also on the *Lexington* was a change from V-4 to V-5 for the ordnancemen. V-5 consisted of those technicians who hung bombs and rockets under the wings of the air group's planes. V-5 also managed the stowage and security of that same ordnance on board the *Lexington*. V-6 was an additional division on CV 16 that separated the arresting gear and catapult technicians from the rest of the V-1 division.[14]

Even with these small variances in division organization, throughout the carrier forces, most of the sailors in V-1, with the exception of the plane captains (PC), were not considered "maintainers" while assigned to the division. Many had completed their training at the NATTC schools, but their job was not primarily about aircraft maintenance or repair. Some of their duties, for instance, included physically moving or "spotting" airplanes on the deck, refueling, operating tractors that moved the planes around the deck, and maintenance of the aircraft arresting gear. The V-1 division had a large role to play in sustaining air operations on a carrier, but the mechanical jobs of repair and preventative maintenance rested with the V-2.[15]

The V-1 flight deck sailors were identified by the color of their jerseys. Each crew member wore a different color shirt that identified his job on the flight deck. Flight deck plane handlers wore blue and positioned the airplanes for the day's flight schedule. The plane directors, who supervised the handlers, wore yellow jerseys. Sailors who were responsible for removing and replacing wheel chocks when launching and parking aircraft, respectively, wore purple. The tow tractor drivers assigned to moving aircraft were also outfitted in yellow. Gasoline crews responsible for refueling did not wear a specific color jersey, but only donned red helmets with their standard dungaree uniforms. The crews or "hook men" who operated and maintained the arresting gear were identified by green helmets and green jerseys. Firemen stood by with carbon dioxide extinguishers wearing red helmets and red jerseys. The flight deck officer, who was responsible for the entire operation, always wore a white helmet and white jersey. The plane captain, who shouldered most of the "on-deck" maintenance duties of an airplane, was often a junior AMM or AM fresh out of A school. His official uniform was a brown shirt and brown helmet, but often it ended up either as a pair of coveralls or dungarees and a white T-shirt.[16]

As the war went on, and carrier operations transformed the nature of naval warfare, the uniforms of sailors also changed. The standard-issue dungarees (blue shirt, denim trousers) became less and less practicable for the technicians to wear on the flight deck or in the hangar. As naval aviation transitioned to a more industrial institution, so did the uniforms. Herringbone twill coveralls were approved for use by aviation technicians on aircraft carriers late in 1943. Requisitions for the olive drab uniforms were permitted beginning in January 1944. CVEs and CVLs were authorized 250 sets in their inventory, and CVs and CVBs were permitted to have 500. More and more, the skilled labor base of the U.S. Navy was transitioning to something akin to the workforce of a manufacturing plant or auto repair shop.[17] A naval aircraft technician became more like the personal auto mechanic to the airplanes on board than just someone who conducted maintenance. They looked the part of a mechanic, and many developed very personal relationships with the aircraft that they worked on, especially the plane captains.

A plane captain was assigned individually to each plane on a ship. He was personally responsible for his airplane's daily servicing and care. The plane captain usually had his name and hometown painted on the nose of the aircraft to foster ownership and pride in his work.[18] His duties typically included cleaning or washing the plane, tying down aircraft properly, inspecting tires and landing gear, ensuring the airplane was properly refueled, checking and servicing engine and hydraulic oil levels, and conducting preflight inspections. When an aircraft needed repair that required an elevator ride down to the hangar, its plane captain worked alongside the hangar deck technicians to schedule routine repair or remedy of a more serious nature.[19]

The importance of a naval aircraft technician in a combat situation is demonstrated by the story of AMM3 Charles W. Devaney. A young plane captain for a F6F Hellcat in VF-31, Devaney was responsible for taking care of that specific plane on a daily basis. As if it were his own, he prided himself in keeping his aircraft in the best condition possible. However, as combat often does, the enemy had other plans for it. On three separate occasions, Devaney's Hellcat came back to the carrier with battle damage. On the first occasion, the aircraft took a few rounds of Japanese gunfire through its engine cowling and wing. Upon landing, Devaney wasted no time tackling the repair and had it patched and ready to fly again in half an hour. The second incident occurred when the airplane took a burst of gunfire through a section of the wing. Devaney quickly repaired the damage and got his plane back onto the flight schedule, fully operational. The final episode occurred when the hydraulic system suffered catastrophic damage after being hit a third time by Japanese fire. This caused a crash landing aboard the carrier, and destroyed the Hellcat's engine. Yet Devaney was not discouraged. He quickly began removing the damaged engine, and forty-nine hours later he had a new one installed. His F6F was ready to get back into the fight.

As a gesture of their appreciation for his hard work keeping their plane operational, the pilots in the squadron painted Devaney's name under the window on its fuselage, a space traditionally reserved for pilots' names. Normally the plane captain gets his name painted on the underside or on a wheel-well cowling. Devaney's extraordinary effort was rewarded with an extraordinary measure. Devaney's Hellcat went on the fight at Kwajalein, Truk, Palau, Saipan, and Guam, flying another 50,000 estimated nautical miles.[20]

The Flight Deck Division performed work that was essential to daily combat operations. The main offensive and defensive capabilities of an aircraft carrier depended upon its efficiency. In order to get the airplane to the deck and ready to launch, all the mechanical systems of the airplane had to be in working order before it was even assigned to the flight schedule. This is where the skilled technicians of the Engineering Department were most valuable.

The Engineering Division (V-2) on the earliest *Essex*-class aircraft carriers, such as *Essex* (CV 9), consisted of 180–200 men.[21] The men were responsible for the maintenance of every airplane aboard the ship. Sailors of the V-2 division were usually graduates of the aviation trade schools, or after 1942, the NATTC schools. It was typical that a routine inspection on each aircraft was performed after thirty hours of flight time. The Bureau of Aeronautics' (BuAer) regulatory 30, 60, 90, or one 120 flight hour inspections on each carrier aircraft were the responsibility of these technicians. This type of inspection involved checking engine

Aviation mechanic's school, metalsmith's class, Great Lakes Training Station, 1918. *Naval History & Heritage Command*

Crew members on the elevator deck of the USS *Langley* (CV 1) with an F2B-1, circa 1928. *Naval History & Heritage Command*

Aviation metalsmiths assemble a Grumman F4F-3 fighter on the hangar deck of the USS *Enterprise* (CV 6), October 28, 1941. The plane bears the markings of Fighting Squadron Three (VF-3), including a Felix the Cat insignia under the cockpit windshield. Note spare airplanes triced up in the hangar overhead, including TBD-1 torpedo planes and SBD scout bombers. *Official U.S. Navy photograph, NARA*

An F4F Wildcat fighter undergoes maintenance on the hangar deck of the USS *Enterprise* (CV 6), October 28, 1941. Note aircraft propellers stowed in the hangar overhead. *Official U.S. Navy photograph, NARA*

Naval Air Technical Training Center, NAS Memphis. AMM students are learning how to conduct propeller maintenance and repair. *Naval History & Heritage Command*

Naval Air Technical Training Center, NAS Memphis. AM students in an aircraft hydraulics course are learning how to maintain landing-gear systems. *Naval History & Heritage Command*

Naval Air Technical Training Center, NAS Memphis. AMM students are getting practice in correctly removing and installing engines. *Naval History & Heritage Command*

Naval Air Technical Training Center, NAS Memphis. This SBD is completely equipped with guns, radio equipment, etc., and is used for plane familiarization in the ARM school. *Naval History & Heritage Command*

Naval Air Technical Training Center, NAS Memphis. Duplicating service operations, trainees perform a thirty-hour check on "live" aircraft. Classroom learning is applied to practical work on the flightline. *Naval History & Heritage Command*

NAS Jacksonville. Three AMM WAVES (Women Accepted for Volunteer Emergency Service) work on an SNJ training plane. All are graduates of NATTC, Norman, Oklahoma, where they spent four months learning to repair and overhaul airplane engines. *U.S. Naval Institute photo archive*

Members of the first class of WAVES to graduate from the Aviation Metalsmith School at NATTC Norman, Oklahoma, July 30, 1943. *Naval History & Heritage Command*

Trainees of the tenth segregated class to graduate from aircraft technician Class A school at Naval Training Center, Great Lakes, Illinois, examine a Wright Whirlwind aircraft engine during their training, September 15, 1943. Black technicians trained separately from White technicians during the war. *Official U.S. Navy photograph, NARA*

First members of the Women's Reserve of the Navy (aka WAVES) and Marine Corps (USMC WR) arrive at Hawaii to survey the territory in preliminaries to the assignment of women in these services overseas. The visiting officers (L to R), Col. Ruth Streeter, Director of the Marine Corps Women's Reserve; Lt. Cdr. Jean T. Palmer of the Naval Women's Reserve; Maj. Marian B. Dryden of the Marine Corps Women's Reserve; and Lt. Cdr. Joy B. Hancock of the Naval Women's Reserve, are greeted at the dock of the U.S. Naval Air Station, Honolulu, by (L to R) Vice Adm. Robert L. Ghormley, Commander, Hawaiian Sea Frontier and Commandant Fourteenth Naval District; Vice Adm. John H. Towers, Deputy Commander in Chief, U.S. Pacific Fleet and Pacific Ocean Areas; and Brig. Gen. L. W. T. Waller Jr., USMCR, Commanding General of Marine Garrison Forces in the Fourteenth Naval District. *U.S. Naval Institute photo archive*

Vice Adm. George D. Murray
NARA

Rear Adm. Arthur W. Radford serving as Commander, Carrier Division 6, ashore at Ulithi Island, March 29, 1945. Radford was named Director, Naval Aviation Training just three weeks before the attack on Pearl Harbor in 1941. *Naval History & Heritage Command*

Capt. A. W. Wheelock (*second from right*), serving as commanding officer of the USS *Essex*, escorts Adm. Chester Nimitz (*center*) through the ship's engine room, March 16, 1951. *Naval History & Heritage Command*

Exterior view of the Aviation Repair and Overhaul Unit-Two (AROU-2) headquarters building at Naval Air Base Samar in 1945. *U.S. Naval Institute photo archive*

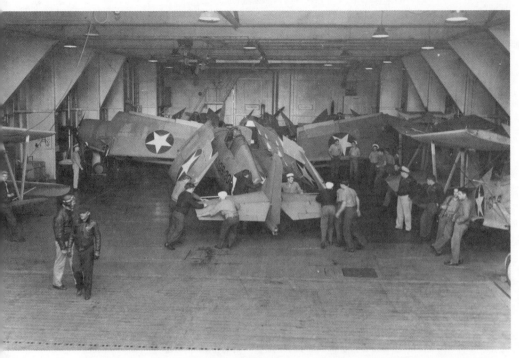

Crewmen spotting a Grumman F4F-4 Wildcat fighter on the USS *Long Island* (AVG 1) hangar deck, June 17, 1942. Several other F4F-4s are present, as are Curtiss SOC-3A Seagull scout-observation planes. *Official U.S. Navy photograph, NARA*

View of planes (F4F-4) on hanger deck of the USS *Charger* (CVE-30) looking aft, October 2, 1942. *Naval History & Heritage Command*

A Grumman F4F-4 Wildcat fighter is lifted on board the USS *Long Island* (ACV 1) from the USS *Kitty Hawk* (APV 1) at Fila Harbor, New Hebrides, August 28, 1942. This plane was en route to Guadalcanal as part of the second group of USMC planes to be based at Henderson Field. *Official U.S. Navy photograph*, NARA

The USS *Enterprise* (CV 6) TBM Avenger torpedo bombers warming up on the after flight deck during operations in the Pacific, circa May 1944. An F6F Hellcat fighter is on the midships elevator, in the foreground. *Official U.S. Navy photograph*, NARA

Rear Adm. Albert Cushing Read Sr., first Chief of Naval Air Technical Training Command *U.S. Naval Institute photo archive*

function, fluid levels, and general condition of the airplane structure. After each thirty hours of flight time, the inspections became more rigorous and lengthier, until the aircraft eventually reached its manufacturer's recommended overhaul period. On average, the normal overhaul period for naval aircraft was every eighteen months in peacetime.[22] Depending on the tempo of flight operations, the time between overhauls would shorten dramatically once the air war in the Pacific began.

The Aviation Engineering Division on board an aircraft carrier was divided into three subdivisions: Engineering (V-2E), Electronics (V-2R), and Shops (V-2S). With the rapid increases in carrier numbers and the size of carrier air groups, however, came the need for further specialization within the Navy's aviation workforce. Therefore, each division was divided even further by type of aircraft. Technicians were assigned to small technical units that were qualified to perform maintenance on only one specific aircraft: fighters, dive-bombers and scouts, or torpedo planes.[23] For example, an AMM in the V2-E division might only be qualified to work on fighters, but not dive-bombers. Therefore, each type of aircraft had a dedicated maintenance team for the duration of deployment. This specialization of labor represented a remarkable change for naval aviation maintenance procedures

Within the V-2E Division, fighter aircraft (VF) technicians comprised the greatest number of maintenance "check" crews, ten in number. Bomber/scout aircraft (VB/VSB) had six and torpedo aircraft (VT) required four.[24] The fighter crews were supervised by a lieutenant (junior grade), who had experience as a pilot or who had aviation maintenance training either through the aviation technical trade schools or a carrier aircraft service unit (CASU), or both. His enlisted counterpart was usually a senior enlisted such as an aviation machinist's mate, chief petty officer (AMMC). The typical check crews normally contained five additional technicians, but the minimum requirement being one AMM1, one AMM2, one AMM3, or an "undesignated" seaman (SN). The other two members could vary in rank based on what was available to the air group at the time. Additionally, all the work completed by the check crews was inspected by two to four AMMs who were split into day and night shifts. The airplane was not considered "safe for flight" after their final inspection and all associated documentation was submitted to the maintenance control officer. Only then would the airplane be available for the following day's flight schedule.[25]

The check crews had to have a supporting network of tools, materials, and specialty technicians to assist when parts needed to be replaced or repaired. This is where the V-2S Division came into play. The aircraft carrier was designed to provide ample maintenance and repair at sea for aircraft. The number of facilities on board was numerous. A metal shop employed forty-two artisans and the hydraulic shop had twelve sailors assigned to it. There were other shops, smaller in size and more specialized: a paint shop was manned by four sailors, while the sparkplug overhaul, propeller, and oxygen transfer shops utilized two sailors each. There were also machine, electrical, radio, radar, and parachute shops. Each required a few enlisted sailors on day and night shifts to support the embarked air group. When repairs, fabrication, or servicing were more complicated than what could be completed quickly while the airplane was in the hangar or up on the flight deck, the check crew would bring the part or parts to the shops for repair or replacement. The V-2S Division also supported flight operations by maintaining the shops for the arresting gear, the catapult machinery, and the torpedoes. All of the technicians aboard were trained on their respective systems before reporting aboard the ship, ensuring the aircraft carrier's labor force continued to become more and more specialized.[26]

Aircraft ordnance and its associated systems, plus aircraft fueling was handled by the V-4, Ordnance and Servicing Division. V-4 typically had 100–110 technicians on board at any given time. These maintainers were responsible for everything from forward-firing fixed aircraft guns and rockets to torpedoes, and refueling airplanes on the flight deck. A lieutenant was in charge, with a lieutenant (junior grade) assisting. Two chief petty officers rounded out the management. One chief was in charge of all aircraft gunnery and the other was responsible for the aircraft-launched torpedoes and bombs.[27]

The relationship between a plane captain and his aircraft was mirrored by the V-4 Division in terms of its ordnance technicians and aircraft weapons. On an *Essex*-class aircraft carrier, a single technician was assigned to each fighter on board. Thus, the number of V-4 technicians utilized in this fashion varied from an average of thirty during the first two years of the war to upward of seventy by the end. These numbers were commensurate with the adjustments in an air group's complement of aircraft during the course of the war.[28] The maintainer was responsible for all gun systems, ammunition, and rockets, if so equipped. Loading and unloading of ammunition, as well as servicing and repair of the gun and rocket launchers, all fell under his responsibility. Airplanes that carried a crew-served weapon (a manually operated rear gun), such as the TBM Avenger, often utilized the same technician who maintained the weapon as the aircrew gunner.[29]

The technicians assigned to the three bomb-loading crews on board were responsible for loading and unloading all air-launched torpedoes and bombs. The torpedoes themselves required considerable maintenance in order to keep them in a constant state of readiness. The internal guidance and fusing of an air-launched torpedo was a complicated feat of engineering and mechanics. The weapon was not something that could be quickly loaded onto an airplane and taken aloft. The torpedo shops employed weapons experts to ensure the detonator, propulsion, and guidance systems were properly set before uploading the torpedoes onto aircraft.

Aircraft maintenance on board the smaller escort and light carriers (CVE and CVL) was similar, although there were a few differences.[30] The four major aviation departments had the same identifiers as those of the *Essex* class, but fueling was managed by the V-2 Division (which was identified as Hangar Operations instead of Engineering) rather than V-4. The most significant material difference, however, was the physical footprint of the air department and its aircraft. Escort carriers nominally operated approximately twenty-two aircraft, split between fighters and torpedo bombers (VF and VT). Scout bombers were not a regular component of the escort carrier.[31]

The division of labor on board the CVE was also different than on the larger *Yorktown*- and *Essex*-class carriers. Most likely due to the smaller number of aircraft, technicians were not divided by type of aircraft as they were on the CV. This meant that on a CVE, maintainers were employed on both VF and VT aircraft simultaneously. For example, an aviation machinist's mate on a CVE had to be qualified to work on both F6F Hellcats and TBM Avengers.

The personnel distribution of the V-2 Division also varied, but a specialized labor force was still the standard. There were four check crews comprised of three-man teams, each supervised by a chief petty officer. The check crews were typically divided into three "day" crews and one "night" crew. Six specialists were available to assist the maintenance crews on a round-the-clock basis. These technicians received special training in aircraft instruments, propellers, carburetors, hydraulics, landing gear, and empennage (tail section) and were designated as such in their ratings. For example, an aviation machinist's mate hydraulics specialist first class would be rated AMMH1. A chief petty officer would supervise the entire group of AMM specialists.[32]

Within the hangar spaces, the V-2 Division had its own network of shops, although much smaller than that on the CV. Three aviation radar technicians (ART) manned the electronics shop, typically an ART1 and two ART2s. The electronics shop supported aircraft radar and radio systems and was also responsible for the rest of the aircraft electrical systems. An aviation electronics mate first class (AEM1) worked with two to three more junior AEMs. The largest shop was metal repair. It was supervised by an aviation metalsmith chief petty officer (AMC) and employed eleven other AMs. As with all aviation ships, there was a parachute loft, but it only contained two parachute riggers (PRs). The CVE's V-2 Division averaged about half as many technicians, between 100 and 120, compared to the larger 180- to 200-man V-2 Division on the CV. However, plane captains and fueling personnel were lumped into V-2 on the smaller carriers, thus bringing the number of assigned personnel closer to 140.[33]

V-4, the Ordnance Division, was divided into three smaller sections, similar to the CV. There were four crews for bomb and torpedo loading, each comprised of four aviation ordnancemen. Each crew was responsible for approximately three of the dozen or so VT aircraft on board. The gun and rocket systems on the fighters were also maintained by a four-man crew. Each crew was assigned approximately three aircraft, the same as the torpedo and bomb crews. The third part of the Ordnance Division was comprised of the Assembly and Hoist Detail. This group was further divided into a nine-man team of bomb handlers and vane-assemblies team. There was also a four-man team that was responsible for torpedo and bomb fusing operations. The entire Ordnance Division on the CVE was approximately one-half the size of the CV's V-4 Division, averaging between forty and fifty aviation ordnance technicians per ship.[34]

Daily operations for the maintenance crews on carriers were similar whether it was a CV or CVE. Each night, aircraft had to be positioned or "spotted" for the next day's flight schedule. The V-2 Division compiled a daily "availability" report that provided planners an idea of how many and what types of aircraft would be available to fly the following day. The nightly report would list the total number of planes that were flyable or in a ready status. This term was shortened to "up." Those planes that were undergoing repair were reported as "down for repair" or simply "down." An estimated time and date of repair completion was added to these aircraft statuses. If an aircraft was approaching a BuAer-mandated hourly inspection, such as a thirty- or sixty-hour inspection, that information was also provided for planning purposes.[35] The goal was always 100 percent availability, but this was rarely achieved. Usually, it ranged from 80 percent to 90 percent, only dipping lower after periods of combat when aircraft were lost or severely damaged by enemy fire.[36]

Carrier aviation technicians faced significantly more challenges compared to their land-based counterparts. They were thus forced to adapt to complex work conditions that did not exist for a land-based airplane mechanic. One such issue was the lack of space in which to work.[37] In the hangar, aircraft were positioned within a few feet, and sometimes just inches from each other, often with their wings folded in order to make room for more. There was little room for technicians to maneuver around parked airplanes. Striking one's head on the side of an airplane or propeller was a common hazard. Work platforms had to be placed with great care and then tied down when in use so as not to hit another airplane when the ship rolled due to heavy seas or maneuvering. Tools had to be accounted for at all times and could not be left lying around. A screwdriver that rolled behind the flight controls could be catastrophic to an aircraft in flight. The constant pitch and roll of the ship required a diligence and attention to detail in how work was accomplished, what tools were used, and where they were placed when not in use. The risk of something such as a replacement engine falling off its work stand as the ship rolled heavily was very real. For the land-based aircraft technician, the stability of their workspace alleviated many of these concerns.[38]

While airplanes were in the hangar, their wings were usually folded in order to save space. Folded wings allowed more airplanes to be stored in the hangar, but it brought with it its own problems that were not easily remedied. For example, as late as January 1944, maintenance crews on the *Saratoga* were requesting a work stand be designed and approved by BuAer that could be hung on carrier aircraft while their wings were folded, giving technicians a safe and stable platform that would save time and labor. Aircraft like F6Fs and TBFs employed wing guns that needed servicing after each flight.[39] The intricacies of a carrier hangar deck called for more innovative measures than many aviation engineers had foreseen.

Trying to maneuver so many aircraft in such cramped spaces often resulted in one airplane striking another while under tow. These "hangar crashes" were usually minor, but they required the attention of artisans and inspectors, even in cases of minor repair.[40] There was less chance of such damage occurring at shore facilities. Additionally, the constant folding and unfolding of an aircraft's wings in order to make space in the hangar or flight deck put additional stress on aircraft mechanical and hydraulic systems. Loose fittings and weak hydraulic hose connections were also a common troubleshooting item for check crews as they discovered leaks and malfunctions.[41]

Other "pilot-induced" damage that was common in carrier aviation was tire blowouts and "prop strikes." Carrier landings in the 1930s and '40s were conducted more as a "controlled crash" than a traditional runway landing. Once his airplane crossed the deck edge, the carrier pilot immediately pulled the throttles back to idle, effectively stalling the engine so the airplane would fall to the flight deck, fifteen to twenty feet below, often causing a blown tire. The goal was to catch the steel hook hanging from the tail of the airplane onto one of the wires horizontally traversing the flight deck and arrest forward momentum before continuing over the bow of the ship and into the sea below. If the pilot applied brake pressure too abruptly at this point, it would often cause a "nose-over," damaging the aircraft's propeller. Only the front landing gear had brake systems, and most aircraft were heaviest forward of the cockpit where the engine was located. Replacement propellers were one of the few items that are actually assembled on the ship. Tires and many other aircraft parts came fully assembled from the manufacturer and were ready for immediate installation.[42]

Sometimes damage or mishaps were due to negligence on behalf of the maintenance department and not the aircrews or the airplanes. Aircraft can malfunction on their own, but sometimes maintenance personnel are a contributing factor. In one instance, a pilot of a TBM-1 began a normal takeoff sequence from a shore station runway. A few seconds after applying takeoff power, the engine's RPM dropped significantly as did the engine's power. Fortunately he was taking off from a runway and not the deck of a carrier. Immediately after the power loss, a bright orange flame erupted from the engine exhaust. At this, the pilot immediately cut his throttle to shut down the engine. This caused the aircraft to swerve on the runway and ended up in a ditch, damaging the landing gear, propeller, and wing section. Fortunately there were no personnel injuries.

The postcrash investigation revealed that the accident was the result of maintenance negligence. The night before, the technician responsible for completing the sixty-hour inspection removed the carburetor stabilizing unit to test for proper airflow. When the test was complete, the technician used the wrong type of gasket to reseat the part. A simple mistake (he used a solid gasket instead of one with cutouts for proper venting), which in turn caused the carburetor to run "rich." Running "rich" or with a higher air-to-fuel ratio than necessary caused the engine to "load up and lose power," resulting in a violent backfire, complete with flames and black smoke—not something a pilot wants to see on takeoff. As with anything, humans are fallible; technicians are not immune from making mistakes.[43]

In a more "passive-aggressive" style of incurring damage, saltwater spray and vapor wreaked havoc on the metal frames of carrier aircraft. Corrosion compromised the structural integrity of airframes and the reliability of active mechanical systems such as engines, landing gear, and armament. Salt buildup on the covering of airplanes roughened what should have been smooth exterior surfaces, which induced aerodynamic drag that could reduce an airplane's maximum speed by as much as ten miles per hour. To combat the salt, the maintenance teams tried their best to regularly rinse down the aircraft, but fresh water was limited due to the other requirements like bathing, drinking, laundry, cooking, and feeding the boilers. Therefore, each part of the airplane that was easily accessible was regularly coated with a corrosion inhibiting oil. This helped somewhat, but it was labor intensive and only provided partial protection from the saltwater elements. After aircraft design transitioned from wooden frames and cloth skin in the 1920s to all metal in the 1940s, the Navy could do little more than mitigate the constant onslaught of saltwater corrosion on its carrier aircraft.[44]

Corrosion on spare parts was also a major concern for aviation mechanics. BuAer took great care in preserving spare parts while in transit or storage aboard the ship. Four preventative measures were considered standard procedures when spare engines and other parts were shipped to and stored aboard carriers. If the part was paintable, a corrosion-resistant paint or enamel was applied. Second, any extraneous material was removed from the parts to allow a preservative coat of oil or grease to be applied to the item itself. The third step consisted of applying a petroleum-based preservative on everything. Finally, the spare parts were wrapped in bags or other air-tight containers to keep humidity low and moisture out. Dehydrating agents such as silica gel placed inside containers or plastic film bags were used to keep the humidity at minimal levels. Even the type of paper used to wrap certain parts was considered in relation to its corrosion inducing properties. Papers containing acids were purposefully avoided since the chemical reaction—if the paper should become damp—would corrode the metal it was supposed to be protecting. Not all of these measures were exclusive to carrier aviation. Land-based units faced similar humidity and environmental concerns in the Pacific, however, the prevalence of saltwater spray on a ship demanded a greater emphasis on corrosion prevention than the Navy or Army had to worry about in land-based aviation units.[45]

The majority of aircraft maintenance was performed overnight since throughout most of the war, combat missions were flown during daylight hours. After the pilots landed, the maintenance crews took over. Aircraft were placed on elevators and lowered to the hangar decks below where they were inspected, repaired, and readied for the next day's missions.

With only a limited number of aircraft on board, naval aircraft technicians were always under a time constraint to accomplish their jobs expeditiously. If unable to complete the required maintenance overnight, the following day's missions would be compromised. The carrier technician's daily routine did not consider overtime, union contracts, or mandatory breaks (although unofficial short "smoke breaks" were very common within the ranks and have been ever since). They worked until the job was complete, or they were relieved by someone else to perform what needed to be done.[46]

Most of the maintenance performed on board aircraft carriers constituted what would eventually be labeled "Class D" maintenance. Class D mainly consisted of engine changes and the installation of components. The Navy had three other classes of maintenance that did not fall under the responsibility of the V-2 Division. Class A was major overhaul work on aircraft and engines; Class B was accessory and minor engine overhauls; and Class C constituted minor structural repairs and engine installation. If a carrier airplane required any unplanned major maintenance or repair while at sea, there was a very real chance that aircraft would be pushed over the side of the ship, according to accounts from maintenance officers at the time. During the latter half of the war, deck space was at a premium and replacement aircraft were plentiful. Repairs were done, but it was usually in conjunction with the installation of new parts. The carrier maintenance teams preferred to install new parts rather than fix broken ones if the parts were of significant size or cost. Even though the labor was very specialized on the carrier, the resources for lengthy, intricate repairs on aircraft were not practical.[47]

✦✦✦

As challenging as the maintenance process was on the carrier, technicians faced many more dangers and difficult situations than just those associated with corrosion, unstable work platforms, or long hours. Life at sea for enlisted aviation technicians was much different than it was for naval technicians on board destroyers, battleships, and other surface ships. Working on the flight deck of a carrier was like nothing "deck" sailors had experienced in previous generations. High tempo and exhausting operations among high-powered aircraft, their lethal propellers, and explosive ordnance marked the average day. Many young sailors grew up very quickly after reporting for duty. Lloyd M. Gilmore, an aviation machinist's mate, left his hometown of Dallas, Texas, and enlisted in the Naval Reserve in August 1942. Upon completion of boot camp and trade school, he reported to the USS *Enterprise* and was assigned to the V-1 Division on the flight deck. Gilmore's primary duty as a petty officer third class was "spotting" airplanes on deck. In layman's terms, a spotter was responsible for parking aircraft to ensure that the most ready and available airplanes were poised for the next mission. As airplanes landed, Gilmore and his fellow V-1 personnel pushed, pulled, or towed airplanes to specific areas on the deck where postflight inspections and future maintenance were conducted. Moving airplanes to different areas on the deck was necessary so maintenance could be accomplished without interfering in current or future flight operations. Most junior sailors, fresh out of school, were initially assigned to V-1 no matter their rating. After spending time on the flight deck, they usually had the opportunity to move to a division more suited to their rating and begin performing the aircraft maintenance they had been trained to do. This was no different for Gilmore.

A typical day during combat flight operations began with reveille at 0430, but sometimes it could start much earlier depending on the day's missions. During August 1945, the fleet was focused on strikes into Tokyo. On the USS *Lexington* (CV 16) a typical day started at 0030 with early breakfast for the V-5 Division personnel; the mess deck opened up at 0200 for general Air Department breakfast, after a 0140 reveille. The rest of the ship was awakened at 0203 and breakfast for officers and pilots was served at 0215. Flight quarters began at 0300 and then general quarters at 0353 in preparation for possible enemy air attacks. First launch was scheduled for 0415, about forty-five minutes before sunrise. A second meal was served to the crew between 0800 and 1100 and a third later that afternoon between 1300 and 1500. General quarters and flight quarters were eventually secured by 1918 and supper was served at 1920. The expectation was that the schedule would repeat itself as long as circumstances dictated.[48]

Gilmore, along with his fellow spotters and plane handlers, maneuvered the planes into a predetermined layout on the deck so each could easily taxi its way to a takeoff position without encountering other airplanes trying to do the same thing. The spotters "stacked" dozens of planes on the aft end of the ship, the fantail, in preparation for the day's first launch. A typical day during combat operations would last until 2130, leaving only about four hours for sleep. Many V-1 personnel chose to sleep topside, on the flight deck, rather than return to their bunks for a few measly hours of rest. Berthing was not air conditioned and the oppressive humidity and heat made life miserable below decks for the exhausted crew, crammed into bunks stacked three high. Gilmore himself would often sleep in the 20-mm antiaircraft gun battery after the last recovery of the night rather than make the unrewarding trek to his bunk below. During sustained combat operations at sea, plane handlers and other V-1 personnel often worked twenty-four hours straight, catching naps when they could and being assigned cleaning duties on the deck when flight operations were secured.[49]

In addition to his spotting and plane handling duties, Gilmore would often "run tailhooks" during recovery operations for extra pay. When aircraft landed on the carrier, it used a tailhook to "catch" a wire secured to a pulley system on either side of flight deck as a way to arrest its forward motion. Prior to touchdown, the pilot released the tailhook via a cockpit lever. The tailhook hung below the tail of the airplane and upon touchdown, the hook end snagged one of the transverse wires across the deck. The airplane rapidly decelerated and eventually came to a stop. At that point the hook had to be released from the wire so the plane could be moved out of the path for incoming aircraft. A simple task at first glance, but 1940s aircraft had no hydraulic mechanism to raise its hook once it was down as modern carrier aircraft do. To remedy this, Gilmore and others would sprint out behind the airplane as it came to a stop, manually disengage the hook from the wire, and reseat it in the tail portion of the airplane. It was a time-sensitive job that required quick reflexes and a willingness to throw yourself into one of the most dangerous environments in the world. The Navy recognized this and rewarded those who "ran the gauntlet" with extra pay every three months.

Working on the flight deck delivered a front row seat to some of the horrors of war for young technicians and Lloyd Gilmore saw his share of gore. In September 1944, he recorded in his diary that one day during the Battle of the Philippine Sea a Dauntless dive-bomber landed after an engagement near Palau. Upon approaching the airplane, Gilmore noticed it had sustained a fair amount of combat damage and a member of the crew had taken the brunt of it. Glimpsing into the cockpit, Gilmore recoiled at the sight: "It was a sad sight. His head was blown open, killing him instantly. Blood and brains were all over the inside of the plane."[50] It was a grim reminder of the violent nature of war.

On another occasion, Gilmore detailed the additional dangers of working on the flight deck during combat operations and around ordnance. In one instance, the .50-caliber machine gun mounted in the wing of a fighter was mistakenly fired while the plane was still on deck. One unlucky sailor was in the way of the round and ended up losing half of his leg four inches below the knee. Gilmore described the scene in his diary: "There was blood and meat everywhere," a description more suited for the jungles of Saipan than the deck of the *Enterprise*.[51]

Forest F. Bruner Jr. chose the Navy to escape that which he enjoyed the least—school. Bruner was bored with high school and decided to escape by enlisting. The idea of moving far from his landlocked hometown of Birmingham, Alabama (and with it the classroom), enhanced the idea of the adventure of going to sea in wartime. Unbeknownst to Bruner, the adventure and excitement of life at sea would have to wait; ironically, Forest Bruner was in for more schooling than he had ever imagined before he would even get a chance to prove his mettle against the Japanese navy. Two weeks after completing boot camp, he was sent to the Aviation Machinist's Mate School in Jacksonville, Florida.[52] He soon discovered this was no ordinary school; it was eight full hours of classroom and hands-on learning followed by hours of required study each evening. Bruner was back in the classroom, but at least he had an end in sight, the flight deck of an aircraft carrier—the USS *Lexington*—in approximately twenty-one weeks.

Bruner's time on board the *Lexington* came during the period of greatest achievements for the Navy in 1944. The air group was successful and the Japanese were losing their ability to match the unprecedented output of the American weapons and personnel. His life on the flight deck was much the same as Gilmore's on the *Enterprise*. Long days and long nights, incredibly dangerous evolutions, and frightening near misses were commonplace. It was a high-risk lifestyle that left little time to dwell on close calls. Bruner recalled the danger that "chock pullers" faced on a daily basis as the air group was preparing for a launch:

> The crewmen who were assigned to be wheel chock men were required to pull three chocks from the plane wheels before leaving the deck. Visualize 50 planes warming up at 5:30 a.m. in the dark. The command is given for standby to launch aircraft. The first row was five planes wide. The chock men wove their way in between the props which were approximately 18 inches apart. They pulled one chock and gingerly carried it to the next row amid the prop wash of the first plane. When three chocks were retrieved, they must be deposited in the catwalks at the edge of the deck. Crew members then returned to the middle of the 50 planes for another three. By the time they were four to five rows deep, you can only imagine the thrust of the prop wash from the front planes. If the chock men stumbled anywhere amid the planes, the chock man would be instantly reduced to Jimmy Dean Sausage. The prop wash can blow a man down the deck like an open parachute. War is hell.[53]

Bruner also saw tragedy result from factors unrelated to maintenance while aboard the carrier. As history has shown, extended periods at sea will sometimes drive sailors to drink . . . literally. Yet for U.S. Navy sailors in 1944 that was not an option—unless you were willing to risk the consequences. The propulsion systems of World War II air-launched torpedoes were powered by alcohol—but not the potable kind. Dyed pink, so as to identify it as such, it was commonly referred to as "Pink Lady." In the minds of some, desperate times called for desperate measures—even if based off of legend and lore. Bruner recalled that several sailors seeking some relief from the daily grind of air combat operations, decided they would take a chance. They showed up one evening with several loaves of bread. Their thought process was that they could remove the toxic ingredients and some of the alcohol content from the torpedo fuel by filtering it through the bread before drinking, thus enjoying a "cocktail" at the end of the workday. They tried, but sadly, their efforts did not pan out as they had hoped. The next morning, two of the sailors awakened their entire berthing compartment screaming, "I can't see! I can't see!" The strength and toxicity of the alcohol fuel had blinded them.[54]

Bruner served out his time on the Lexington and was shipped home shortly after the Japanese surrendered aboard the USS Missouri in Tokyo Bay on September 2, 1945. While at home on leave in the spring of 1946, just four months prior to his official discharge, Forest Bruner walked into a Birmingham General Motors automobile dealership looking for a job. He introduced himself and applied for a position as a mechanic "trainee." The timing worked out for both employer and employee, and when Bruner moved home for good in August 1946, he began work at the Drennen Motor Company installing floor mats and antifreeze. It was a far cry from servicing Hellcats and Devastators, but it was a job. The expectation was that he would move up to the heavy mechanical shop when a position opened up. After two months of no movement, and seeing others move to the head of the line in front of him, Bruner decided he had had enough. With a two-year statute of limitations on his GI Bill, he was running out of time to gain experience and training as an automobile mechanic, so he left the job at the dealership in search of other opportunities.

Shortly thereafter Forest Bruner Jr. found a job at Davis Electric and Carburetor Company. It was here that he built upon the training and experience received in Jacksonville, on the flight deck, and in the hangar. Bruner completed the two-year auto mechanic program and like many other discharged naval aviation technicians, continued in the business of maintenance and engine repair, but without looking over his shoulder every day for fear of seeing a Japanese Zero on a strafing run or kamikaze dive toward his workstation.[55]

Aviation technicians like Bruner and Gilmore had to face more than just operational dangers from flight deck operations. The maintenance department on board carriers were naturally located within the "high-value target" area for attacking enemy aircraft. The crew of the USS Franklin (CV 13) was one of those who experienced the tragedy of war at sea. On March 19, 1945, the Franklin, or "Big Ben" as she was affectionately known by her crew, was struck by two bombs from an undetected Japanese dive-bomber as during the second launch of the day, at 0708 in the morning. The first bomb penetrated the flight deck and detonated in the forward portion of the hangar deck with devastating consequences. Fires spread throughout the hangar spaces and engulfed parked airplanes and their maintenance crews with no warning. Most of the planes in the hangar were already loaded with ordnance, which soon began to cook off and cause even greater chaos and destruction. There was no escaping the flames and searing heat that incinerated everything in its path. Everyone in the vicinity of frame 82, where the bomb hit, was killed within a few minutes.

A second bomb struck aft of the first, about frame 133, but did not penetrate the flight deck. However, while in the middle of a launch cycle, the planes, pilots, and technicians working the flight deck were all extremely vulnerable. Fires quickly spread to many of the planes turning up for launch, the propeller wash and winds over the deck creating a natural incendiary environment that left nothing and no one unscathed. The explosion blew up the aft elevator and flipped it completely onto its side. As the airplanes began to burn on the flight deck, their ordnance began to cook off as those below deck had. A dozen of the fighter-bombers on deck were armed with a relatively unstable 11 ¾-inch mini-rockets called "Tiny Tims." As these rockets were exposed to the searing heat and fires that engulfed the airplanes, the Tiny Tims began to cook off sending a deadly hail of projectiles across the flight deck. The collateral damage from the rockets added to the chaos and pandemonium already on the flight deck, and quickly added to the number of personnel who lost their lives in the attack.[56]

Albert Antar, a twenty-year-old enlisted technician aboard the USS *Yorktown* in 1942 during the Battle of the Coral Sea, witnessed firsthand the dangers of working on the flight deck of the carrier during his first combat experience. While working on his airplane in the hangar, a single Japanese bomb struck the *Yorktown* just aft of the island, almost directly above his workstation. It penetrated the wooden deck and continued to pierce through the steel flooring below until embedding itself in the fifth deck down where it exploded. The path of the bomb passed twenty feet from where Antar was standing. It left a trail of more than sixty dead sailors due to the initial explosion and the secondary fires from the ruptured fuel tanks. Antar walked away without a scratch and would continue to serve throughout the war. He retired from the Navy after twenty-four years of service.[57]

Other hazards that came with the job of working on the carrier deck included airplanes "jumping chocks" while engines were being warmed up prior to pilots arriving for preflight inspections. Often ground personnel, junior enlisted technicians, were qualified to start engines for warm up or other maintenance procedures. However, as carrier operations increased in late 1943, the experience levels of such technicians were lacking due to the massive influx of technicians, airplanes, and carriers hitting the fleet. Simple actions such as inspecting the placement of wheel chocks and applying sufficient brake pressure while adding power to engines above idle were sometimes overlooked. This could result in the airplane pushing itself over the wheel chocks and causing injury to ground personnel working around the plane, or mechanical damage to the airplane itself.[58]

There were times when the dedication of the enlisted technicians seemed beyond comprehension. On May 8, 1942, the final day of the Battle of Coral Sea, the *Lexington* was under attack. She took direct hits from five torpedoes and two bombs dropped by Japanese aircraft. The damage and ensuing fires eventually forced the crew to abandon ship. The "Lady Lex" was rendered unrecoverable after fires continued and worsened throughout the day. Ultimately, she was sunk by two "mercy" torpedoes fired by the destroyer USS *Phelps* fired at a range of 1,500 yards. But leading up to that, the crew managed to keep the ship operating even in the midst of multiple fires below deck. The air group was still trying to get planes into the air, thus the maintenance crews were still on duty. Before the order to abandon ship was given, many tried to salvage as much of the fighting capabilities as possible, which meant flying as many planes off onto another carrier in the vicinity. In one instance, the air group commander had his men gathered around him on the fight deck where he was opining on the fortunes and misfortunes of war. Meant to be an inspirational talk, it stirred one young mechanic to speak up about his latest endeavor—replacing an oil pump on his airplane. The commander commented that it seemed to take him a long time to complete the relatively simple task. The sailor replied, "Yes sir . . . had to draw it from stores and had an awful job getting to it. There's a terrible fire down there."⁵⁹ While this vignette seems humorous, it is a vivid example of the dedication these young men had for their airplanes while fighting the war.

It is no secret that the war created a heroic and skilled labor force for both the military and civilian aviation sectors. Having trained more than a third of a million aircraft technicians in four years, the Navy released most of them following the Japanese surrender. After their honorable service the Navy owed them some guidance on where to find their next employment once naval aviation entered a peacetime draw-down of forces and operations. Training technicians to support combat aviation operations had to translate to support for peacetime and civilian operations. By June 1945 the "writing was on the wall" for naval aircraft technicians. NATTC understood there would be a mass exodus of its technical cadre, so it began providing guidance early rather than waiting for an armistice.

According to BuAer guidance there were in excess of two hundred peacetime jobs waiting for a naval aircraft technician after discharge. An aviation machinist's mate might do well as an operator of power and hand tools in a machine shop or factory. He or she could also work as a drill press technician, bolt threader, or hydraulic field serviceman. As was the case with Forest Bruner Jr., an engine service mechanic on automobiles was a natural fit, but AMMs could also find postwar employment as an aircraft service mechanic, tractor mechanic, airplane inspector, or aircraft factory worker as well.

The aviation metalsmith could likely find employment as a welder, sheet metal worker, plumber, steam fitter, coppersmith, or press operator. Many of these jobs carried with them apprenticeships and qualification exams that the ex-sailors could easily navigate due to their former training and experience. An aviation electrician's mate could obviously find work as an aircraft technician, transformer assembler, general electric wiring technician, refrigerator serviceman, electrician, telegraph installer, telephone wire chief, or telegraph repeater attendant.

Even an aviation ordnanceman had options in the peacetime workforce. They could find a job as a general instrument repairman, electrical assembly worker, spray gun or projector assembler, gunsmith, or even a radio mechanic with the skills learned in the fleet.⁶⁰

"Keeping 'em flying" may have been their primary mission, but naval aircraft technicians were well suited for employment outside the naval service once the war was over. Rear Adm. H. S. Kendall, commander of the Naval Air Technical Training Command in 1945, remarked during an interview with *Naval Aviation News*,

> These men to whom the Navy has given thorough training in electronics, combustion engines, specialized training in all fields of aircraft maintenance and repair, are the men who will return to civilian life well qualified for good peacetime jobs. Predictions of developments to come following the war are staggering to the imagination but they have one quality in common: they require advanced technical knowledge in many fields, if they are to be realized. Many of them will be realized. And I am sure that well forward in the ranks of tomorrow's most valued and honored technicians, will be found the men who today are serving their country as air and ground crewmen in Naval Aviation. In time of war they are being trained for the peace we all desire and cherish.[61]

✦✦✦

During the interwar years, the *Lexington*-class carriers were designed to operate with one particular air group and its associated squadrons. These squadrons were organized into a self-sufficient unit, complete with maintenance capabilities. The air group was assigned to a specific carrier and embarked its squadrons, as needed. The small numbers of carrier aviation units, along with the minimal operational requirements that existed in the 1930s, did not require a permanent footprint of technicians and their associated matériel on board the carrier unless the air group was embarked. Therefore, every time a squadron embarked or disembarked, a massive undertaking was required to load or unload all the support equipment, tools, and administrative and maintenance personnel.[62]

Once war with Japan began, the time and labor required to transfer the maintenance divisions on and off the ship hampered the readiness of both the air group and the carrier. Carrier pilots were required to maintain their training even when the ship was in port for extended periods.

Thus, the air group would fly their aircraft off the carrier and onto a naval air station when the ship was in homeport for long periods. Aircraft carriers also had to maintain the ability to deploy for combat operations on short notice. The time and cost of embarking and reembarking the air group's maintenance department was prohibitive. Due to the likely urgency off operational demands, the massive numbers of carriers and air groups that would eventually fight the war, and the cost of moving hundreds of men and supplies on and off made the existing procedure impractical.[63]

The Navy had to change its carrier aircraft maintenance practices. Thus, the carrier aircraft service division (CASD) was established and became a permanent fixture on aircraft carriers whether an air group was embarked or not. It soon shortened its name to the "air department."[64] The technicians assigned were aviation rated technicians, but were considered part of the ship's company. This explains why when researching squadron personnel rosters from air groups during the war, only the pilots and aircrew are listed.[65]

Once the "V" divisions became a permanent fixture on the CV, there had to be a unit ashore to maintain the aircraft when they left the carrier to operate from island or shore bases. This unit was designated a carrier aircraft service unit (CASU) in February 1944. CASUs were loosely defined as shore-based air group service outfits designed to support the flight operations of air groups. The CASU was responsible for the operation of its own local facilities and its primary duty was to support naval aviation in the operating area. As far as airplane maintenance, the CASU was capable of servicing, rearming, completing minor repairs, and routine upkeep. CASUs did not have any organic maintenance equipment, but relied on the ACORN units to provide them with the necessary items to do its job. The CASU concept allowed carrier air departments to streamline their maintenance operations into flight-related tasks only, transferring responsibility of all major maintenance duties to shore-based maintenance units.

Dozens of CASUs were established throughout the South Pacific Islands for the duration of the war, as well on U.S. coastal bases including Pearl Harbor. The primary job of the CASU was to support the carrier squadron by way of maintenance when its mission brought the aircrew and planes ashore for extended periods. Forward deployed CASUs took the place of carrier maintenance departments on shore where well-equipped naval air stations did not exist. The CASUs were mobile units that could be quickly stood-up in one area and then quickly transferred to another as ground forces secured small islands across the Pacific. A CASU had maintenance, medical, welfare, ordnance, supply, and other administrative personnel assigned to it. Its primary task was to maintain and repair carrier aircraft, but it was not meant to, nor equipped to complete major overhauls. A&R facilities still handled the majority of Class A, B, and C maintenance.[66] There were nearly seventy CASUs in commission throughout the Pacific during World War II.[67]

The CASU averaged 17 officers and 516 enlisted men, but it varied in size depending on location. Some of these units could be as large as 1,500 enlisted with 89 officers—depending on the number of aircraft they were assigned to support at once: 45, 90, 180, 270, or 360. Hot, humid, and primitive locations were the norm. Even in a moderate climate, the work could be challenging. The CASU technicians operating in the Pacific dealt with bright skies, strong sun, and oppressive heat and humidity throughout the year. One of the more difficult problems to remedy was the glare in their eyes while working on airplanes. BuAer came up with a solution to reduce the glare and sunburn on their faces—baseball caps. In late 1944, BuAer authorized each CASU 175 blue caps for designated engineering crew, 150 for ordnancemen, and 150 for flightline operation crews.

Previously, BuAer had approved a brimmed hard-shelled headgear, which was called a "sun helmet" for use in the CASU operations. But technicians soon found the sun helmets were unsuitable to wear while working in or around airplanes. Based on feedback from the CASU and fleet units, BuAer designed the new caps for its maintenance crews. The idea was so popular though, BuAer eventually made the baseball caps available to any aviation unit who desired to outfit its technicians in the caps. Even pilots caught on to the idea and soon khaki colored ball caps with long, long brims were issued to pilots as well.[68]

CASUs also acted as a forward staging area for replacement parts, aircraft, and squadron personnel rotating into the combat zones. On occasion, it also took on the task of technical schooling for sailors who did not receive any or all of the NATTC training before being transferred to forward operating areas. The CASU would often have a ground school set up to train new recruits how to work on the three types of carrier aircraft (fighter, bomber, torpedo) in lieu of what they would have learned at an NATTC technical school. Many times, they would develop their own training courses designed to sharpen or refresh a technician's skill set.[69] CASUs were wartime-only units that were initially designed to support the carrier war in the Pacific.

However, as the strategic picture of the war changed, so did the mission of a CASU. In late 1944 operations throughout the Pacific required more than just support for the carrier air groups. Tactical air bases with extensive maintenance facilities were needed to support two-engine and four-engine bombers, patrol planes, and Army aircraft that were integral to the amphibious operations against entrenched Japanese forces throughout the island chains. Thus, while the CASU program began as support for carrier aircraft only, the strategic circumstances of the war required the commander, Naval Air Forces, Pacific Fleet (COMNAVAIRPAC) to modify CASU maintenance responsibilities to include land-based aircraft in addition to carrier aircraft. In October 1944 the definition of the acronym CASU was changed to combat aircraft service unit (forward). From that point forward, the CASU (F) serviced both carrier and patrol aircraft, to include Army Air Corps and Allied units.[70]

During the second half of 1942 another significant change in aircraft maintenance operations occurred. The increase and intensity of aircraft operations in the Pacific after the battles of Wake Island and Midway Atolls made it clear that the Navy needed an aircraft engine overhaul facility in the South Pacific. The CASUs alone were insufficient to complete the increasing number of overhauls. Aircraft engines that required major overhauls had to be shipped three thousand miles from the South Pacific to Pearl Harbor due to the inability of the CASUs to keep up with the demand. This took up valuable shipping space on merchant and naval vessels and placed the units out of commission for weeks or months.[71] Ironically, the duration of labor involved on a major overhaul was only a matter of a few days to a week. Recently promoted from chief of BuAer to commander, Air Forces, Pacific Fleet and awarded a third star, now-Vice Admiral Towers endorsed a request sent to the Navy Department for an overhaul facility in the southern Pacific operating area. He commented on the necessity for such a capability on the front lines:

> Experience during the past several months has clearly demonstrated the immediate necessity for establishing in the South Pacific overhaul facilities for aircraft engines, propellers, and power plant facilities. . . . Action is necessitated by lack of sufficient pool of spare engines to permit the rotation of engines for overhaul between the South Pacific and established facilities at Pearl Harbor or the West Coast. . . . The need for prompt action is shown by the fact that more than three hundred and fifty (350) replacement engines have been shipped to the SoPac whereas only about fifty (50) have been returned to overhaul bases to date. The drain on the engine pool, if continued, may soon result in critical shortages which will hamper operations.[72]

By December 1942, the Navy had called two officers to Washington, DC, to begin planning what would become the Navy's aviation repair and overhaul units (AROU). Cdr. Thomas D. Guinn and Lt. Cdr. Seraphin B. Perreault were ordered to the Office of the Vice Chief of Naval Operations. They soon brought three other officers in to assist with standing up the new unit. Lt. F. A. Celler, USNR, was nominated as the aviation repair officer, Lt. J. V. Koch, USNR, was placed in charge of personnel duties, and Lt. R. S. Jennings, USNR, was assigned as supply officer. Their goal was to design a system that could complete a hundred major overhauls per month while positioned in the forward operating areas of the Pacific. The concept of an AROU began to take shape and units began forming within a few months.[73] AROUs were commissioned at various times throughout the 1943–44 period.

AROU-1 was commissioned in August 1943, but did not forward deploy into the Pacific until April 1944. AROU-1 was given orders to transfer from Alameda, California, to the Admiralty Islands, located just to the north of Papua New Guinea.[74] Another smaller repair unit, designated AROU-2, was requested in February 1944 by Admiral Nimitz, who had been promoted to commander in chief, Pacific Fleet (CINCPAC-FLT) after the attack on Pearl Harbor. AROU-2 was commissioned in

March 1944 with Cdr. Norman O. Anderson as its first and only wartime commanding officer. AROU-2 was assigned to Roi, Kwajalein Atoll, in the Marshall Islands.[75] The Navy commissioned a total of five AROUs throughout the South Pacific during the war.

An AROU was completely self-sufficient, similar to a CASU, but on a much larger scale. More than 1,000 sailors were assigned to AROU-1, with approximately four-fifths, or around 800, being aircraft technicians or part of the Supply Division within the AROU. Some large units, such as AROU-5, had 2,200 sailors assigned when operating at maximum capacity.[76] The rest of the sailors attended to the administrative duties and other nontechnical ratings such as laundry, cooking, commissary, morale and welfare, shore patrol, firefighting, medical care, and religious duty. Other AROUs varied in size, such as AROU-2, which had about half as many personnel—492 enlisted and 15 officers.[77]

The primary role of the AROU was the assembly and repair of Pacific Fleet carrier aircraft. Major engine overhauls were only completed at select AROUs. AROU-2, for instance, was not designed to have an engine overhaul division within its force structure.[78] Hundreds of technicians were handpicked from the naval air stations in the United States to serve in the technical divisions of the AROU. Furthermore, the AROU's labor force was subdivided by specialization, similar to the aircraft carrier maintenance divisions.

The Assembly and Repair Department was composed of the following divisions: Planning and Matériel, Engine Overhaul, Accessories, Repair, Overhaul, Aircraft Pool, Ordnance, Radio-Radar, Propeller and CO2, and the Parachute Loft. Within each of the divisions, the technicians were further grouped by subspecialty. The Repair Division had its own carpenter shop, a paint shop, a fabric shop, a welding shop, a landing gear shop, and a machine shop. The Aircraft Pool Division divided its technicians into smaller groups like structures, hydraulics, preservation, turn-up, electricians, flightline, and flight maintenance. Within the Engine Overhaul Division, technicians were grouped into carburetors and pumps, mock-up, test stands, inspection, and minor overhaul. Specialization of labor was critical to the success of the AROU.[79]

Overhauled engines at the AROU were preserved for future replacements or for shipment out to aircraft carriers in the vicinity. Once the engines were deemed serviceable and all required maintenance or repair was complete, they were coated with an anticorrosion agent and placed in a moisture-proof bag. A dehydrating agent was then added, the excess air removed with a vacuum pump, and the bag was sealed. These engines were shelved and then delivered to the fleet or placed into aircraft as necessary.[80] The processes were in accordance with BuAer's guidance on the proper way to preserve aircraft spare parts.

The Aircraft Pool Division was tasked with readying newly delivered aircraft from transport carriers for transport. When "factory-new" aircraft were off-loaded from transports at the AROUs, they were often in pieces, disassembled for shipping. Most of the time new aircraft were shipped by section in crates or other containers to save space in transit. The division technicians' daily routine was one of feast or famine. The division's job was to "unwrap" the new planes, assemble and "de-preserve" any parts that might have been disassembled for shipment, make the final adjustments, perform functional checks, and wait for a squadron to show up that would ferry the airplanes to the carrier. Their job was to make preserved and overhauled planes combat ready in the shortest amount of time possible. The average time allotted for this task was 350 man-hours per plane.[81] Between mid-September 1944 and January 1, 1945, the aircraft division of AROU-1 furnished approximately 800 combat-ready aircraft to the fleet.[82]

Of the five AROUs commissioned by the Navy during the war, the oldest unit—ironically designated as AROU-5—was completing its first engine overhauls in June 1943. Its first month output was only 7 overhauls, a far cry from their goal of 100 per month. But by January 1944, AROU-5 technicians reached their goal with 103 and never looked back (see Table 5.3).

An analysis of Table 5.3 supports the argument that the Navy's air force was not fully prepared to go to war when it did. As the backlog of engines in 1942 raised concern with Towers and other naval leadership, the lack of maintenance infrastructure and available labor did little to assuage their worry. The U.S. Navy's victory at Midway served as an indication of what was to come in terms of necessary aircraft maintenance. Perhaps the Navy realized the effort it would take to keep the carrier fleets at full strength when so many aircraft were engaged in combat?

Table 5.3. AROU-5 Summary of Engine Overhauls, July 1943–February 1945 [1]

MONTH	MAJOR OVERHAULS	MINOR OVERHAULS	TOTAL
June 1943	6	1	7
July 1943	36	5	41
Aug. 1943	80	2	82
Sept. 1943	58	3	61
Oct. 1943	62	21	83
Nov. 1943	66	30	96
Dec. 1943	55	12	77
Jan. 1944	70	33	103
Feb. 1944	85	42	127
Mar. 1944	97	20	117
April 1944	110	36	146
May 1944	125	34	159
June 1944	150	60	210
July 1944	120	47	167
Aug. 1944	142	46	188
Sept. 1944	105	33	138
Oct. 1944	161	22	183
Nov. 1944	176	31	207
Dec. 1944	163	7	170
Jan. 1945	185	17	202
Feb. 1945	132	59	191
Total (21 Months)	2,184	561	2,755

[1] "Aviation Repair and Overhaul Unit 5," Appendix B. It should be noted that of the 2,184 "major" overhauls in Table 5.3, 1,003 were on the Pratt and Whitney R-2800 engine, predominantly used in the F6F Hellcat fighter. The remaining 1,181 were conducted on the R-2600 and R-1820 models both built by Curtiss. These engines were used in various Navy and Army aircraft, but predominantly in the SBC Helldiver, the Brewster F2A Buffalo, the Grumman F3F, and early models of the F6F. The focus of effort by the AROU was the Navy's carrier aircraft. The number of engines undergoing overhaul at just one of these units is indicative of the wear and tear fleet operations were having on airplanes. See "Aviation Repair and Overhaul Unit 5."

More combat missions equaled more overhauls. It was not until a year later that the AROU began completing engine overhauls and six months after that before their production surpassed one hundred per month.

The timing with which the AROU began to deliver large quantities of engines was consistent with the timing at which naval aircraft technicians were graduating at the highest rate since Lieutenant Commander Wheelock overhauled the trade school programs.[83] It also coincided with the opening of the Naval Training Centers in Norman and Memphis in September 1942. The six-month average for each rating's course of study places the largest numbers of available around the same time that the AROUs were completing the most overhauls. The skilled labor that made up the AROUs and CASUs were graduates from the aviation trade schools managed by Lieutenant Commander Wheelock's Technical Training Division in BuAer from 1940 to 1942.[84]

AROU-5s monthly production of overhauled engines was representative of the other four AROUs forward deployed in the Pacific. The number of engine overhauls completed each month in 1944 supports the notion that the aircraft technician played a substantial role in the strike missions of the Fast Carrier Task Force. The Navy's fast carrier doctrine was as much dependent on the aircraft technician as it was on the officers and technology of the U.S. Navy. If the engines and airplanes were not available when needed, the carriers were worthless.

A "major overhaul" was routinely conducted after 500 flight hours.[85] An average sortie could be anywhere between 2 and 3½ hours, depending on the mission and aircraft. A standard combat mission for an F6F was usually 3 or 3½ hours.[86] Therefore, 500 engine hours equated to somewhere between 140 and 250 flights, or 5 to 9 months assuming a limit of just one sortie per day. However, in 1944 and 1945, the average number of flights per aircraft per month for fighters was 15 and 17, respectively, based on reports after the war from the Fast Carrier Task Force.[87] This equates to approximately 45 hours per month. At this rate, an aircraft engine would reach its overhaul limit in about 11 months. Therefore, if the engines started arriving for major overhaul at the AROUs in late 1943 or early 1944, then it is plausible that it was not until

Specialization of Labor 147

after Midway—perhaps early 1943—that the Navy started increasing its flight operations to its highest since the war began. What significance did this have in terms of aircraft technicians?

Importantly, it correlates with the period of highest graduation rates of the NATTC trade schools: November 1942 through March 1943 (see Table 3.1). The timing of the increased output of the trade schools combined with the establishment of NATTC, plus the ever-increasing aircraft carrier construction and associated aircraft deliveries throughout 1943 made it possible for the Navy to modify its operational doctrine. By then, the maintenance support was in place to support intensified flight operations and eventually implement the fast carrier task force concept.[88]

While the Navy had carriers in operation in 1942 and 1943, the majority of aircraft carriers were constructed in 1943 and commissioned in 1944. Overall, carrier flight hours were much lower in the 1942–43 time frame as compared to that of 1944–45. Just 6 percent of the Navy's carrier-based aircraft combat sorties occurred during the first twenty-four months of World War II. This equates to 7,381 of the approximately 116,000 combat or "action" sorties flown by air groups assigned to aircraft carriers before January 1, 1944.[89] The number of engine overhauls that the AROUs completed were also lower in 1943 than in mid-1944 or 1945.[90] The higher rate of flight hours correlated directly with the timing of increased aircraft carrier inventory. The correlation was of a matériel nature; more planes and more carriers equaled more flight time. More flight time equaled more overhauls. But the data hints at another contributing factor behind the dramatic jump in overhauls and flight hours than simply matériel availability and doctrinal change. It suggests that the availability of a well-trained and sufficiently sized technical labor force directly affected the Navy's ability to engage in a protracted naval air war in the Pacific.

The naval air war against Japan did not achieve sustained success until enough technicians were in place to support the doctrine of the Fast Carrier Task Force. Based on BuAer's development of technical training from 1940 through 1942, the U.S. Navy did not have enough manpower to back a high operational tempo of flight hours and fast carriers. But the general timing of qualified technicians reaching the fleet in mass quantities in 1943 does appear to coincide with a shift in the Navy's strategy and increased success in the Pacific. Although this was not the sole reason for the shift, it should not be ignored.

Even with the numerous CASUs and AROUs, three years into the war it was evident that the Pacific Fleet needed a more mobile repair unit for its fast carrier task force. The closer the Navy got to Japan, the quicker its carrier groups moved and shore-based repair facilities could not always keep up with the demands. BuAer had seen this coming and tried to plan for it earlier in the war, but the Navy could not afford to give up any of its ships for such a limited mission as aircraft repair. Amphibious operations in both the Atlantic and Pacific were stretching all resources to the max. By the end of the war when the United States had gained the upper hand, the Navy made good on BuAer's plan to deliver a floating aircraft repair shop to the fleet.

Floating support vessels for aviation operations was not a new concept in 1944. Aircraft tenders had been around since the *Langley* was taken out of combat service early in the war. However, it wasn't until versatile amphibious landing ships (LST) were no longer needed en masse for amphibious landings in Europe or Pacific beachheads that the Navy was able to free up four "to be built" vessels and convert them into floating aircraft assembly and repair shops that would serve the invasion forces in the Pacific.

The four assembly and repair vessels (ARV) were built at the American Bridge Company shipyards in Pittsburg, Pennsylvania. Integrating the design and capabilities of the LST for this mission was especially useful and innovative. An LST hull could sail directly up onto the beach, as it had done so many times before in support of amphibious landings, and provide a semipermanent repair shop that could service fighters and bombers in the invasion area until landing strip and forward airbase facilities were constructed (or secured from the Japanese as in the case of Henderson Field on Guadalcanal). The four ARVs were commissioned with names uncommon to American fighting ships in the 1940s, names drawn from Greek and Roman mythology: the *Aventinus* (son of Hercules), *Chloris* (goddess of flowers), *Fabius* (son of Hercules by a nymph), and *Magara* (daughter of Hercules).

Each of the ships was built to accomplish a certain repair mission. Both the *Fabius* and *Magara* were designated ARV (A) as they were equipped especially for airframe repair and maintenance. The other two ARVs—the *Aventinus* and the *Chloris*—were built to handle engine repair, thus designated ARV (E). The ARVs deployed as a team, one (A) and one (E) landed on the beach in unison, and established A&R shop for the air support elements of the invading forces. The ARVs could not be used until there was at least a rudimentary airstrip for airplanes to land close by. The labor and complexity of laying down a combat airstrip in the middle of a relatively uninhabited island in the Pacific paled in comparison to constructing a repair shop and the logistics of transporting all of the support gear and the spare parts. Once an airstrip was secured, the ARVs dropped anchor at the beachhead.

ARVs were not kept at the invasion site indefinitely. They would arrive on station with convoys and pull into the beach after ammunition and food ships had unloaded their cargo. In tandem, the ARV was big enough to provide satisfactory specialized maintenance, while the Acorn units were setting up the CASUs for general aircraft support. ARVs would sometimes stay on the beach even after the CASU was up and running to assist. Eventually they were withdrawn for their own resupply and reoutfit, in expectation to follow the next amphibious landing. Often this resulted in the ships staying "on location" for several months.

The capability of the ARV ships to make repairs was impressive: "ARVs contain shops which can fix almost anything that goes wrong with aircraft in action."[91] Each class of ship had specific workspaces, or shops, that handled very defined tasks. The A-model ships were built with the following shop spaces aboard: airframes, carbon dioxide transfer, paint and dope, fabric and upholstery, instruments, landing gear and hydraulics, machine, oxygen transfer, plating and anodizing, radio and radar, tie rod and cable, welding, heat treatment and metal, woodworking, sandblasting, and metalizing. The different shops aboard E-model ships were: accessories, aviation electrical, engine quick-change and buildup, inspection, machine, ordnance, propeller, and storage battery. Just as the technicians were directed into very specialized labor fields through the new rating systems put in place throughout the war, the ARV contained a specialized labor force capability within. No more was there a need to interchange shops or their technicians to cover another technician's job.

The ARV teams established themselves on the beach and worked together to complete the mission. One way it ensured efficiency in its work was through effective communications. Not only were the ARVs landed adjacent to one another, once secured on shore a communications cable (aka "landline") was strung out between the two ships. This provided the ability for the units and shops to coordinate with each other on an instant and regular basis. This was necessary to transition the capability of each individual ship to a single unit that acted in the same manner a shore facility would.

The significant problem with the ARVs facilities was their location. While it was convenient to have the side-by-side ARVs on the beachhead of the invaded island, if the landing strip was not in the immediate vicinity of the ships, there was still the problem of getting parts to and from the airstrips. To solve this problem each ARV ship deployed with a variety of vehicles designed to transport parts to and from each ship. Aboard each ARV was the following: one mobile machine truck and trailer, a welding shop truck, two line maintenance power supply jeeps (to provide electrical power to the aircraft and repair vehicles on the flight line), one cargo truck, one radio/radar maintenance truck, four general cargo trucks, four weapon carriers, eight jeeps, six tractors, four jeep trailers, and two portable floodlight trailers. They also arrived with four air compressors, six power units, two thirty-six-foot boats to serve as ferries to and from supply ships, four forklift trucks, two rearming boats, two propeller trailers, one torpedo-topping compressor, and twelve engine transportation stands. The fleet of vehicles and mobile units aboard the ARVs made the job of getting parts to and from the flight line nearly seamless.

Inside the ARV also amounted to an engineering feat. Throughout the interior of the ship was an overhead crane that traversed the enormous forward compartment (originally designed to carry tanks in the LST hull). The individual repair shops line either side of the compartment, opening into the vast open space. On an E-class ship, the engine test stands, engine shop, and carburetor test shop were built on the main deck house, itself an innovation on the LST frame. On A-class vessels, the main deck house contained auxiliary machinery, boiler and evaporator, laundry, a dope and drying room, and the wing shop. The ARVs had oversized water purification units for the crew's fresh drinking water and the boilers. The ARV had a larger crew than a typical LST, thus the need for more fresh-water production.[92]

Designed by BuAer and BuShip engineers, the ARV was an engineering feat forced upon the fleet by the circumstances of the war. Delayed by the necessity of LSTs for amphibious landings in both Pacific and Atlantic theaters, it was not until very late in the war that the ARV made an impact. It was another innovation that addressed major changes to U.S. naval forces brought on by carrier aviation. While an ARV was not designed to support aircraft carriers directly, the aircraft used to support amphibious invasions in the Pacific were initially brought into the area of operations via aircraft carrier. Carrier aviation and the nature of the war in the vast Pacific island regions had forced innovation once again.

Significant and sustained carrier operations did not occur until the Guadalcanal campaign (August 1942–February 1943). This, combined with the lower sortie rates and flight hours in 1942 and 1943 compared to the last two years of the war, suggests that the Navy was not ready to fight a protracted war at sea until its carrier aircraft technicians were trained and in place. Likewise, a more robust supporting infrastructure was not a singular event but was established over time. Thus we must reconsider the completeness of the arguments that have claimed it was the technology behind the planes and carriers, or the bravado of the pilots and admirals that was most responsible for the United States' naval victory in the Pacific. Without enough trained technicians to manage the repairs, overhauls, and replacements that a carrier task force required, and a sufficient logistics chain to supply and support the naval air war, the effectiveness of the fast carrier doctrine implemented in 1944 would have been severely limited.

Chapter 6

Supplying a Throwaway Culture

While carriers deployed with a complement of spares, due to space constraints, a logistics train from stateside to the Pacific was still required. During the first half of the war in the Pacific, carrier task forces routinely returned to Pearl Harbor to refuel and resupply stores, parts, aircraft, aircrew. While underway replenishment was a fairly regular occurrence, it could not satisfy the needs of a modern aircraft carrier in terms of aircraft specific replenishment. All of this changed in January 1944 in preparation for the attack on the Marshall Islands and the Allied thrust to fully secure the central Pacific.[1]

Fleet anchorages in the Pacific, managed by floating mobile base units designated "service squadrons," afforded the task force the ability to continue its forward deployment rather than returning to Pearl Harbor when in need of resupply. Service squadrons that operated in the vicinity of carrier combat operations required much more support than just that of escort carriers and aviation supplies, thus they were comprised of a myriad of ships. For the Okinawa campaign (March–June 1945), Service Squadron Six utilized seventy-three ships in support of Task Force (TF) 58: one light carrier (CL), seven escort carriers (CVE), twenty-eight destroyers, two cargo ships, twenty-four oilers, five ammunition ships, four fleet tugs, and two distilling ships.[2] The ability of a fast carrier task force to remain at sea for lengthy periods during combat operations can be attributed directly to the service squadrons. During the Okinawa campaign, the three fast carrier groups comprising the Fast Carrier Task Force remained at sea for forty-two, sixty-two, and seventy-seven days, respectively.[3]

Of all the methods and vessels used to transport spare parts within the service squadrons, the escort carriers were the most prolific. The service squadrons were not intended to supplant the carrier aircraft service units (CASUs); rather, they operated in conjunction with each other. While CASUs were responsible for making replacement aircraft available to the carrier groups, they did not necessarily have the ability to deliver new or repaired airplanes. The escort carriers were instrumental in filling this gap. The CVE delivered aircraft, aircraft engines, and aircraft parts to Pacific Fleet. CASUs and other commands stood up in the Pacific atolls, such as Kwajalein also benefiting from the CVE mission. Planes could be flown directly from a CVE to the Fast Carrier Task Force as a one-for-one replacement for either a damaged or lost aircraft, often including a fresh pilot. Other methods included static off-loads via crane to either a fifty-ton self-propelled barge or directly to a pier.[4] This was most common in situations where new aircraft were not yet flyable as they were often shipped with wings and other parts removed in order to save space in transit.

Depending on the tempo of operations, the size of aircraft pools situated on land bases in the Pacific could reach 1,500 airplanes at once. These airplanes were not intended solely for the use of the Fast Carrier Task Force, but also replacement of land-based units such as Marine Corps squadrons and Navy inshore patrol squadrons. Even though the CASUs and service squadrons were firmly in place by early 1944, there was still a need to transfer new aircraft built in the United States to the logistics units in the Pacific.[5] The hub of such operations was Pearl Harbor and the workhorse of those transfers was the escort carrier. As the Navy began its "island hopping" campaign in earnest, the USS *Copahee* (CVE 12)—a *Bogue*-class escort carrier under the command of Capt. Dale Harris—was one such vessel.

In preparation for the Marianas Islands campaign (aka Operation Forager), Captain Harris watched as 86 aircraft, 390 passengers, and 196 cases of equipment were onloaded to the *Copahee* in Pearl Harbor. On

April 17, 1944, he gave the order to cast off all lines and began steaming westward. The ship was designed to carry no more than 24 operational aircraft, but innovations in storage and shipping methods permitted the *Copahee* (and others like her) to carry many more. In less than one week, the *Copahee* arrived at the recently acquired Majuro Airfield in the Marshall Islands, quickly off-loaded her cargo, and prepared for a return journey to Pearl Harbor.[6] Only this time, her cargo was not new parts and planes, but 23 damaged planes, 2 aircraft engines, and 312 passengers on their way back to U.S. territory for much needed R&R. After delivering her damaged and "worn-out" matériel, the *Copahee* was assigned another load of aircraft and parts to deliver to Majuro. This continued throughout the Marianas campaign, bringing the total number of replacement aircraft delivered into the operating area to greater than 200.[7]

The *Copahee* remained in the vicinity of the Marianas throughout the campaign, including the famous "Marianas Turkey Shoot" on June 19, 1944, in which Navy pilots shot down an estimated 600 Japanese airplanes, losing only 123 of their own. She would make regular runs between Marianas and Eniwetok, replenishing her supply of airplanes, pilots, and parts. The daily routine of a CVE in the Pacific varied depending on what the operational demands were. As was the case during the Marianas campaign, there were days when the CVE was quite busy and required to complete the complicated task of launching and receiving multiple aircraft to and from multiple carriers. On the eve of Marianas D-day, June 14, the *Copahee* completed the following deliveries: four fighters and one torpedo plane to the *Cowpens*; one fighter, one torpedo plane, and three SB2C bombers to the *Hornet*; four fighters to the CVL *Bataan*; five fighters, five torpedo planes, and seven SB2C bombers to the *Yorktown*; and four fighters, two torpedo planes, and two Avenger pilots to the *Belleau Wood*.

Captain Harris' crew then received a number of what were commonly referred to as "flyable duds," or aircraft that could take off and land, but were not capable of combat operations. The *Copahee* continued to receive and deliver aircraft throughout the campaign on an as-needed basis by the Fast Carrier Task Force. There were days when thirty or more airplanes were flown from the CVEs to the CV and CVLs, and other days when flight operations were nonexistent. On rare occasions, CVE cargo would even cause the casual observer to question the origin of its load out. On July 7, in a twist on routine operations, the *Copahee* onloaded a number of captured Japanese aircraft for transfer to Pearl Harbor and eventually the mainland for research and development purposes.[8]

During massive campaigns, such as the Battle of Leyte Gulf in October 1944, there were days when task forces needed resupplies in greater quantity than a single escort carrier could manage. Such was the case on October 11 when TF 38, under the command of Vice Adm. Marc Mitscher, required a replenishment in preparation for an attack on Formosa. Not one, but three escort carriers were sortied to deliver a total of sixty-one replacement planes, three pilots, and eleven air crews to Mitscher's Fast Carrier Task Force in a single afternoon.[9] Less than twenty-four hours later, Mitscher's task force began a three-day effort to eliminate as much enemy airpower on Formosa as possible and deny the Japanese the island's use as a staging base for combat planes. TF 38's airplanes were ready to launch an hour before sunrise, thanks to the efforts of the plane captains and other technicians working through the night. Throughout the first day, 1,378 sorties were flown from the four carrier groups. The second day saw just under 1,000 sorties flown by noon. Over the course of the three-day assault, American pilots shot down more than 500 Japanese airplanes, sunk dozens of Japanese freighters and smaller craft, and did vast amounts of damage to ammunition dumps, hangars, and industrial sites.[10]

It was not only the CVE that provided the requisite spare parts that the Fast Carrier Task Force needed. Undesignated cargo ships such as the *Fortune* (IX 146) were an integral part of the logistics force in the Pacific as well. The *Fortune* operated out of Kwajalein and was gainfully employed. She did not deliver planes, but did supply spare parts to the carriers during periods of underway replenishment. These ships were generally converted merchants whose cargo was slung along a cable-pulley system from her deck for transfer to the carrier while steaming in formation; the ships were separated by a mere few dozen meters. These operations were about much more than just aircraft parts. Underway replenishment included everything from fresh fruit, vegetables, food stores, ship stores, ship engine parts, fuel, oil, and pretty much anything else a modern warship needed to stay at sea and fight.[11]

More than 2,000 aircraft, 600 vessels, and 300,000 personnel participated in the Marianas campaign in 1944. The concept of carrier aircraft and parts replenishment by the CVE and other vessels was an entirely new concept in terms of naval aviation. Such missions did not even exist when the Japanese bombed Pearl Harbor. This was a logistics operation that was developed concurrently with the construction of aircraft carriers and aircraft over the first two years of the war. Carrier replenishment at sea was unique to the Pacific war due to the nature of combat in this theater, the distances traveled, and the scope of operations. Naval air combat losses were minimal in the Atlantic theater, thanks to a lack of Axis carrier operations. The real fight for naval air supremacy was in the Pacific and the Fast Carrier Task Force could not afford to pause operations due to a dearth of planes, pilots, or parts. The replenishment carriers such as the *Copahee* and cargo vessels like the *Fortune* were crucial to Allied victory in the Pacific.[12]

+++

Getting the planes and parts out to the task forces was one thing, but getting the planes and parts onto the supply ships and into the logistics chain was another. The U.S. Navy was far from prepared to handle such a demand at the outset of the war, even with the support of a sizeable commercial manufacturing infrastructure.

Aircraft production facilities in the United States adjusted their own operations as the war progressed. Beginning with relatively small output, factories gradually increased their capability and numbers of aircraft and parts increased rapidly after 1942. Prior to Pearl Harbor a purchasing committee managed the purchase of Army and Navy aircraft. In April 1941 this group became officially known as the Joint Aircraft Committee (JAC). The JAC was the principal agency for scheduling aircraft and aircraft supply purchases. Airframes, engines, radars, radios, and support equipment all fell within the bailiwick of the JAC; each member of the committee, whether Army or Navy, was authorized to approve or disapprove contracts for its respective service.[13]

By 1941 the Army had already begun pursuing and executing contracts for various models of aircraft. In keeping with President Roosevelt's "Germany First" policy, the procurement of Army Air Corps matériel took precedence over that of the Navy. As soon became evident, the Navy's system of delivering aircraft to the fleet would have to adapt to rigorous demands along with its methods of training vast numbers of aircraft technicians adapted to the needs of the fleet.

It was only after the first year of the war that aircraft production contracts and deliveries to the Navy began to take shape. The supportive relationship between the Army and Navy aviation departments aided in this, in that it relieved some of the pressure associated with how to deliver training and trained pilots to the fleet. Before December 7, 1941, America saw Hitler as the greatest threat, thus Army aviation received the bulk of support and preparedness efforts. As a result, the Army had acquired a surplus of training airplanes that they were willing to part with. Many of these aircraft were transferred to the Navy and this initial boost to the training fleet allowed the Navy to concentrate its resources on production of combat aircraft. By the fall of 1942, deliveries of naval combat aircraft had increased fourfold over the previous year.[14]

The Navy's eventual windfall in terms of aircraft deliveries was not without its challenges. The more hours Navy aircraft flew, the more they required spare parts; naval aircraft used spare parts faster than any other single machine in the Navy's weapons arsenal. High percentages of grounding of fleet aircraft were common in the leadup to war and the earliest months of combat. As the threat of U.S. involvement drew closer, FDR's requests for more airplanes and carriers brought with it the realization that the Navy was going to be flying more hours than it ever had. There would surely be a need for more spare parts to "keep 'em flying."

In late 1941, Navy procurement officers worked with manufacturers to alleviate the problem, effectively reducing the need to cannibalize spare parts from other airplanes or fashion makeshift parts from discarded and unused materials. When the Navy realized that a lack of spare parts would hamper fleet operations, contracts were revised to deliver spares at a much higher rate. Prior to this, determining the need for replacement parts was left to the manufacturers. As the number of aircraft contracts and deliveries increased, the level of effort to manage the naval aviation supply chain followed suit. The Navy then established the Aviation Supply Office (ASO) to assume this role.

The ASO was chartered on October 1, 1941, in Philadelphia. Its purpose was not to enter into the business of aircraft acquisition, but to oversee the management of spare parts throughout the fleet. The ASO operated under the guidance of the Bureau of Aeronautics (BuAer), but also coordinated its efforts through the naval Bureau of Supplies and Accounts (BuSandA). In essence, this was a joint venture conducted between two bureaucratic subagencies of the Navy. Certain materials, such as sheet metal and paint, were considered "standard stock." It was much more efficient for the Navy to purchase these items in bulk and ration them out than to have the ASO enter into its own purchase contracts. Supplies and parts that were specific to naval aviation were managed specifically by the ASO under the auspices of BuAer. This was material that was quite literally being "handed over the counter" at various naval air stations and carrier maintenance spaces. The technical expertise and experience within naval aviation made these types of operations specific to BuAer and its ASO personnel. Therefore, BuSandA steered clear of the finer details of aviation supply. It was the BuAer officers and technicians who formulated the systems of stock numbering, inventories, and forecasting future requirements to maintain the highest degree of readiness. BuAer had the experience with aircraft operations, the data that pointed to types and quantities of spares that would be needed in a wartime effort, and the supply systems that were responsible for actual delivery of the matériel to the Navy's ever-increasing carrier air groups and naval air stations.[15]

Once requested items were manufactured, they were sent from the contractor directly to large warehouses in Philadelphia. This location became known as the Aviation Supply Depot (ASD).[16] The ASD was responsible for distributing aircraft parts to the fleet upon request. Problems arose as variants and quantities of aircraft rapidly increased throughout 1941 and into 1942. As the models of aircraft increased over time, the cataloging of parts became more and more cumbersome.

Additionally, as multiple manufacturers built identical parts and even identical airplanes in some cases, part numbering and nomenclature was challenging at best. The ASD instituted a part numbering system in which all interchangeable parts were renumbered according to their use rather than their manufacturer. This eliminated any confusion when ordering replacements. For example, by renumbering the interchangeable parts for the various versions of Pratt and Whitney engines, a technician could quickly reference the replacement part needed without multiple cross-references to verify that he or she was ordering the correct part.[17]

ASD personnel were instrumental in creating a catalog that contained pictures, descriptions, and ordering instructions for all parts. Simple drawings were provided showing interchangeable and substitute parts in case the particular part desired was not available. Even in the case of minor parts, it was accepted that some items might be limited and a technician would have to order the larger fully assembled unit and then remove the needed part. Specific instructions for ordering replacement parts from the supply chain were also laid out clearly and simply throughout the different sections. Multiple sections of the catalog were issued at multiple times. Aircraft technicians were instructed to check all available sections, and to cross-reference for data on certain parts. Overall, the catalog system was highly successful in keeping the supply chain operating smoothly and minimizing the time that many airplanes were in a "down" status.[18] The hefty *ASO Catalog* resembled the voluminous Sears catalog of the day.[19] It aided in identifying and requisitioning any aeronautical materials, spare parts, and related equipment needed by aviation commands.

The *ASO Catalog* was an immediate star in the world of aircraft maintenance. Feedback from aviation units was overwhelmingly positive on its usefulness in the workplace for identifying parts and ordering replacements. NATTC trade schools also utilized the catalog and folded it into its training courses. Students and instructors commented after each new publication was introduced, "Please expedite all possible sections as this Catalog is the nucleus of the course of instruction at this school"; "The *Catalogs* have arrived and are of immense help"; "One of our greatest troubles is to insure [sic] proper identification of material"; and "The most valuable Navy publication so far as this squadron is concerned."[20] The *ASO Catalog* was a multivolume document intended to be placed into the "hands of personnel who have the job of identifying parts and drawing up requisitions."[21] This included A&R shops, technical training schools, naval air stations, supply depots, or squadrons.

The primary users of the *ASO Catalog* were those sailors who wore the aviation supply clerk (SKV) rating. The SKV rating was established in August 1943. By January 1944, the first school for training aviation storekeepers was opened in Alameda, California. Another school was opened later that year in the Jacksonville, Florida Naval Air Technical Training Center. The Navy recognized the need for a specialized school when the volume of parts was keeping pace with the increased influx of new aircraft. The fleet's air forces grew in earnest over 1943, and parts distribution and supply went from an afterthought to the forefront of planning concerns.

Prior to the school's opening, the Navy used the general rating of storekeeper (SK) to maintain the supply and distribution systems. As aviation supplies became more technical and more advanced, the Navy decided to specialize its supply clerks, just as it had specialized its technical labor force in the form of aviation technicians. With new models and multiple variants of combat and training aircraft entering into service, the job of a supply clerk became more than simply sending and receiving parts.

The school quota at Alameda was considerably small, only permitting ninety-nine students at one time, while graduating thirty-three every two weeks. Alameda began with only two pay clerks, two chief storekeepers, and two aviation machinist's mates as instructors. Much of the curriculum that was used to train future SKVs was developed in Alameda during the inaugural period of instruction.[22]

Having a much larger footprint and capacity in comparison to Alameda, Jacksonville called for a class of 122 students entering on a biweekly basis. Students were sent by their parent commands via BuPers and the commanders of either the Pacific Fleet or the Atlantic Fleet. Prospective students were expected to be vetted by their own commands before being sent to SKV school—this was not a "nice to have" opportunity. The training that these sailors received was nothing short of college-level course work. Students who were awarded billets at SKV school had already graduated from Class A storekeeper school. Once they completed the six-week course of study, they were designated SKV3.

Each instructor at the school was himself a prior graduate of the school with an average of two years' experience in the aviation supply business. While the school might not have been around that long, the instructors had accrued "on the job" training and were chosen according to their performance and reputation. Throughout the course, each student received training in procurement, receipt, salvage, storage, preservation, packing, shipping, and properly marking parts for restocking, striking, or repair. Students were required to demonstrate a level of knowledge in addition to that of general naval storekeeping. In order to wear the SKV rating badge as a petty officer third class, a sailor had to be able to instantly identify through visual means, any airplane part or accessory and maintenance materials as well as the requisite tools to install them. A supply clerk was also required to have a working understanding of aeronautical nomenclature—that is, rudder, vertical and horizontal stabilizers, ailerons, gyro, flaps, magneto, and the like.[23]

The general idea the Navy had in mind with the SKV rating was that a maintenance technician could walk into the aviation supply shop, lay a broken part on the desk and say "Get me one of these gadgets," and the SKV could identify and supply the needed item . The mechanic may not know the part number or identifier to tell the SKV, but the goal of an aviation storekeeper school graduate was to recognize the part and know exactly where to find a replacement in the *ASO Catalog*—the fleet didn't want any delays in getting planes back into the air. The faster and more accurately the supply system could get new parts to the hangar or flight deck, the better the naval pilot's chance to defeat the enemy.[24]

Time is of the essence in naval aviation in wartime. On the carrier, it mattered even more because there was an enemy just over the horizon trying to be first in getting his planes off the deck to attack the American carrier forces. There was little room for error or delay. While the seemingly mundane subject of supply has received little attention in the historiography of naval aviation in World War II, it should be abundantly clear that it is a critical element of one's understanding and appreciation of its key role in securing victory in the war in the Pacific.

✦✦✦

As with the *ASO Catalog*, the naval aviation community relied heavily on the written word to facilitate communication across its community. While the supply aspects of aviation maintenance constituted a large portion of that communication, ingenuity and innovation played a considerable part as well. Beginning in the mid-1930s, the Bureau of Aeronautics published a biweekly newsletter called *Naval Aviation News*. The publication was designed to disseminate relevant information to pilots, flight crews, and technicians across the fleet. These newsletters, marked "Restricted" and only available to Navy personnel, were meant to inform and educate through articles or vignettes sent in from the fleet. *Naval Aviation News* included everything from "lessons learned" from pilot errors to tips on survival if shot down behind enemy lines—it also covered common hazards and technical difficulties experienced by maintenance personnel on the flight line.

Not all information was of a negative nature. One section of the newsletter was devoted to improving the work in the maintenance department. Each issue dedicated a page or two to a section titled "Technically Speaking." Here, BuAer published information about the latest innovations for naval aviation technicians as well as helpful technical data for flight crews. Most of the material published in this section was aimed at the technician, but pilots were wise to read through the material since it offered insights into aircraft operation and maintenance procedures. This was an active program designed to promote ingenuity in the hangar and on the flight deck, often lauding the achievements of the technicians themselves.

The Office of the Chief of Naval Operations advertised its desire to publish and promote new ideas among its technical personnel and flight crews. "That little gadget of yours, that idea or hint worked out in combat, may be the simple solution another squadron is groping for. It may be the extra advantage needed to down a *Betty* or *Messerschmitt* . . . save a life!"[25] From our modern perspective, it might seem odd that the Navy was so open to new ideas from the deck-plate leaders within the enlisted ranks, but grass-roots innovation and ingenuity have been and always will be a part of the technician-oriented culture of the Navy.

As World War II began there was little need to challenge "the way it has always been done," or look for better ways of doing things in the maintenance and repair stations. Naval aviation was still a relatively new concept, especially on board an aircraft carrier—it was often up to the technicians to figure out ways to make their jobs easier and more efficient. As airplane designs were advancing at a breakneck pace, the Navy could barely keep up with the support equipment needed to keep the fleet in the air.

In a particularly wise move, the Navy encouraged technical personnel to utilize their creative thinking to improve the way naval aviation did business. Officially known as the Beneficial Suggestion Program, this initiative (which was also open to civilian government employees) highlighted innovative ideas that proved useful and applicable to the naval aviation service. Participation was encouraged through official recognition and, more often than not, a cash prize. The program eventually became colloquially known as "Benny Suggs" and was routinely mentioned in *Naval Aviation News*. Cash prizes for useful ideas varied from $25 war bonds to awards of more than $5,000. The Navy based the value of each Benny Sugg primarily on its potential monetary savings for the Navy. There were reportedly 48,460 ideas submitted by technicians working in shipyards, ammunition depots, and other shore establishments in 1944 alone. Of those, 8,420 were adopted. Benny Suggs were estimated to have saved the Navy $30 million.[26]

Benny Suggs varied in size and scope, as well as specificity. For example, Aviation Chief Machinists' Mate (ACMM) David Henriques, assigned to CASU 33 fabricated a unique compression wrench. The tool evenly distributed torque between blade halves when installing blades and bearings on Curtiss electric pitch propellers. This reduced the need for pounding on the unit while installing new bearings. The new compression wrench virtually eliminated the age-old practice of hammering new bearings in and risking damage to the blades or bearings themselves.[27]

Seemingly simple jobs, such as moving an aircraft around the deck of a carrier without power from its engine, were often labor intensive. For example, one procedure called for locking the tailwheel of a TBF model aircraft in the forward position once the aircraft was parked on the flight deck or in the hangar. If left unlocked, the tailwheel was free to swivel and the aircraft could sway back and forth during rolling seas or when taxiing into position. Unfortunately, performing this task required from six to eight sailors manually lifting the tail while a technician reached underneath and set the locking pin in the tailwheel. S1 Charles R. St. Johns, a sailor on the USS *Bogue* designed and fabricated a jack that could raise the tail high enough for a single sailor to perform the entire operation.

Locking or unlocking a tailwheel at the wrong time could cause damage to the tailwheel assembly. Before taxiing, the tailwheel was to be unlocked, but for takeoffs and landings it needed to be locked. Not doing so at the appropriate time was one cause of damage that was prevalent enough to prompt *Naval Aviation News* to print a cautionary note:

> Tail Wheel Trouble: A considerable number of reports are being received of tail-wheel caster lock damage caused by towing or taxiing planes with the tail-wheel locked. As pointed out in several BuAer publications, lockable caster tail-wheels should be locked only for take-offs and landings on airfields and for take-offs from carriers. They should be *unlocked* for landing aboard carriers and for *all towing operations*; also for most taxiing, the major exceptions being to save brakes in strong cross-winds or long taxi-ways where clearance is assured by the tower or signalman.[28]

In another instance, a maintenance shop at an AROU in Guam was experiencing less than satisfactory results in applying plasticized lacquer, commonly referred to as "dope," to aircraft skin due to the high humidity, which sometimes reached 70–90 percent during the day. Dope was required to be applied to aircraft fabric to tighten and strengthen the material, it also provided waterproofing. When applied correctly, especially in the right environmental conditions, dope increased the lifespan of aircraft material and associated components. The AROU crew knew the humidity inside their Quonset hut shop was compromising the integrity of the final product. They requisitioned a standard carrier refrigerator unit through the supply chain and installed it in the Quonset hut. Cracks and openings in the hut were sealed as best as possible and proper venting was installed for the exhaust system. After installation, humidity inside the hut dropped to between 38 and 45 percent. The refrigerating unit routinely removed seventeen pounds of water from the air on a typical day. Not only did the lowered humidity positively affect the doping and painting chores, the technicians enjoyed a much more pleasant working environment.[29]

On the escort carrier USS *Kasaan Bay*, the flight line crews and maintenance department teamed up to design a dolly for removing damaged airplanes from the flight line, specifically those that had lost their landing gear during a crash landing. They needed a device with the capability of transporting an aircraft across the flight deck without getting stuck on pendants and landing cables. The dolly also had to be low enough to the deck that it could slide under the fuselage of a wrecked airplane. Their prototype dolly utilized six old TBF tailwheels that had been removed for excessive wear and tear. They were attached to the underside of U-shaped cradle structure that only required a two-inch clearance. The sheet metal design was low enough and wide enough to slide under the fuselage of any model of aircraft then in use in the fleet. Once the plane was resting on the dolly, it could be easily maneuvered around the deck, either to a suitable storage area or to an area where it could be jettisoned over the side.[30]

Positioning an airplane for safe maintenance was an ongoing challenge for carrier technicians. Procedures that were simple and straightforward at a shore base in a noncombat region looked much different at sea. For example, changing a tire was a common occurrence in the daily routine of an AM. But on the carrier, tires blew or were damaged at a much greater rate than at an air station landing strip due to the harsh conditions associated with landing on a carrier. The Navy provided wing jacks to the carrier maintenance departments, but due to space constraints on the CVE and CVLs, they were stored in the hangar spaces. Large carriers like CV and CVB could pre-position the jacks on the flight deck to be utilized at a moment's notice. In the case of a CVE, when an aircraft blew a tire on landing, either the larger jack had to be hauled up from below on the elevator or the plane had to be taken down. Both processes sacrificed crucial time that could not afford to be lost in the midst of a combat operation.

To remedy this dilemma, Ens. E. W. George, designed a "rim" jack on board the USS *Suwanee* (CVE 27) that was designed to work especially with F6F wheel assemblies. If a Hellcat had a flat tire, it was essentially a "down" aircraft. Not wanting to use a large wing jack to raise the entire plane off the ground, technicians attempted to use standard automobile jacks for tire changes. Unfortunately, the design of the F6F wheel would not permit it, and there was a risk in damaging the rim when doing so. Ensign George designed his jack to work from the wheel rim, raising it enough so the automotive jack could be leveraged against the axle. Then the plane was raised just enough on that side to change the tire, very similar to how the operation is performed on an automobile. The rim jack was very small and could be easily moved around the flight deck to parked aircraft—even those parked on the edge. This permitted technicians to change tires while flight operations continued, causing no delay in the cycle. The airplane being worked on was quickly returned to the flight schedule in an "up" status. George's primitive but valuable invention was made of scrap channel iron, angle iron, and pipe, and only required a cutting torch and an arc welder.[31]

Benny Suggs were sometimes diminutive. PO F. R. Koch, an AM stationed at NAS San Diego, designed a small clamp for use with plastics. It was a substitute for the traditional "C" clamp that could easily damage softer materials, such as plastic. Unlike other clamps, Koch's variant was designed to sit flat on the machine table and had padded surfaces to protect plastic materials. The newer clamp allowed technicians to secure sheet plastic on a router, shaper, or saw table without additional tools and risk of damage to the material.[32]

Sometimes a technician's resourcefulness and quick thinking could save a plane from a dire situation, even if it was not a permanent Benny Sugg that was incorporated into fleet maintenance practices. AMM2 J. W. Rosenkranz, an aircrewman, was serving as a gunner during a strike on Truk Island. While returning to the carrier his pilot realized the wheels would not lock in the down position for landing. They were flapping up and down in the slipstream. The hydraulic system had failed due to a leak and there was not enough pressure in the system to lock the wheels into place. The pilot continued to circle the carrier trying to pump enough hydraulic pressure into the system to get the wheels to lock, but it was hopeless. Too much fluid had leaked out to build up enough pressure. Rosenkranz, thinking unconventionally, suggested to his pilot that he pour some water from his canteen into the hydraulic reservoir as a temporary measure and then try to pump some pressure into the system. Sure enough, Rosenkranz's idea worked and the pilot got the wheels to lock after pumping enough fluid through the system. The plane landed safely and no damage was done to the aircraft; all that was needed was a hydraulic system flush during the postflight maintenance.[33]

While small inventions and workarounds like these may seem minor in the bigger scheme of a naval war, the opposite is true. Each aircraft in the Navy's inventory was touched daily by the hands of naval technicians; automation was nonexistent in the world of servicing and repair. If a sailor could design a tool or procedure that expedited the job without sacrificing safety or quality, it was a win. The culture of naval aviation has always embraced innovation and creative thinking. Benny Suggs and other clever, creative troubleshooting ideas have been, and will always be, valued by naval aviation.

✦✦✦

Just as a constant supply of aircraft and ship supplies were necessary to "turn the tide" in the war against Japan, a ready supply of trained technicians was equally crucial to winning the war. When President Franklin Roosevelt requested that Congress declare war on Japan on December 8, 1941, the Navy entered into an air war for which it was ill prepared. The trajectory of the war did not suddenly shift in the summer of 1942. Academic arguments that only cite specific battles or campaigns as turning points in the war neglect to acknowledge the complete picture behind carrier aviation in World War II. Further, giving sole credit to the Navy's accomplishments in combat fails to recognize the remarkable contribution that naval aviation maintenance had on the outcome of the Pacific war.

The aviation technician contributed immensely to American naval success, but as the war moved into its closing stages, aircraft repair at sea became less crucial. As aircraft and shipbuilding companies on contract with the Navy realized their full production potential by 1944, it was easier to just exchange damaged airplanes with replacements in order to keep the carrier's air group at full strength. With so many spare airplanes available, the Navy could simply off-load aircraft that were not mission-capable, and replace them with new ones awaiting delivery from a local CASU. In essence, U.S. naval aviation transitioned to a "throwaway" culture in the last phase of the war due to the abundance of available replacement aircraft.

There is a direct correlation between the timing of increased technician manpower and the numbers of aircraft delivered from factories.

The timing of this surge correlated with an increased supply of spare parts and aircraft through standardization and improved technology. The rate at which the Navy expended its allocated aviation funds on aviation also coincided with the expansion of its aviation labor force. Three sets of statistics—inventories of personnel, aircraft, and aircraft carriers—deliver a solid backing to the argument that technicians had a critical role in the development of the Navy's carrier warfare doctrine when studied in aggregate.[34]

First, by analyzing the number of nonflying aviation personnel (which can be reasonably inferred as mostly technicians) alongside the number of carrier aircraft the Navy had on hand, a collateral ramp-up is evident. A year before the war, the number of active-duty enlisted aviation personnel was approximately 7,000. That number doubled to 14,000 by the end of 1941, and more than quadrupled to 63,000 in 1942. In 1943, it increased more than twice, reaching 144,000; a year later the strength of the enlisted aviation ranks stood at 215,000 sailors. By August 1945, the Navy claimed an enlisted aviation force of 248,000 men and women.[35]

Though the active-duty enlisted aviation ranks in 1942 had grown exponentially over the 1941 numbers, this only represented a numerical increase of about 50,000 personnel. Still, no other year during the war saw such an explosive rise. BuAer and BuPers also completed the biggest revisions to its aviation technical training programs during that year. In March 1942 the trade school at NAS Jacksonville adjusted the timing of its school day to handle two groups of students by implementing a two-shift schedule, doubling its graduation rates. Construction on NTC Norman and NTC Memphis was soon completed and courses began in September 1942. Basic naval aviation technical schools were geographically consolidated from nine locations down to four. The greatest change to the system of aviation technical training was bringing all administrative control under one roof when NATTC was established with Rear Adm. A. C. Read in command.[36]

After NATTC took over the education of the enlisted technician, the ranks of maintainers headed to the fleet continued to grow, increasing a little over two times, amounting to some 80,000 additional sailors. At the same time, aircraft carrier and airframe deliveries also rose. The

Navy's total aircraft carrier inventory doubled in 1942 and then tripled by the end of 1943. Simultaneously, by December 1943 the number of naval fighter aircraft on hand increased tenfold since the start of the war. The vast increases of aviation matériel in 1942 and 1943 coincided with a similar rise in personnel availability. As aircraft and ship manufacturers were producing multitudes of airplanes and carriers, BuAer and BuPers were struggling to keep up with delivering their own product to support the war effort—the aviation technician (see Table 6.1).

If this data is depicted in graphical form, it is apparent that the rise in aviation personnel was followed closely by an increase of both aircraft and carriers, as shown in Figures 6.1 and 6.2.

The slopes of the VF and CV lines begin their sharpest rise on the horizontal axis in late 1942 to mid-1943. In both Figures 6.1 and 6.2, this occurs less than a year after the personnel numbers begin their upward trend in the summer of 1942. The comparable rise of new aircraft carriers and aircraft coincided with an associated surge of trained aviation technicians.

The first major increase in the number of carriers did not begin until after June 1942. The introduction of the escort carrier (CVE) is the main reason for changing the slope of this graph in 1942, as U.S. inventory went from two to twelve carriers in a period of six months. Note the concurrent rise in personnel during that period (Figure 6.1).

Similarly, fighter procurement makes its first minor upward swing at the same time. The Navy began contracting with Grumman for the F4F Wildcat fighter in 1940 and continued renewing the contract as new and improved variants were developed. The first operational F4F was delivered to the Navy in December 1940. From then on, airframe deliveries began at 10 per month and increased to 27 per month by the end of the year. The year 1942 brought with it a further increase in the production rate to an average of 40 to 50 per month. Some models of the F4F were produced at a much higher rate, amounting to 130 per month at the end of 1942. In total, the Navy purchased 1,714 F4F Wildcat fighters for a combined total of $79 million, not including complete spares or spare parts.[37] When placed side by side, the surge of technicians correlates with a similar expansion of aircraft and aircraft carriers by the end of the war's first year (Figure 6.2).

Table 6.1. USN Aviation Personnel and Matériel on Hand, 1940–45[1]

	12/40	6/41	12/41	6/42	12/42	6/43	12/43	6/44	12/44	6/45
Aviation Personnel	7,204	10,439	14,848	26,947	63,521	104,858	144,198	182,872	215,739	240,303
VF	245	349	514	736	1,253	2,246	5,281	10,037	11,849	13,940
CV	6	6	7	5	4	7	10	13	16	20
CVE	0	1	1	2	12	19	35	63	65	70
CVL	0	0	0	0	0	5	9	9	8	8

[1] "Annual Report of the Secretary of Navy: Fiscal Year 1945," 21, 31, 55. Fighter data is total number owned by the Navy, not total deployable. Aircraft carrier inventory determined how many aircraft could be put to sea at one time.

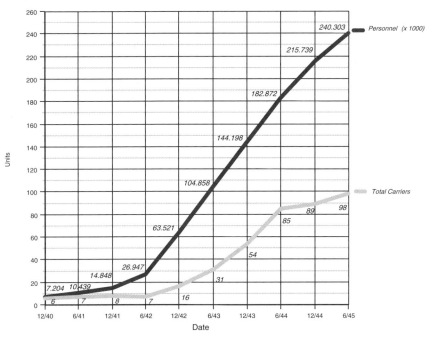

Figure 6.1. Aviation Personnel vs. Aircraft Carriers over Time

Source: "Annual Report of the Secretary of Navy: Fiscal Year 1945," Appendix A.

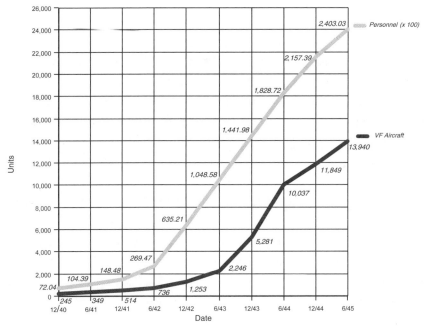

Figure 6.2. Aviation Personnel vs. Fighter Aircraft (VF) over Time

Source: "Annual Report of the Secretary of Navy: Fiscal Year 1945," Appendix A.

✦✦✦

Matériel expenditure factors also support the argument that labor and material costs affected the way carrier maintenance was performed. Similar to buying a new car, airplanes came with options—and price adjustments to go along with those options. The Navy's aircraft contracts were broken down by basic airframe, engine, propellers, radio and radar, instruments, armament, and miscellaneous equipment. Within each group, there was a price for installation of the part, a price for a complete spare, and another price for the spare parts associated with each system. Table 6.2 lists the average costs associated with the F4F-3 and F6F-3 fighters as of January 1944.

The unit price varied depending on mission capabilities within each model, but Table 6.2 shows the average cost determined by BuAer in 1944. For example, an F4F airframe alone ranged from $26,000 to $53,000 (engines, propellers, and spare parts not included.)[38] It was not until the summer of 1943 that the Navy saw the massive deliveries of fighters to the fleet with the introduction of the Grumman F6F Hellcat. At $30,000 to $45,000 more per aircraft, fiscal considerations began to impact maintenance practices.

The last contract for the F4F Wildcat was signed in March 1942 for 70 airplanes at an airframe-only price of $37,900 each. Grumman delivered all 70 that August. Over the next three years, a total of almost 14,000 newer F6F Hellcats would show up in the Navy's inventory, ranging in price per unit between $37,000 to $63,000, depending on the model. Of course the price per airframe decreased as the number ordered increased (economy of scale). Work on the first F6F, began on Christmas Eve in 1941, under a contract for 1,263 aircraft at a unit cost of $63,600 each. Aircraft deliveries varied by month, but averaged 80 over the two-year period of performance A second contract for 7,139 F6Fs in August 1942 lowered the price to $39,100.[39] The airframes promised in this contract were delivered throughout 1944 on an average of 500 per month.[40]

As with any machine, spare parts are essential. When purchasing airplanes from Grumman, the Navy contracted for spare parts as well. Specifics on what parts were considered in the package is not available, but the percentage of parts included is. The F4F contract included an

Table 6.2. Average Unit Aircraft Prices, Navy F4F vs. F6F, January 1944 [1]

PART	F4F-3, -4 ($)	F6F-3 ($)
Airframe	25,500	53,500
Airframe Spare Parts	7,650	16,050
Engine (Installed)	15,283	19,228
Engine Spare	7,642	9,614
Engine Spare Parts	8,253	8,268
Propeller (Installed)	4,199	2,215
Propeller Spares	2,519	1,329
Propeller Spare Parts	1,209	638
Radio-Radar (Installed)	2,600	4,450
Radio-Radar Spares and Spare Parts	2,600	4,450
Instruments (Installed)	1,120	1,100
Instrument Spares	338	310
Instrument Spare Parts	112	100
Armament (Installed)	3,321	5,025
Armament Spares	699	1,073
Armament Squadron Equipment	90	91
Miscellaneous Equipment (Installed)	1,470	1,600
Miscellaneous Spares	500	560
Miscellaneous Spare Parts	230	240
Complete Aircraft (no spares or spare parts)	53,583	87,209
Complete Aircraft (with spares and spare parts)	85,335	129,841

[1] "Bureau of Aeronautics Average Unit Contract Prices—Navy Airplanes," January 1, 1944, 1, Carriers Collection, Box 13, NHHC.

average of 22 percent spare parts with each plane, meaning that much of the airplane was available for replacement by technicians. That same figure dropped to 16 percent in the newer F6F contracts.[41] What caused this change?

There are several possible reasons for the change in the percentage of spare parts, but it is difficult to ascertain which is most responsible. Initially, I would surmise that as with anything in the weapons industry, technology improved over time and the airplanes became more reliable as they were developed. The average addition of spare parts for an F4F was $32,000. A spare parts kit for the F6F averaged $43,000. Fiscally, it made sense to order fewer spare parts with each unit, because on the whole the number of F6F deliveries were nine times more than the F4F and cost about $34,000 more for the basic aircraft priced at $53,583, compared to $87,209.[42]

Another possible reason is that with such a large contract on the F6F, and with the planned number of aircraft to be delivered, BuAer preferred to scrap a broken plane than spend the labor man-hours to fix it. With the number of fighters that the Navy was planning to have in reserve, why spend the money on spare parts when it would be easier to push the broken plane over the side and bring up a new one from the hangar or fly a new one in from a CASU? As far back as 1927, the Navy had toyed with the idea that replacing carrier airplanes was a better investment in time and money than fixing them. In a letter from Rear Adm. William V. Pratt, then president of the Naval War College, to Chief of Naval Operations Adm. Edward W. Eberle on the subject of "Airplane Carriers," Pratt stated that he concurred with BuAer's recommendation for the next generation of aircraft carrier design to consider that carrier maintenance crews only conduct minor aircraft maintenance while underway: "Shop facilities—Concur in Bureau of Aeronautics reasoning, to provide for only top maintenance. The essential thing is to get planes in the air at the critical time. Let repairs come later, or abandon planes."[43] The Navy knew then that planes in the air were more valuable than planes in repair. However, the logistics of making such recommendations a reality would take more effort than simply words on paper. Supporting a maintenance program that was consistent with such a policy required a fully mobilized aircraft industry outside the Navy and an efficient supply chain within the Navy—neither would be available until at least the second year of World War II.

The last consideration is the impact of the technical schools at the time a contract was written. On the F6F, the first contract was written in May 1942 and included 22 percent spare parts. In December 1943, that dropped to 16 percent and in February 1944, it was only at 10 percent.[44] When NATTC was established in September 1942 and took over the technical training program, the numbers of technicians available to the fleet increased dramatically. I believe there were two possible but mutually exclusive reasons for the decrease in spare parts in relation to NATTC training.

The most conservative, or what could be deemed "positive," reason would have been a result of the internal operations of the schools. Once technical training was standardized and centralized under NATTC, BuAer's expectation very well might have been that the quality of training and overall technical skills of the graduates would have improved. Thus, better trained technicians would inevitably have an immediate impact on keeping airplanes flying. This would mean fewer replacements. After all, the mark of a good mechanic is one who can diagnose and fix a problem, rather than just replace a part. According to BuAer's Training Division, the newly trained technicians would be better than those of previous years. LCDR Wheelock offered this as early as January 1942 when he included comments to that effect in his lecture on how BuAer was managing the new training requirements that accompanied the increased size of the fleet and the number of naval aircraft. In effect, "instruction must not only be as good as it was before, but it must be better . . . text books are supplements by visual and aural aids which, we hope, will guarantee that the required subjects are learned one hundred percent."[45] Perhaps in the mind of the BuAer acquisition team, as the technical training program matured, carrier aviation maintenance would improve altogether.

Yet, when studying the situation a year later, it is more believable that BuAer realized in order to keep up with the increased pace of the war in the Pacific, it would have to err on the side of caution—repair less and replace more. One tangible fact that supports this suggestion is that in 1943 BuPers lowered the minimum GCT scores for entry into certain aviation ratings.[46] Lowering the minimum standardized score entry criteria would no doubt inflate the number of students and thus graduates. But it might also be damaging to the effectiveness of the overall labor force. The minimum score for entry into the AMM rating declined from sixty-two to fifty-two. The AO rating dropped from seventy to fifty-two.[47] BuPers may have reduced it to increase acceptances, but even so, BuAer might have seen this as having far-reaching impacts. It is very reasonable that BuAer saw this as a downgrade in technical acumen of its incoming technicians. Therefore, if the financial means were there, why waste time repairing aircraft when it could just as easily replace them? That way, technicians could focus on routine service and maintenance for everyday flight operations.

According to spending reports, BuAer did have the funds to procure many more aircraft in 1942–44. Buying more aircraft would ultimately require less repair and fewer spare parts. The increased dollar value on fighter aircraft deliveries alone in the twelve months between December 1942 and December 1943 grew by a factor of over six as shown in Table 6.3.[48]

Table 6.3. Semiannual Value of Navy Fighter Aircraft Deliveries to June 1945 [1]

DATE	DOLLAR VALUE	VF AIRCRAFT DELIVERIES
Dec. 1940	$3,711,000	64
June 1941	$8,566,000	153
Dec. 1941	$10,911,000	189
June 1942	$29,141,000	520
Dec. 1942	$56,933,000	874
June 1943	$132,327,000	1,622
Dec. 1943	$316,533,000	3,823
June 1944	$449,206,000	6,616
Dec. 1944	$413,641,000	5,459
June 1945	$510,901,000	6,182
Total	$1,921,148,000	25,362

[1] "Bureau of Aeronautics Average Unit Contract Prices — Navy Airplanes," January 1, 1944.

Carrier aircraft served no purpose when they could not fly. Similar to rounds left in a chamber, they were of little use other than deterrence when sitting on the deck of an aircraft carrier in a "hot" war. In 1943, the Navy contracted with Grumman to receive nearly 600 new F6F each month. The most F4Fs delivered per month was 209, which occurred only in the last three months of 1942. The remainder of 1942's monthly deliveries hovered around fifty each.[49] The question that undoubtedly troubled Wheelock, Radford, and perhaps Towers in 1942 was whether or not the Navy's aviation technicians could keep that many new fighters flying, let alone the additional obsolete aircraft such as F3Fs that were still in service. With little concern for funding, the most reasonable solution was to spend less on spare parts, save money and labor hours, and use those funds on entirely new airplanes.

✦✦✦

The technicians on the carriers were intended to spend their time on Class D maintenance, engine changes, and component installations.[50] Engine changes were normally routine after a certain number of flight hours, or if a simple repair was not possible. A few hours of labor to remove a malfunctioning engine and replace it with a new one out of the box made the most sense. Each airframe contract from the manufacturer came with a specified number of replacement engines. Developing a maintenance philosophy that removed the burden of repair on the at-sea technician and shifted emphasis toward replacement gave the Navy an edge. Removing the trouble of major engine and airframe repair from the carrier-based maintainers and moving it to the land-based CASU and AROU was crucial to the efficiency of the Navy's aviation maintenance program. But in order for these units to function effectively, supply had to be sufficient to meet the demands of the fleet.

In June 1943, twice-retired Admiral Henry E. Yarnell was recalled to his third tour of active duty in the Office of the Chief of Naval Operations.[51] His first task (and arguably, the primary reason for his hire) was to conduct a fleet-wide survey of aviator and nonaviator officers as to the status of naval aviation. Yarnell titled the subject of his findings in a memorandum under the subject "Report on Naval Aviation." The stated purpose of the survey was to receive "comment, constructive criticism, and suggestions as to means and methods by which the efficiency of naval aviation could be improved."[52] The subject of aviation logistical support had forced the Navy to look closer into the ways it was conducting "business."

Yarnell solicited responses from 300 officers but only received 127 replies. Although the response was less than 50 percent, Yarnell claimed to have received valuable information from those that chose to respond. As far as aircraft maintenance was concerned, one of the many subjects he was tasked to report on—supply chains and spare parts availability—stood out as the most critical issue affecting carrier air group's readiness. Yarnell summarized the general reaction of the aviation community concerning supply by stating that "There was much criticism in the letters concerning the supply system, lack of spare parts, slowness of delivery, etc. This has resulted from lack of production of adequate spare parts, and slowness in their distribution. The result is that many planes are out of service due to lack of spares. This situation should be remedied as quickly as possible."[53]

Yarnell's report was long in coming. The logistics quandary was addressed a year earlier when Vice Admiral Towers, COMAIRPAC, had called for establishing overhaul and supply pool facilities in the South Pacific in support of carrier and land-based aviation operations. His comments pointed to an established deficiency in naval aviation's supply chain: "Action is necessitated by lack of [a] sufficient pool of spare engines to permit the rotation of engines for overhaul."[54] Yarnell's report showed little improvement in the nine months since Towers had spoken out.

One unnamed flag officer (the surveys were completed anonymously) responded to Yarnell's query by asking "Who is responsible for logistics to the extent for insuring that aircraft suitable in numbers and types, armament, equipment and supplies are available and maintained in quantities successfully to establish a war plan? Obviously, the answer is 'No one.'" A more measured response from one junior officer stated "The system of supply is very deficient, especially in the procurement and distribution of spare parts. In this particular squadron, three planes have been out of commission for over a month due to the shortage of propellers." Another disgruntled lieutenant offered, "We have to use every trick we can think of to get what we want from supply when they should be doing everything in their power to anticipate our needs and get it to us. I'm now scheduling flights for a thirty-six plane squadron. Twenty-four planes are the most I can count on. This is only 66 percent." Another lieutenant argued, "A great number of our planes are kept grounded for lack of spare parts, either because the parts are not manufactured in quantity, or because of poor distribution."[55] Spare parts and the logistics of getting them to the squadrons at war were a challenge during the 1942–1943 period, but 1944 saw a better system emerge with the establishment of the CASUs and the AROUs throughout the Pacific.

The CASUs and AROUs provided ready aircraft and spare parts to fleet units as a supplement to the spare parts loaded on the carriers. Before these units were in place, technicians aboard the carrier had to make do with what they had on hand in terms of spare parts and repair. By the time Towers had called for a better logistical support infrastructure throughout the Pacific, BuAer most likely realized that repairs on the carrier were more trouble than simply replacing an airplane with another that was prepositioned somewhere in the Pacific. If major repair or overhaul was required, after 1943, the Navy could rely on its own capable maintenance staff at the AROUs and CASUs to complete such labor-intensive work, for it was then that the Navy began to see modest gains in overcoming the deficiencies associated with a lack of trained aviation technicians in the fleet. As previously shown in Table 6.1, the greatest increases of available technicians occurred in late 1943 and throughout 1944.[56]

The year 1943 also brought with it a great advance in the technological sophistication of U.S. Navy carrier aviation with the introduction of the F6F Hellcat fighter. The airplane engine alone was an engineering marvel. To put it into perspective, up until this point in the war, aircraft carriers had been deploying with a mix of the Brewster F2A, the Grumman F3F, or the Grumman F4F. The F2A and F3F were each powered by a Wright R-1820 engine. The version installed in the F3F, an older aircraft, had a rating of 950 horsepower (hp). The R-1820 in the newer F2A produced 1,200 hp. In 1940, Grumman teamed up with Pratt and Whitney (PW) and used the PW R-1830 as the power plant for its newest fighter. Less than three years later, Grumman again subcontracted with PW for the F6F and installed the R-2800 engine, which delivered a much more powerful 2,200 hp capability.[57] The rapid advance in horsepower alone would be enough to challenge even the best veteran engine mechanic, which the Navy was short of in 1942.

As with engine upgrades, Grumman engineers did not stay with a single Hellcat airframe design throughout the War. The engineering behind the airframe was a dynamic process. After the initial lot of Hellcats entered service, Grumman responded to feedback from the pilots and BuAer, making various changes. What became identified as the F6F-5, differentiating it from the older F6F-3 model, began operating from carrier air groups in 1944, just one year after the F6F initially entered service.

The most obvious change to the previous Hellcat was the paint on the -5 model. While the -3 was given a rough coat of paint thinking it would lessen the chance of reflected flashes of sunlight. After testing in battle, it became clear to all that the silhouette of the airplane was just as visible during the daylight hours with or without a rough paint scheme. Thus, Grumman delivered the new -5 models with a waxed, highly polished coating of glossy paint that reduced drag, increasing airspeed. The dark blue color was chosen for camouflage against the ocean's surface from above. The -5's engine cowling was also redesigned to be more aerodynamically streamlined and visibility improvements were made in the windshield. The ailerons, along with a stronger tail and stabilizer structure gave the new plane better maneuverability. The pilots especially appreciated the larger sheet of armor plating that was built in behind the cockpit for protection. Even as the nomenclature for the F6F Hellcat stayed virtually the same, changes among the models were necessary to keep U.S. naval aviation technologically superior to that of the Japanese.[58]

Just as the flight deck of a carrier is a dynamic environment, so is the technology behind it. For pilots, there was a learning curve to transitioning from one model to another, but usually that transition was in a controlled environment such as flight school. A maintainer already on the carrier did not have that luxury. He had to learn "on the fly" because when new planes landed, they needed servicing. No commanding officer was going to send all, or even part of his maintenance department back to the States for a refresher class on the new model Hellcat that just come aboard from the CASU.

Perhaps BuAer recognized the gravity of the situation and planned accordingly, preferring an overabundance of planes to spare parts. The contract that was signed in mid-1942 called for two lots of F6Fs, a total of 1,333 airplanes. The next lot of airplanes were contracted in December 1943 for a total of 7,139. The final F6F contract was let in February 1944 for 3,000 units.[59] The Navy ordered a total of 11,472 Hellcats in under two years. Even if each carrier embarked only F6Fs (which never happened), the number of Hellcats outweighed the amount of available deck space the Navy had on all of its carriers combined by the end of the war by a factor of three.[60] The massive number of aircraft ordered was leading naval aviation maintenance to assume a more throwaway culture than it had ever embraced before. Perhaps BuAer was correct in their assumptions back in 1926 that suggested the Navy's aviation technicians would be better utilized in routine maintenance and servicing rather than making time-consuming major repairs.[61]

It seems as though someone in BuAer recognized this and adjusted accordingly. In a brief given by the BuAer Planning Division on July 5, 1944, it was stated that an average carrier air group consisting of ninety-one planes required an average of sixteen replacement planes per month to sustain combat operations. Nine were to replace aircraft losses—either operational or from combat—and seven were for worn-out aircraft based on number of combat deployments. This was a mix of attack planes (bombers/torpedo) and fighters, but over a typical multi-month deployment, it was a significant amount no matter what model aircraft it was.[62]

An "operational loss" was defined as something other than an aircraft being destroyed by enemy action.[63] Therefore, this might include pilot error, but it also could include aircraft malfunction. In the case that the pilot did save the aircraft in a malfunctioning situation and make the landing aboard the carrier, there was always a chance that it would still get dumped over the side and written off as a loss. In total, BuAer determined that 66 replacement airplanes were required to support an active carrier air group while engaged in combat operations during the war.[64]

As noted earlier, the more F6F fighters the Navy bought from Grumman, the less expensive each unit cost. One could liken this to buying "in bulk" today. But the implications of this is what I believe encouraged a "throw away" culture among the carrier navy more than anything else. Labor cost for the Navy to make repairs on carrier airplanes were minimal compared to the cost of an airplane or a replacement engine. For example, in 1943 a petty officer second class working as an aircraft technician aboard an aircraft carrier overseas was paid a salary of $115.20 per month. If assigned to a shore command, his monthly pay was $96. But if he was also on flight orders (i.e., aircrew gunner or radioman) he would receive an additional 50 percent of his base salary, which equaled $57.60 more if assigned to a carrier.[65] Assuming a twelve-hour workday while at sea and not a qualified aircrewman, the labor cost for an AMM2 was about forty-six cents per hour.[66] If, at maximum, ten petty officers third class worked eight hours to replace a bad engine, the labor cost would only be about $20. However, the spare engine itself cost around $9,600.[67] If that engine was needed before it had reached its maximum flight hours, would it really be worth the time and effort to remove a bad engine and replace it with a new one aboard the carrier?

The amount of time technicians would be unable to tend to routine maintenance duties if required to conduct multiple engine changes at sea would undoubtedly have a negative impact on the readiness of the air group's planes. In war, days engaged in combat are not always scheduled in advance. It was imperative that the carrier's air group was ready to fly with minimal notice. If sixteen replacement planes were delivered on a monthly basis to the carrier, then why not dump the broken aircraft or at least get them to an AROU or CASU for repair? Hangar and deck space on a carrier were at a premium. Keeping unflyable aircraft on board did not make sense in the combat-intensive conflict fought in the Pacific against the Japanese.

✦✦✦

When the *Essex*-class carriers were first designed, the aircraft complement was intended to be 83 airplanes.[68] By the end of the war, some carriers were deploying with 102 or 103 aircraft as a standard load-out.[69] An additional 20 aircraft most likely left little room for maintenance or extra spare parts. This would also have an impact on supplies and is another reasonable explanation in the reduction of spare parts ordered with the newer F6F fighters. The last four contracts written on the F6F included a spare parts percentage of 16, 10, 9, and 11, respectively. All of these contracts were written after December 29, 1943. The last four contracts for the F4—written years earlier, between November 1940 and June 1942—included spare parts percentages of 15, 28, 30, and 30.[70] The mindset of the acquisition officers at BuAer during the first two years of the war must have envisioned a shift in the methods of naval aviation maintenance once they realized the potential of carrier warfare. Not until after the Guadalcanal campaign and the introduction of the F6F did the Navy begin lowering the spare parts percentages on fighter contracts. At the same time, aircraft deliveries increased exponentially (see Table 6.3). Therefore, if funding was not a serious concern, as it seemed not to be by the middle of the war, why not spend less on spare parts and more on completely new airplanes and keep readiness at a consistently high level?

As previously stated, the biggest change in enlisted aviation personnel occurred between June and December 1942. The number of available technicians to the fleet increased sharply over the next two years. President Roosevelt had called for an increase of 15,000 planes in the naval air fleet and eventually moved the target to 30,000 after the United States entered the war. Authorizations for more airframes went up throughout the war, and by 1945 the Navy had accepted just over 71,500 new aircraft.[71] BuAer planners such as Lieutenant Commander Wheelock saw the need coming for more aircraft technicians than the Navy had ever employed before and accordingly reworked the technical training program to meet such a demand. Thus, it is apparent that the Navy did its best not to put the proverbial "cart before the horse." This should not be a shock to the casual observer. Surprisingly, most naval historians to date have neglected to recognize this, nor have any seriously commented on the importance of aircraft maintenance in terms of the development of carrier warfare.

✦✦✦

During the war, the annual budget for naval aviation was comparable to that of the Bureau of Ships (BuShip) and the Bureau of Ordnance

(BuOrd). In total, BuShip had the largest authorization from Congress with $40.2 billion between July 1940 and August 1945. BuAer was authorized $26.1 billion and BuOrd $23.1 billion. Of these authorizations each bureau only allocated and spent a portion of the funds. BuShip appropriated $38 billion but only expended $30.6 billion of that allocation. BuAer appropriated $23.9 billion but only spent $15.7 billion. BuOrd came in with $22.6 and $13.8, respectively.[72] These figures show that for each bureau, funding was not a significant problem.

Funding was practically unlimited for the Navy during the war. It did not matter how many or how much, the Navy got what it asked for. The only limit was that of productive capacity. Contracts and deliveries were limited by civilian production lines, not fiscal restraints. Actual labor costs for the Navy to repair damaged aircraft might not have amounted to much, but the time it took to do so was priceless. Therefore, it made sense, in terms of combat readiness, to replace the inoperable plane as quick as possible with an operable one. It is worth noting the dramatic change in the Navy's culture in this regard compared to the restricted budgets of the early to mid-interwar years.

Table 6.4. Cost of Equipping a Carrier Air Group, 1929 and 1944 [1]

1929 *Saratoga*	Without Spare Parts		With Spare Parts	
Type Aircraft	Unit cost	Total	Unit cost	Total
(36) F4B	$13,830	$497,880	$33,856	$1,218,816
(12) O2U	$13,180	$158,160	$47,053	$564,636
(32) T4M	$19,739	$631,648	$54,595	$1,747,040
Total (80)		$1,287,688		$3,530,492
1944 *Essex*				
(36) F6F	$87,209	$3,139,524	$129,841	$4,674,276
(36) SB2C	$106,393	$3,830,148	$158,894	$5,729,184
(18) TBF	$105,710	$1,902,780	$156,699	$2,820,882
Total (90)		$8,872,452		$13,215,042

[1] "Cost of Equipping a Carrier Air Group," n.d., Carriers Collection, Aviation, Box 13, NHHC.

Another way to analyze this is to look at the overall cost of equipping a carrier at different points in history. As we know, early carrier aviation had relatively fewer technicians available to the fleet, but a much smaller number of carriers and aircraft as well.

Thus, the cost to supply a carrier air group with complete sets of spares and associated spare parts increased by 375 percent in fifteen years. Outfitting a carrier without spares and spare parts was dramatically cheaper, but the cost still inflated by nearly 400 percent during the same period. Even though the cost per aircraft and the cost of spare parts drastically increased, the nearly $10 million rise in spare parts per air group cannot be taken lightly. If that money were put aside and spent on new F6F fighters instead of spare parts, the Navy would have had more than a hundred new F6Fs to send to the fleet instead of parts that required downtime for the squadrons. This would positively affect the readiness and availability of the air group to carry out its assigned missions. During the war, mission-ready aircraft mattered most. Maintenance and repair were suitable for peacetime, but in war, fleet commanders needed their assets ready for combat, not awaiting maintenance.

Exactly which assets are best suited for carrier combat forces was an early question that operational and planning staff officers faced. As early as February 1942, the question of what was the proper or most advantageous load-out of airplanes on a U.S. carrier surfaced. As Bull Halsey took the *Enterprise* on a mission into the Marshalls, he did so with Capt. George D. Murray in command of the ship. Murray had been at the helm of another numbers crunch three years earlier at BuAer as the question of proper manning at the bureau was a heated point of discussion between Towers, Mitscher, and Nimitz. As ironic as it was, Murray would be part of another shift in policy due to the war, but unfortunately, he would not see its results as an O-6 in command of a carrier.

Immediately after the Pearl Harbor debacle, Halsey was adamant that the U.S. Navy needed to go after the Japanese who were most likely staged near the Marshall Islands. However, his orders from Pearl Harbor were to steam north and east of Oahu, searching for enemy submarines. He complied, and as if to reward his obedience to Nimitz's orders, airplanes from the *Enterprise* quickly found and sank a Japanese submarine. While this was an obvious win for the Americans, jubilation did not last long. Wake Island soon fell with little resistance, and the *Saratoga* took a Japanese torpedo in her side as she was recovering airplanes. With this much bad news, Admiral Nimitz, the new commander of the Pacific Fleet, knew he had to go on the offensive.

Nimitz knew that it was critical to hang onto Midway Island, as well as maintain the communication lines from Pearl through Samoa and Fiji into Australia. To accomplish this, he could not let the Japanese remain untouched in the Marshall Islands. He surveyed his options and chose Halsey and the *Enterprise* task force (TF-80) to carry out the mission with the *Yorktown*'s task force on a similar mission to the area. Halsey departed Samoa with Rear Adm. Frank "Jack" Fletcher in the *Yorktown*, headed toward the Marshalls.

On January 31, 1942, Halsey and Fletcher split and took separate routes to their intended targets 500 miles away. The next morning, beginning at 0443, the *Enterprise*'s Air Group 6, under command of Cdr. Howard L. Young, launched thirty-six SBD Dauntless dive-bombers, nine TBD Devastators, and twelve F4F Wildcats for a strike at the Japanese airfields, runways, hangars, seaplane bases, and any naval vessels in the vicinity. Only six Wildcats were left to provide cover for the carrier as CAP (Carrier Air Patrol) in the event Japanese forces were able to slip past the attacking Americans, and threatened the *Enterprise*.

The relatively inexperienced Navy dive-bomber and torpedo bomber pilots from the *Enterprise* did well in their first combat mission. Multiple hangars and airplanes were damaged at Roi airfield, and numerous ships and submarines were damaged at Kwajalein Island. It was by no means a "knockout blow," but enough to rattle the nerves of the Japanese. Minimal resistance was put up by the Japanese, mainly in the form of antiaircraft guns and a few Mitsubishi A5M Claude fighters that were launched for air defense.

The *Enterprise*'s F4Fs were directed to Wotje Atoll and Taroa airfield. They too met enemy resistance from the Claudes, who were scrambled at the first notice of attack. The Claude had much greater maneuverability and climbing ability than the Wildcat, but the Americans had the advantage in speed. The Navy pilots avoided dogfighting, as they were able to keep their distance from the Claudes and still deliver ordnance on the airfields. As the initial damage reports came in over the radio, Halsey realized the need for dedicated bombing support on the enemy bases. He authorized two additional waves of attacks by his SBD. The dive-bombers delivered 500-pound bombs onto the vulnerable Japanese targets but were met with ample resistance from Japanese Claudes. Halsey realized that by remaining almost within visual range of the islands, he was risking his flattop should the Japanese pilots get behind his fighters and engage his CAP. By 1300 that same afternoon, Halsey, recognizing that he had accomplished what he had intended, decided to "retire" and steam east at high speed. But not all the Japanese airplanes had been destroyed at either Roi or Taroa, and soon six Mitsubishi G3M "Nell" bombers were inbound for the *Enterprise*.

Air Group 6 Wildcats were behind in intercepting the Nells and they found the *Enterprise* within range. Multiple bombs were dropped close-aboard to the "Big E," but Captain Murray's agile maneuvering kept his ship free from any direct hits, with the exception of some machine gun fire from the Japanese gunners and a near miss by one very brave Japanese pilot in a burning aircraft. All of the Nells that approached were destroyed by either antiaircraft fire from the carrier or the F4Fs on CAP.

Yet, the entire time the attack was underway, the naval technicians continued to do their job readying the *Enterprise*'s recovered planes for another launch. Postflight maintenance duties did not stop during combat, and neither did the mechanics. In one instance, a maintainer working on an SBD had to answer the call of duty "above and beyond" his duties as an aircraft technician. As a Nell took multiple direct hits from the carrier's antiaircraft guns, the pilot, Lt. Kazuo Nakai, a veteran of fifty combat missions in China and six at Wake Island, steered his bullet-riddled and burning airplane toward the deck of the *Enterprise*. Almost as if planned, but long before the desperate concept of kamikaze would take hold among Japanese fliers, Nakai put his airplane on a collision course with the flight deck and dozens of parked U.S. Navy aircraft.

The young technician, realizing his day was about to get much worse if he froze, summoned the courage to scramble into the rear seat of his SBD and swung the double barrels of the Devastator's Browning

7.62mm machine guns toward the incoming Japanese bomber and pulled the trigger. The direct hits to the canopy and fuselage were enough to either wound or kill Nakai and cause the plane to drift to the left. It flew directly up the flight deck, almost as if on an approach, but from the bow. Nakai's aircraft missed every plane and structure on deck except one—the SBD that the maintainer was firing from. As the Nell passed by, Cdr. E. B. Mott, the *Enterprise* gunnery officer, could clearly see Nakai's body slumped over the controls. When the plane hit the water, Mott was hit in the face with a splash of gasoline that would have turned into a raging inferno on the carrier had the Japanese pilot successfully impacted the ship instead. Unfortunately for the heroic mechanic manning the SBD gun, his airplane was no longer flyable after the Nell severed its tail as it passed over the edge. But he walked away unscathed, albeit shocked. But it was a small price to pay for saving dozens of airplanes and personnel, and possibly the entire ship.[73]

One of the outcomes of this operation was the realization that the present number of F4F fighters on board to support CAP operations, was less than ideal. After the attack on the Marshalls, Commander Young brought his opinion forward to Murray and Halsey. He argued that the fighter compliment on board the carrier was insufficient for situations such as what they had just experienced, and it was more luck than tactics that had kept the carriers safe. Young argued that the current compliment of eighteen fighters should be increased to twenty-seven. His justification was that the low performance capability, sluggish handling, and relatively slow speed of the SBDs and TBDs made them vulnerable to enemy fighters. Fortunately for the American pilots during the raid on the Marshalls, very few Japanese fighters intercepted the sluggish American planes. Losses were extremely low for Halsey on the *Enterprise* and Fletcher on the *Yorktown*—only twelve overall. In an almost clairvoyant fashion, Young claimed, "Fortunately in this action, VT-6 encountered no air opposition, but it is certain that their mission would have [failed] . . . had they been intercepted by enemy fighters which were in the near vicinity."[74] Young's desire would be acknowledged, but not acted upon for a few years. It would not be until Grumman began delivering hundreds of fighters a month, after the *Essex* class began to join the fleet, and the numbers of technicians supported the influx of matériel that the Navy would be able to adjust the number of fighters on the carrier flight deck to Young's desired twenty-seven or more.

✦✦✦

In 1944, a board headed by Rear Adm. Arthur Radford, fittingly known as the Radford Board, submitted its findings on the nature of present-day aviation planning and recommendations for forecasting as the war moved into its latter stages. Radford's findings also considered peacetime aviation operation for postwar consideration. Based on the board's findings, the Navy developed a plan that was designed to improve the overall maintenance and supply program for naval aviation as well as modify maintenance practices at sea. What became known as the Integrated Aeronautic Maintenance, Materiel and Supply Program (IAMMSP) relegated major repair and overhaul of naval aircraft to the continental United States. It also provided for replacements of completely new aircraft rather than the return of renovated aircraft to combat areas.[75] More simply, the plan ensured new aircraft were assigned to combat units. Those that needed reconditioning or major overhaul were sent back to the United States for repair and reassignment to training commands as necessary. In general, aircraft were retired from operational service after two combat tours to save on costly maintenance at sea and ashore.[76] This practice reduced the workload not only on the carrier aircraft maintenance departments but also on the CASUs and the AROUs operating in the Pacific. New aircraft required little more than routine maintenance to keep in the air. Thus, the service units could focus on the routine overhaul maintenance and minor battle damage repairs, rather than struggling to keep up with the "normal wear from hard use" in combat.[77] It made sense fiscally and in terms of how much would be required from the Navy's labor force.

During the first two years of the war, aircraft manufacturers operated with magnificent production capability, almost effortlessly supplying the fleet with enough aircraft for its pilots to fly. Manpower and industry met the demand from the Navy easily at first, but by the end of 1943 as carrier and pilot production increased, the Navy was running into problems managing the flow of airplanes into the carrier air groups. Supply was meeting demand in early 1944, but there was little structure as to how the system was supposed to operate. The Navy needed a program to systematically deliver new planes to the combat crews on the front line, provide what one might refer to today as "new-used" aircraft to the training commands in the continental United States and manage the process of salvage and cannibalization of aircraft parts from airplanes not flyable or useful to the fleet anymore.

Thus, in April 1944 the Radford Board was tasked with solving the problem of supply and maintenance in the new era of naval aviation during the war, and in preparation for a transition to peacetime force. Along with Radford as senior member, other board members included Rear Adm. L. B. Richardson, Col. A. D. Cooley, USMC, and Navy Supply Corps Capt. C. W. Fox as executive members. The board began meeting the same day its precept was released. It met for a total of fifteen sessions that month and delivered its first report and recommendations to the Chief of Naval Operations, Adm. Ernest King, on May 4, 1944. If enacted, Radford promised his plan would achieve better "support functions of naval aviation ashore and afloat."[78] King quickly approved the board's recommendations on improving the nature of present-day aviation planning and recommendations for forecasting demand as the war moved into its latter stages. The board reconvened in October to review the progress of the IAMMSP. It found that through instituting a more accurate reporting system, BuAer could better manage the intake and exhaust of new and used aircraft to the fleet.

The Radford Board suggested following a plan that was designed to improve the overall maintenance and supply program for naval aviation as well as modify maintenance practices at sea. The central tenant of the IAMMSP was shifting all major repair and overhaul of naval aircraft to the continental United States. It also provided for replacements of completely new aircraft rather than the return of renovated aircraft to combat areas.[79] More simply, combat units were given priority when allocating new aircraft—the squadrons on the front lines would receive brand new airplanes at regular intervals. Those planes that needed reconditioning or major overhaul after serving a prescribed period in combat were sent back to the United States for repair and reassignment to training commands as necessary. In general, aircraft were retired from operational service after two combat tours to save on costly maintenance at sea and ashore.[80] This practice reduced the workload not only on the carrier aircraft maintenance departments but also on the CASUs and the AROUs operating in the Pacific. New aircraft required little more than routine maintenance to keep in the air. Thus, the service units could focus on the routine overhaul maintenance and minor battle damage repairs, rather than struggling to keep up with the "normal wear from hard use" in combat.[81] It made sense fiscally and in terms of how much would be required from the Navy's labor force. The IAMMSP was designed to control the allocation, use, repair, and distribution of planes and spare parts.

The IAMMSP stressed using the newest combat airplanes in the western Pacific against Japanese naval forces and then retiring it to noncombat duty. The retired planes could be better defined as "matured" as the planes were by no means obsolete or unreliable. But considering the delivery rate of such fighters as the F6F were hovering around four to five hundred a month throughout the latter half of 1944 and into early the following year, the Navy could well afford to keep its fast carriers full of the newest, shiniest, most technologically advanced airplanes on the planet.

The Radford Board determined that there were six primary factors that constituted the service life of a combat airplane: design, materials, manufacturing, new military developments, use, and maintenance. What had changed since the first two years of the war was the control needed of the latter three factors—new military developments, use, and maintenance. Technology had changed along with the tide of the war. The missions changed from defensive to offensive, seeking a longer strike capability, and trying to meet the threat of the very capable and agile Japanese Zero. New weapons such as forward firing rockets were strapped onto wings, and fighters were no longer only used in the air-to-air role, but were performing duties as bombers as well. The increased number of flight hours on each plane also affected its ability to fight effectively. The more use, the more maintenance was required. The more involved that maintenance was, the more time each aircraft was off the flight schedule.[82]

In simple terms, the IAMMSP was a refined planning program for U.S. naval air forces in the Pacific based on accurate maintenance reporting. It ensured the future needs of naval aviation could be forecasted several months in advance. Pools of aircraft were created based on the forecasts so losses could be covered immediately. Likewise, the IAMMSP emphasized keeping enough parts on hand at advanced stations to make minor repairs on planes which did not yet require reconditioning. The IAMMSP also kept a continuous check on flying hours and condition of every plane in combat so that it can be retired from battle before lack of major repairs and loss of military advantage such circumstances created hardship on the pilot. It was also emphasized that those aircraft retired from frontline combat service should be returned to the United States for further use in noncombat roles. Cannibalization was also authorized within the confines of the IAMMSP. Cannibalization from used airplanes that were not considered worth reconditioning was now permitted at any of the advance units such as CASUs, AROUs, and even aircraft carrier hangar bays. This gave individual technicians lots of leeway in determining what was worth fixing and what was not. Working aircraft parts could be salvaged and used on other planes in making the minor repairs necessary to "keep 'em flying."[83]

A key to IAMMSP's success was its diligence in reporting the status of all aircraft in service. These reports were taken on a monthly basis beginning on August 31, 1944. A squadron maintenance department filled out a detailed "Monthly Report of Operating Aircraft" or NAVAER 1872 form, as of midnight (local time) on the last calendar day of each month. The report was sent via air mail no later than five days later to the CNO's office for filing and dissemination to applicable departments. The report itself provided the following information: total aircraft on hand as of the previous month's report (section A), number of aircraft gains since the last report (section B), total number of allocated aircraft that month (section C), aircraft losses since the last report (section D), and total aircraft on hand at the end of the month (section E). The form used a simple formula to derive its final numbers: $C = A + B$ and $E = C - D$.[84]

NAVAER 1872 also provided a detailed account of the status of each aircraft in the squadron. With less than two dozen aircraft per squadron, it was not an insurmountable task, but rather a routine update each month. The form tracked how many months each airplane was in service, total flight hours, how many hours it flew over the last month, whether it was reconditioned or not, and when it was gained or lost.

"Lost" was defined as damaged beyond repair or destroyed by any means. BuAer also tracked from where it was received, whether or not it was recommended to be stricken from service at the end of its "combat life," and if considered a loss, what were the factors in its loss.

The engine of the airplane was also part of the overall equation. If an engine was considered inoperable or had reached its service life, then the plane would no longer be useful to the frontline units. Therefore, the total number of hours since it's last overhaul and whether it was recommended for striking at the end of its service life, were also annotated on form 1872. The IAMMSP also removed the requirement that carrier squadrons and CASUs conduct such maintenance.

Striking an aircraft was more than simply pushing it over the side of the deck. There was a method in which squadrons could designate a plane for striking. There were three categories for striking aircraft: Class I, II, and III. If a plane was damaged beyond "economical" repair, it was designated a Class I. This was the only situation where a squadron or ship could dispose of the airplane on-site. Typically, Class I were results of enemy fire or a crash landing. If a plane was determined to be overage under Navy directives and thus considered "unserviceable" because it could not be repaired in an economically realistic fashion, then it was labeled a Class II strike on the 1872 form. A Class II stricken aircraft usually resided in the training command in the continental United States rather than at sea. Airplanes that fell into the Class III strike category were those that were defined as "excess" per the CNO's directives. A Class III was placed in storage for either reconditioning and further use in noncombat operations, or placed in a status of long-term storage for parts.[85]

Striking aircraft became more than just a paper drill because of the implications that accompanied it. The Navy was permitted a certain number of aircraft, or a "ceiling," as determined by Congress. If a plane was struck, then it was no longer counted against the ceiling, and a new airplane was then allocated in its place. But if reporting was late or did not occur, then the squadron would not receive a replacement, thus hampering their ability to complete its combat mission. Since 1940, the Navy had been authorized by Congress to have *no fewer* than 15,000 planes in service at any one time. The Radford Board's IAMMSP anchored itself in maintaining a constant level of new aircraft in the combat units while using the worn out and reconditioned aircraft in the rear echelons of training and supply.

The IAMMSP provided the fleet with a yardstick of sorts to measure the ability of each individual aircraft to meet its mission requirements. Simply put, the newest combat airplanes were placed into frontline carrier combat units. As each aircraft matured, it was cycled back into the ashore training programs in the continental United States. The IAMMSP declared combat units would deploy with new planes only, while training units would fly with those reconditioned or repaired. But determining the exact service life of each aircraft rested on six elements: design, materials, manufacturing, new military developments, use, and maintenance.[86]

It is helpful to understand what variables were considered when determining the age of each aircraft. To be considered eligible for inclusion into a combat unit, or "1st period" assignment, an airplane had to have the following: high operating efficiency, greatest military advantage, low repair needs, and minimum spare part needs. If it did not meet these criteria, then the following criteria was considered for it to be sent back to the United States as a trainer: did it have at least "good" operating efficiency? Was its military advantage still existent, albeit low? The airplane was showing increased repair needs, along with increasing spare part needs. If it met these criteria, then it was a candidate for a training command. When it was determined to have a low operating efficiency, no military advantage, high repair, and part needs, then it was abandoned, or stricken from the inventory. For those airplanes that had no value in recondition, repair, or cannibalization, their aluminum parts were salvaged and melted down into ingots for future parts manufacturing at naval and civilian aircraft factories.[87]

Prior to the IAMMSP, the "old" system of distribution split new aircraft deliveries across all units. New airplanes flowed from the manufacturers in equal distribution to forming units, the Pacific pool, and training units. Forming units consisted of squadrons that were being stood up to support new aircraft carriers; they were not yet part of frontline combat forces. The Pacific pool was the supply of airplanes poised on the forward operating areas of the Pacific, ready to be delivered to aircraft carriers on an as-needed basis. Training units were squadrons located ashore in the continental United States, where young officers earned their "wings of gold" before joining the air groups at sea. Each of these units had a similar number of new, old, and older aircraft. It was equitable across the spectrum, but not necessarily beneficial.

The problem with the old way of doing business was that on any given day, frontline combat squadrons might find themselves with a few new airplanes, but a majority of its supply was filled with late models and some that needed reconditioning. Technology was changing so fast in the aviation world that each time a new plane rolled off the assembly line, it most likely had a technological advantage, better weapon system, and faster than current fleet aircraft. To Radford and his board, it made sense that the best airplanes go to the frontline fighter units. Why not keep the new airplanes for pilots flying sorties day in and day out against the Japanese and give those who were in the noncombat/training units older and reconditioned aircraft? Having the "military advantage" over the Japanese was only beneficial if it occurred where combat was occurring. Placing faster, more heavily armed, and more maneuverable fighters and torpedo bombers on the fast carriers was the sensible thing to do in order to bring the war to a faster end. Training pilots who were in noncombat elements could be satisfied by older, reconditioned airplanes.[88]

The IAMMSP not only affected the allocation and delivery of new aircraft, it also changed the nature of repair. The Radford Board observed the various repair facilities servicing the fleet in 1944. From a fully equipped A&R shop ashore to a remote, or what were known as "shade tree" maintenance facilities dotted throughout the western Pacific island chains, overhaul and major repairs were taking place anywhere they could. Thus the board brought forward the recommendation that all general reconditioning should be limited to facilities in the continental United States. The United States had numerous well-equipped and technically sound facilities in the United States that could complete the tedious work safely, efficiently, and using the latest technology in parts and processes.[89]

The IAMMSP gave the Navy a fascinating and starry-eyed story to tell. Reporters and historians on the decks and bridge-wings of the carriers saw young pilots launching in shiny, new aircraft that looked as though the paint had hardly dried. Older planes were rotated out of the squadrons on a regular basis and new ones were flown in with green pilots rotating out from CASUs or CVEs on delivery duty. The problem with this appearance to the casual observer was that it neglected the true nature of the program. As the program's name—*Integrated*—implied, it was not a singular concept that could be lauded for success. Maintenance, material supply, manufacturing, and accurate bookkeeping all had a role to play. If one or more of these pieces fell behind, the value of Radford's program could not live up to expectations. Much like the mechanical pieces of a classic aviator's watch, it took the work of multiple gears to keep the program running on time.[90]

However, unlike a timepiece, the IAMMSP was designed to vary in speed as determined by circumstances. When operational tempo and combat was slow, flight hours went down and so did the rate of striking and maintenance problems. When the war heated up, and combat operations were sustained over long periods, the IAMMSP had to be ready to deliver replacements at a much greater rate. The IAMMSP's signature element was the ever-present supply of ready aircraft pre-positioned throughout the Pacific. The CVEs delivered aircraft to CASUs whether they were of immediate need or not. The Navy, understanding war seldom follows any sort of plan, roadmap, or structure, ensured they had enough planes on hand to supply the fleet at a moment's notice. This policy, almost in itself, contributed as much as any other factor in defeating the Japanese.[91]

✦✦✦

Once Radford's IAMMSP was in place, there was no longer a need to keep as many aircraft spare parts on the carriers. This allowed more space in the hangar for airplanes, which had a ripple effect. Additionally, by 1944, aircraft and aircraft carrier production were at their peak. More airplanes and aircraft carriers were available, and air groups were provided replacement planes on a regular basis. And since the maintenance department did not have to hold as much in the way of spare parts as previously, the hangar had more space available for additional aircraft. Therefore, by reducing the footprint of spares and spare parts aboard the carrier, the Navy could replace it with additional squadrons and aircraft. I believe that the changes in maintenance policy and procedures after 1943, particularly those associated with the IAMMSP, contributed directly to an increase in the overall complement of aircraft per air group, in addition to aircraft and aircraft carrier modifications.

The percentage of spare or reserve aircraft incorporated into the design of each aircraft carrier varied over the years and affected the size of the air group. The *Ranger* (1934) was designed to carry a margin of only 10 percent (eight spares) in addition to its operational seventy-five aircraft.[92] Plans for the *Wasp* (1939) called for a 50 percent reserve of a similar complement of seventy-five aircraft.[93] According to the initial design requirements of the *Essex*-class carrier, the Navy had built the ship to sail with the capacity for stowage of "50 percent of complement aircraft, as spares, disassembled" similar to that of the *Wasp*.[94] In 1940, that equated to space for approximately forty airplanes disassembled in the hangar, based on the original plan for eighty-four aircraft per air group. By 1943, newer *Essex*-class carriers like the *Yorktown* (CV 10) operated with the equivalent of just 25 percent of its total aircraft strength stowed in the hangar spaces.[95] That meant a more powerful striking force in flyable aircraft. Therefore, the diminishing percentage of reserve aircraft per carrier resulted in larger-sized air groups, eventually culminating in a hundred-plus airplanes per carrier. These fluctuations served as an indication of peace and wartime influences on naval planners. Forthcoming changes in maintenance policy regarding the decision to replace more damaged aircraft rather than repairing them, would be a factor in determining the number of spare airplanes on board.

After Pearl Harbor, it became essential that BuAer keep the Secretary of the Navy up to date on aviation requirements in support of the war effort, especially after the fiscal year estimates were submitted months or years ahead of time. As operations dictated, the specific requirements were extremely dynamic. BuAer revised its estimates on an "as-needed" basis in response to combat losses and updated ship completion estimates in a "Summary of Objectives" document. As of October 31, 1942, BuAer had determined that the proper percentage of spare combatant aircraft was 33.3 percent of the total air group.[96] In terms of a CV air group, this meant that for every three aircraft assigned to a carrier, a single "ready" spare was required. This did not necessitate the CV carrying an extra three dozen aircraft, but BuAer ensured that all parties were aware of the large quantities of "extra" airplanes that would need to be purchased over the course of the war to meet this requirement.

The numbers do, however, line up nicely with the later configurations of the *Essex*-class carrier air groups, which by August 1944 were listed as embarking 96 aircraft, and by June 1945 embarking with 102 to 103 aircraft.[97] While not exactly a 33.3 percent addition to the original 83-plane configuration, it certainly explains the ability and reasoning behind increasing the complement of airplanes. If BuAer believed that approximately one-third of its combat planes would need replacement during the war—and understanding the nature of logistical challenges of getting new planes to an aircraft carrier in the middle of the Pacific—why not deploy with as many of the extra planes already on board? Rather than toiling with repairs or aircraft deliveries, the Navy simply reconfigured the *Essex* air groups to meet the requirements of carrier warfare.

The aggregate numbers of late 1944 delivered an even more replacement-minded view of carrier aviation. According to the briefing given on the overall state of naval aviation on July 5, 1944, the percentage of spares that were to be made available to carrier air groups was even bigger than the 33.3 percent mentioned a year before. As discussed previously, sixteen replacement planes per month were required on average for an *Essex*-class carrier air group. Table 6.5 is a reproduction of BuAer's Production Planning Division's projected requirements for all carriers at sea or in production as of 1944.

Clearly, the impact that spare aircraft had on fleet operations was significant. By June 1944, most carrier groups were allocated a contingent of spare planes that accounted for approximately 40 percent of the total of all aircraft assigned (see Table 6.5). This meant that for every ten operable airplanes on the carrier's flight deck, four more were ready spares located either in the hangar or prepositioned at a CASU or naval air station.

By 1944 naval war planners had apparently accepted that the Pacific air war would be one of attrition. Aircraft in repair would do little to support combat operations, but rapid replacement of damaged or malfunctioning airplanes would. One should not interpret this as a lack of confidence in the Navy's aircraft maintenance program, but rather in response to the nature of the war. The vast distances in which the carrier task forces were operating made logistics to and from the continental United States very

Table 6.5. Aircraft Distribution for Carriers, June 1944[1]

SHIP TYPE	SHIPS TO BE COMMISSIONED BY 12/31/45	NO. UNITS	PLANES PER UNIT	TOTAL OPERATING PLANES	SPARES	TOTAL PLANES
Heavy Carrier (CVB)	2	5	121	605	412	1,017
Medium Carrier (CV)	23	43	91	3,913	2,666	6,579
Light Carrier (CVL)	9	19	33	627	427	1,054
Escort Carrier (CVE) *Sangamon*	21	38	33	1,254	854	2,108
Escort Carrier (CVE) *Kaiser* & C3	62	61	24	1,464	997	2,461
Night Fighter Groups (Shipboard)	0	28	12	336	229	565
Miscellaneous		1	117	117	80	197

[1] "The Program for Naval Aviation."

difficult. The time and expense of shipping damaged airplanes back to the West Coast of the United States, or even Pearl Harbor, was impracticable. The Navy could not afford to wait weeks at a time for replacement parts or aircraft while amphibious forces were fighting their way through Japanese-held island chains throughout the South Pacific.

The air group had to defend the task force, support the ground units fighting through the islands, or strike enemy combatants from above. It was the job of the maintenance division aboard the carrier to keep planes in the air. Aircraft losses were common throughout the war, as one would expect due to the frequency of operations and the ferocity of Japanese resistance. However, aircraft losses due to reasons other-than-combat were also quite high—in fact even more than combat-related losses. While the specifics of what constituted an operational loss is not defined, one can reasonably associate it with both mechanical failure and pilot error (see Table 6.6).

Table 6.6. U.S. Carrier Aircraft Losses in Combat and Noncombat Operations[1]

CAUSE OF LOSS	NO. VF (FIGHTER)	% VF	NO. VB/VT (ATTACK)	% VB/VT
Enemy Action	1,463	36.1	1,025	37.7
Combat not Enemy Action	30	0.7	30	1.1
Friendly Fire	128	3.1	91	3.2
Operational Accidents	2,390	58.9	1,547	56.8
Other	45	1.2	30	1.2
Total	4,056	100	2,723	100

[1] "Operational Experience of Fast Carrier Task Forces in World War II," 72.

The number of operational accidents is staggering in both fighter and attack aircraft. Even when adding all other types of losses, operational accidents still outweigh all other losses by a ratio of nearly two to one.[98] Within these statistics, one can infer that the biggest threat to U.S. Navy pilots was not the Japanese navy, but rather themselves and their own aircraft. But how much of that can be attributed to faulty aircraft systems, unsatisfactory maintenance, or in-flight errors by the pilots?

Exact answers to such questions are elusive, but looking even closer at the postwar analysis of the Fast Carrier Task Force, it is apparent that within combat situations the Navy did delineate one cause of loss from the next. Over the course of the war, diligent records were kept for aircraft losses that occurred while the carrier task forces were engaged in combat missions. Surprisingly, within that subset, losses caused by enemy action and operational loss are almost identical.[99] From December 1941 through August 1945, the carrier-based VF community lost 1,078 airplanes to enemy action and the attack aircraft (VB/VT) losses of the same sort numbered 756. During that same period, operational losses that occurred during carrier-based combat missions numbered 1,221 for VF and 656 for VB/VT aircraft (see Table 6.7).

The total number of enemy-induced and operational losses were 1,834 and 1,877, respectively. But aside from land-based antiaircraft guns, the biggest threats to USN carrier aircraft were pilot error (577), then

Table 6.7. Losses by Carrier Aircraft on Combat Mission by Cause of Loss [1]

CAUSE OF LOSS	VF	VT/VB
Enemy Actions		
Aircraft	302	107
Ship	84	183
Land Antiaircraft	691	457
Other	1	4
Enemy Action Total	1,078	756
Operational Losses		
Mechanical Failure	354	173
Pilot Failure	440	137
Fuel Exhaustion	114	167
Other	308	179
Operational Total	1,221	656

[1] "Operational Experience of Fast Carrier Task Forces in World War II," 74. Statistics herein are subject to a 10 percent margin of error according to the document (p. 75).

mechanical failure (527), and lastly the elusive "other" category (487). Enemy aircraft followed behind all of these with 487 losses attributed.

Carrier aviation maintenance only had a stake in one or perhaps two (depending on what "other" entailed) of these causes. The better that the technician did his job on the flight deck, the less chance there would be of mechanical failure. However, considering the *replace* versus *repair* culture at the time, it is quite possible that the influences of later maintenance policies such as the IAMMSP may have affected these numbers.

Until 1944, carrier operational losses due to mechanical failure were extremely low. The year 1942 reported only 16 and 1943 only 28. In 1944, the number jumped to 199 and then in eight months of fighting in 1945 mechanical losses numbered 284.[100] The number of sorties, aircraft, and aircraft carriers were much lower in 1942–43 than in 1944 and 1945.

However, the introduction of the IAMMSP into the Navy's aviation maintenance practices in the second half of 1944 was conveniently situated at a point where the rates of loss are at their height.[101]

Understanding the impact that revised maintenance procedures and committing newer aircraft to the fleet on a regular basis during the second half of the war is best seen in what was termed aircraft "availability." This number differed from the aircraft aboard, usually a few short. Unavailable, or "down" aircraft due to repair or routine maintenance counted against readiness percentages. It was the job of the carrier's maintenance team to have as many available aircraft as possible when needed. The goal would be to have maximum aircraft availability during periods of sustained combat operations.

There is archival evidence to support the argument that the revised maintenance policies after 1943 had a positive impact on aircraft availability when the Navy needed it most. From April to June 1945 Carrier Division 22, consisting of 4 CVEs, reported that its average availability of VF airplanes was 88 percent or 69 out of a 78-airplane complement. The torpedo bomber models (VT) averaged 43 of 47 available, equating to 91 percent in support of the occupation of Okinawa. The division averaged a striking force of 78 fighters and 47 attack aircraft divided among four escort carriers. Of those, an average of 69 fighters and 43 torpedo bombers were available for combat. When data from two additional carriers attached to the division on a temporary basis is included with the reporting, 26 of the 30 aircraft on hand were combat ready on a daily basis. The average number of airplanes on board each CVE in the division was 29.5 and the average number available was 25.9. This equated to an overall availability of 87.8 percent, which is representative of the last two years of the war.[102]

From January 10-16, 1945, Task Force 38, which consisted of the *Hornet*, *Lexington*, and *Hancock* battle groups, conducted combat operations in the South China Sea with an initial complement of 942 aircraft. On day one of combat operations, Task Force 38 reported 850 of 942 (90 percent) aircraft available. This included 607 of the 657 fighters assigned to the three air groups. By the end of the operation, availability had dropped to 81 percent due to combat losses only.[103] The IAMMSP was fully integrated into the Fast Carrier Task Force by 1945 and it enabled carrier groups to keep its availability percentages in the 80–90 percentile for the duration of the war.[104]

As we have seen, the Navy began replacing worn out aircraft with brand new ones in earnest by 1944. Simultaneously, the naval aviation's labor force, the enlisted aviation technician, reached its peak strength. Carrier production was also peaking at the same time. Fiscally, the Navy had the funds to supply each air group with new planes at the rate of sixteen per month.[105] Technicians were filling these billets within the carrier aircraft maintenance divisions as well as the CASUs and AROUs. Overhauls were at peak production around the same time. Once the Radford Board submitted its recommendations for a new maintenance policy that argued for a better system than had been in place the previous two years, why wouldn't the Navy embrace it? Perhaps it was Radford's reputation as a previous director of aviation training for the CNO in 1941, or his experience as a carrier division commander in 1943, or his tenure as a carrier task force commander in 1944—one can only surmise. What is apparent however, is that the Navy embraced his aircraft maintenance policy recommendations wholeheartedly.

I cannot simply say that naval aviation maintenance embraced a throwaway culture solely based on Admiral Radford's recommendations, but as we have seen, there is ample evidence that such a mindset did exist in some degree from 1944 onward. "Keep 'em flying" might have been the motto of the Navy's aviation maintenance departments, but perhaps that really only applied to six- to twelve-month-old aircraft? More realistically, in order to keep even the newer airplanes available, the need for nonemergent daily maintenance on board carriers was so great that aircraft technicians were fully utilized, even in a throwaway culture.

Ultimately, it was the aircraft technician who kept the Navy's carrier aircraft in the air when needed most. There was a shift midway through the war in numbers of available aircraft, spare parts, and technicians. As if it was planned, even though it was not, numbers of new planes and personnel went up and percentages of spare parts went down. Policy changes within the institution adapted to the needs and available assets of the time. The role of naval aircraft technicians might have changed between 1940 and 1945, but nevertheless they remained an integral part of the Navy's success in the Pacific air war. Bob Hope best summed up the importance of the naval aircraft technician in the war when he said,

> You know it takes more than good airplanes to make an aircraft carrier or a Naval Station and more than a good pilot to get a plane over the target and bring it back home safely; it takes men behind the pilot. Men trained in Radio. Mechanics who are able to man a machine gun or make repairs in mid-air. Machinists Mates back on the carrier or on the ground to repair the latest motors, Metalsmiths to sew up those broken wings. Ordnancemen to make sure that a plane's guns will always bark at the right time. . . . And when these men come out of this training center, they're ready to do all this and more, ready to pitch and play third base on the Navy's major league team of air and ground crewman. Yes, sir, folks, when you think of General MacArthur's famous words "I'll Return," add a word of thanks to fellows like these who helped make it possible for him to say, "I have returned!"[106]

Conclusion

The defeat of the Japanese navy in the Pacific came largely from the decks of the U.S. Navy's Fast Carrier Task Force. Advances in technology no doubt played a pivotal role, however, without concomitant achievements in technical education, labor methodology, and logistical innovation, victory would have been delayed, at the very least. The ability of the Navy to provide the requisite number of trained aircraft technicians and supply the U.S. fleet with enough matériel to achieve its strategic objective was integral to its success. The war between the world's two largest aircraft carrier fleets and ultimately the Navy's ability to project power cannot be fully comprehended without identifying the critical role of the aircraft technician. In the same manner, one could argue that America's rise to an eminent sea power was forged on the backs of the naval aircraft technician, not just the aircraft carrier. Could one have existed without the other? Very unlikely, but for the last seventy-plus years, naval historians have told their tales of the war in the Pacific without acknowledging the dungaree or coverall-clad young aircraft technicians working up to eighteen or more hours a day—at sea or ashore—to keep planes in the air. Recognizing the complete picture from the outset of aviation technical schooling to the everyday challenges that carrier aircraft technicians faced at sea throughout the war is an important contribution to the historiography of the U.S. Navy in World War II.

The narrative behind the U.S. Navy's development of a large technical workforce in order to support a new era of carrier warfare is a complex history of institutional change. No longer was the striking power of a navy limited by the range of a battleship's guns. Carrier-based aircraft could travel several hundred miles farther and deliver more ordnance than any shipboard naval gun. By the end of the 1930s, it was evident to some that the potential striking power of the aircraft carrier would eventually supersede the notion that its principal contribution to the fleet would be an auxiliary force to the battleship and surface navy. Yet, it seemed as if no one in naval leadership fully understood the ramifications of building a new navy around the aircraft carrier.

The ability of the U.S. Navy to fight a protracted war throughout the Pacific Ocean was not solely the result of technology, tactics, or admiralship—naval aviation maintenance played a major role in the U.S. victory and indeed constitutes a significant historical subject. In order to better understand the full dimensions of modern naval war in the age of the aircraft carrier, it is essential to consider all elements of the military institution, not just those that made headlines. And what constitutes the critical mass of an institution? Its people. Without people, what use is a Hellcat or an *Essex*-class aircraft carrier? This book has opened the door to studying the role of the aircraft technician in the Pacific war. The history of naval warfare in the earliest age of aircraft carriers is not just about the airplane and the aircraft carrier. If there is no study of the personnel who labor to keep those weapons at the ready, or the schools and commands that train them ashore, how can we understand the complete history of the greatest naval war in U.S. history?

In order to understand the institutional changes that took place within the U.S. Navy during World War II, it is essential to ask the right questions. It is common knowledge that there was an immense buildup of people, planes, and ships, but how was that massive effort sustained operationally? More specifically, how did the naval aviation community transform thousands of new and often untrained recruits into an effective force of skilled technicians? In doing so, how did the character of this achievement affect the conduct of operations? To what degree did the Navy's success in creating a new technical workforce change its culture?

Naval aviation leadership throughout the interwar period focused on the improvement of technology and tactics rather than training a new, and in the event of war, necessarily large cohort of enlisted personnel. Aircraft maintenance was an afterthought for much of the era because of the small number of carriers and aircraft. Until 1939, aircraft maintenance did not garner much attention, for it had always been sufficient. Yes, there was some grumbling about not having adequate personnel, but nothing serious enough to warrant any real change. However, when the United States realized a two-ocean naval war was imminent and a drastic increase in the size of its aviation fleet was ordered, the Navy was forced to reconsider its earlier practices and forge new policies and processes.

First, the Bureau of Aeronautics (BuAer) had to revise its personnel and technical training policies in order to manage the colossal buildup of personnel and planes. Recruiting individuals with technical acumen and the activation of Naval Reserve personnel with maintenance experience became a high priority. The bureau modified its internal administrative structure in order to manage the rapid influx of recruits and transform them into competent aviation mechanics.

In addition, the incoming recruits had to be trained how to maintain naval aircraft. Technical trade schools were built, a curriculum for different aircraft systems was developed, and field experts were brought in to produce academic material. Standardizing curriculum and filling classrooms with qualified instructors was a challenge. By 1941 the schools were managing to graduate a satisfactory number of candidates, but the increasing burden of the administrative and logistical requirements became too much for BuAer to handle.

The naval bureaucracy had to restructure in order to best accommodate the complex training requirements. Consolidating all technical schools under an independent command was the adjustment that naval aviation needed. The Naval Aviation Technical Training Command took control of all technical training in 1942 and never looked back. Formalized vocational training was established at major naval installations throughout the United States. Additionally, various levels of technical training were made available to enlisted personnel based on their proficiency and experience. For the first time in American history women and Black sailors were given opportunities to serve in aviation technical ratings in the U.S. Navy. Periods of instruction were streamlined so the trade schools could deliver more aviation technicians at a faster rate. Specialized ratings and qualifications were also added to sailor's service records so supervisory personnel could place each technician into a job where he or she would be most productive.

The structure of naval operational maintenance programs also required modification. At sea, aircraft maintenance on the carrier transitioned to a full-time, integrated workforce. Enlisted aviation technicians were fully integrated as permanent members of the ship's crew. The aircraft maintenance division on board the carrier no longer belonged to the air group, but were now a full-time component of the ship's Air Department. The more training that technicians received while assigned to technical training commands (trade schools), the more the carrier's maintenance team could specialize its workforce.

Specialization of labor within the workforce was critical to the efficiency of overhaul and repair facilities on and off the carrier. Most overhauls and major repairs were completed at shore establishments where the specialized technicians were readily available. Many technicians received advanced training on specific mechanical and electrical aircraft systems in addition to the general knowledge gained from A schools. These experts soon permitted the maintenance department to minimize aircraft system troubleshooting and repair time. Specialization with the carrier's Air Department reduced aircraft "downtime" because minor problems could be corrected on the spot, and airplanes could be placed back onto the flight schedule. If the repair was more labor-intensive, it was completed at a shore-based facility somewhere in the Pacific island chains—at either a Carrier Aircraft Service Unit (CASU) or an Aviation Repair and Overhaul Unit (AROU).

In developing the forward-deployed servicing and overhaul units, the Navy was implementing a division of labor on the macro level. Carrier maintenance was no longer required to complete the intensive labor associated with overhaul and major repair. Task forces were deployed to fight, not to fix; therefore they could delegate the labor-intensive overhaul work to the CASU and AROU units and focus on having available aircraft for each day's flight schedule.

Conclusion

The division of labor concept, exemplified by the CASU and AROU model was a breakthrough in the naval war against Japan. By 1944, naval aviation had developed its skilled labor forces to levels sufficient to fill the personnel needs of both the carrier task forces and shore-based overhaul units. Simultaneously, the war industry reached its highest levels of production of naval aircraft and aircraft carriers. Admirals and aircrew had the latest technology, and lots of it. Fully trained technicians did "keep 'em flying," which allowed aircrew and admirals to utilize their weapons to the maximum extent possible.

The commercial aircraft industry's massive production of naval aircraft solved many of the supply problems that plagued carrier aviation early in the war. In doing so, however, it also altered the culture of aviation maintenance that had been in existence since the 1920s. Prior to 1944, aircraft technicians did their best to minimize aircraft losses and down-time due to mechanical or structural malfunctions that could be repaired. Often this meant an aircraft would be unavailable for the flight schedule for an extended period. After 1944, the Integrated Aeronautic Maintenance, Materiel, and Supply Program (IAMMSP) further changed how the Navy conducted its aircraft maintenance.

When the IAMMSP was introduced into the Navy's aviation maintenance departments, it had an immediate and lasting effect on the culture of aviation supply and maintenance. The IAMMSP directed that major overhaul and repair would only be conducted in continental U.S. facilities. CASUs and AROUs would be dedicated to supporting the forward-deployed carrier air groups. Broken or malfunctioning aircraft were no longer the problem of the carrier air departments, CASUs, or AROUs. Most importantly, the IAMMSP dictated that combat aircraft would be retired after serving two deployments in support of combat operations and replaced with new airplanes from the factories. Prior to 1944, the expectation was that carrier aircraft would serve as many as five years in operation before replacement. The culture within naval aviation maintenance shifted from one of repair to one of replace.

Some might define this as a throwaway culture, which has a negative, materialistic connotation about it. However, this was the best course of action based on the protracted war of attrition that the Navy was engaged in. Repair consumed valuable man-hours and placed the air group at a disadvantage. Having a "down" aircraft meant one less bomb on target, or the possibility of Japanese bombers finding their way to the U.S. carriers. Carrier technicians were best trained in routine servicing and minor repair on board the carriers. The problem of supply and logistics was remedied through various means, particularly the CASUs and AROUs. The Navy implemented a plan to deliver sixteen new airplanes per month to each air group. This accounted for aged-out planes and those damaged or lost in combat. It also relieved the pressure on aircraft technicians at sea by minimizing the extra workload that older aircraft often required. The culture that many long-standing professionals among the enlisted ranks of aircraft maintainers had grown accustomed to was a product of a fiscally conservative era of peace. The war years were very different, and the Navy was compelled to adapt accordingly.

The social culture of the Navy also changed with the increased emphasis on naval technicians. Considering the impact that Waves and their Marine counterparts had on the ranks of the Navy and Marine Corps, one cannot overlook their agency in the outcome of the war. While it hasn't always been a smooth road for women in the Navy, female aircraft technicians proved that technical labor is not gender-specific. Women may not have served on carriers during the war, but they did the same jobs as men and oftentimes more at shore air stations. The Navy has never looked back from women in the ranks since 1943. The role women played in the Navy and Marine Corps was much more than being limited to administrative-yeoman types of jobs. The need for aircraft technicians during the war necessitated the gender barrier to be breached and the culture of the naval service was changed forever.

Black men were also given new opportunities. The Navy opened ratings for Blacks other than mess cooks, stewards, stevedores, and other unskilled jobs. Trade schools opened their doors to Blacks and gave them jobs on the flight line and in the hangars. While it was not a fully integrated concept, it was a step in the right direction. Some of the schools were for Blacks only, while others claimed to be racially integrated. However, many of these still segregated the classrooms, requiring Blacks to attend class in the evenings, while daytime classes were for Whites only. Nevertheless, it was a step in the right direction and better than being relegated to just a few ratings that had nothing to do with the technology of the war. Blacks could now strive for aviation machinist's mate or aviation metalsmith, and with the skill set such ratings provided, postwar careers in the technical trades were now a possibility.

There is no question that the Fast Carrier Task Force contributed to the defeat of the Japanese navy. Aircraft availability averaged between 80 and 90 percent throughout the latter half of the war. Task group commanders were supplied the appropriate number of "up" aircraft when necessary. Aircrew had planes to fly and bombs to drop. The aircraft technician on the flight deck and in the hangar was proficient and rarely short of work. Even without the burden of overhaul and major repair, aircraft maintenance on the carrier was nonstop. Daily maintenance and servicing of aircraft was time-consuming and critical to the success of each strike made by each task force. The Naval Air Technical Training Command referred to World War II as "The Technicians War."[1] While this was most likely intended as a motivational slogan, it was not far from the truth.

Some of the changes in naval aircraft maintenance practice had lasting effects. For one, this period ushered in the establishment of many of the naval aviation maintenance policies and procedures currently in existence. Specialization and division of labor is commonplace in the modern Navy's enlisted workforce. The maintenance department is still divided into work centers identified by their ratings. The number of ratings available to enlisted men and women have been reduced, but the opportunity to seek specialized qualifications in many technical fields still exists.[2]

Maintenance procedures that came into existence during World War II continue to be an integral part of naval aviation. The battle against corrosion is still being fought. Derivatives of the liquid preservative compounds that were used to protect metal aircraft parts in World War II are in use on naval aircraft today. Corrosive-inhibiting agents are commonplace in every U.S. Navy squadron.[3]

This study underscores the importance of education in the process of creating an effective modern military. The BuAer made the hard decision to embrace change in order to meet the needs of the fleet. Educating aircraft technicians in the same methods that had been done for years would not suffice for what was recognized to be imminent war. Navies today (and the military overall) rely on technology more than ever to fight wars. It is not enough to simply sign young men and women up at the recruiting stations. It takes a vast network of internal organizations to bring that new recruit through basic training, then an A school and follow-on schools in some cases. The trailblazing efforts of Austin Wheelock, Daniel Brimm, A. C. Read, and Arthur Radford in relation to the technical training programs of naval aviation have gone largely unnoticed. If one examines the structure of the U.S. Navy's aviation technical training today, little has changed since 1943.

In a broader context of the war, my research has emphasized the lack of preparedness throughout the U.S. Navy until 1943. I believe the situation that the U.S. Navy faced in 1941 was very similar to what the Soviet Union faced in 1939. Even with a strong industrial and personnel base in 1939, the Soviet Union lacked a highly trained, well-organized, and skilled labor force that could match the Nazi war machine.[4] Likewise, the U.S. Navy had a strengthening industrial base in ship and aircraft production, but for the first two years of the war, it lacked the skilled labor necessary to sustain a protracted carrier war in the Pacific. This was evidenced by the large quantities of aircraft engine overhauls that were backlogged by the second half of 1943, the limited number of combat flight hours flown before 1944, and the great swell of technical ratings introduced into the fleet after the first year of war. My argument does not discount the impact that the Fast Carrier Task Force of 1944–45 had on the outcome of the war. However, it was the introduction of a specialized workforce and the skilled technicians who labored on the hangar decks that constituted the final piece of the puzzle.

Further historical work in the field of naval aviation maintenance is needed. The "battle piece" has been exhaustively studied, but the narrative of "machines, men, manufacturing, management, and money" as it applies to World War II naval aviation maintenance is wide open for further exploration. My hope is that my findings will challenge other historians to look below the flight deck, outside of the cockpit, and inside the trade schools to further enhance our rich history of naval aviation.

The study of World War II aircraft maintenance should also encourage questions outside the limits of naval aviation and carrier warfare. There is much to be said about the nature of sustaining labor and capital

Conclusion

in a protracted wartime environment based on the conflict between Japan and the United States. A number of recent wars or armed conflicts have been over within a few months or even weeks. This is especially true when major combat units such as carrier strike groups or Marine expeditionary forces are actively engaged with other large-scale organized military units.[5] What happens when the fighting continues past a few months and into years? Are protracted wars a thing of the past? What lessons are there to learn from the unlimited spending that produced thousands of technologically advanced weapons, but did little at first to provide the skilled labor necessary to maintain such weapons. Are twenty-first-century militaries prepared to obtain the skilled labor necessary to fight a multiyear war over large geographic distances? Perhaps this book will encourage those decision makers at the forefront of national defense policy and strategy to ask pertinent questions like these. What will the next Great Power conflict look like, and what role will naval aviation play? The naval aviation community has never seen combat like it did from 1942 to 1945 in the Pacific. Were America to enter into a war where aircraft attrition and combat losses were even a tenth of the World War II numbers, could it support protracted operations? Have the Navy's training commands prepared, or at least considered a plan to ramp up technical education and training for a wave of airplane and helicopter technicians that would be necessary to sustain another protracted air war? Defense leadership, along with historians, should consider these questions as they determine the future training and sustainment policies of carrier warfare. Relationships between skilled labor, industry, and capital in modern protracted warfare are not purely theoretical. These issues became all too real in 1941, arguably, much to the surprise of U.S. Navy leadership. It is my greatest hope that this study and others that follow will prompt government and military policy makers to consider the hard lessons of the past when making plans for the future.

Notes

Introduction

1. See U.S. Navy BuAer *Annual Report of the Bureau of Aeronautics* for years 1934–36.
2. "Extracts from the Annual Report of the Bureau of Aeronautics as Submitted by Rear Admiral A. B. Cook, U.S. Navy, to the Secretary of the Navy, for Fiscal Year 1937," November 12, 1937.
3. Office of Deputy Chief of Naval Operations (Air), "Aviation Personnel, 1939–45," in *United States Naval Administration in World War II* (Washington, DC: U.S. Government Printing Office, 1959), 22: 323–25, 338.
4. "Aviation Personnel, 1939–45," 150–52.
5. "Annual Report of the Secretary of Navy: Fiscal Year 1945" (Department of the Navy, 1946), A-55.
6. Naval History and Heritage Command, "U.S. Navy Active Force Ship Levels, 1945–1950," last modified November 17, 2017. https://www.history.navy.mil/research/histories/ship-histories/us-ship-force-levels.html.
7. This figure is derived from an estimate of a hundred aircraft per CV, thirty per CVL, and thirty per CVE.
8. "Annual Report of the Secretary of Navy: Fiscal Year 1945," A-77.
9. "Annual Report of the Secretary of Navy: Fiscal Year 1945," A-21, A-49.
10. A. R. Buchanan, ed., *The Navy's Air War* (New York: Harper, 1947).
11. Some of the most valuable data relevant to quantifying the impact of aircraft maintenance on the carrier during wartime operations is found in the unpublished study.
12. Jon T. Sumida and David A. Rosenberg, "Machines, Men, Manufacturing, Management, and Money: The Study of Navies as Complex Organizations and the Transformation of Twentieth Century Naval History," in *Doing Naval History: Essays Toward Improvement*, ed. John B. Hattendorf (Newport, RI: Naval War College Press, 1995), 25.
13. John Keegan, *The Face of Battle* (London: Penguin, 1978).
14. The USS *Langley* (CV 1) was converted into a seaplane tender in 1937 and saw combat against the Japanese during the first months of the war. On February 27, 1942, it was attacked by Japanese aircraft and suffered irreparable damage. The *Langley* was scuttled by U.S. forces shortly thereafter rather than risking the ship falling into enemy hands.
15. The Washington Naval Treaty of 1922 put a limit on combined aircraft carrier fleet tonnage at 135,000 tons, and individual ships could not displace more than 27,000 tons each (although the limits were often exceeded during construction as seen in the *Lexington* and the *Saratoga* at 36,000 tons each). The *Ranger* was designed in 1925 as a smaller version of the *Lexington* class (14,000 tons), similar in size to the

Langley. The three *Yorktown*-class carriers (the *Yorktown*, *Enterprise*, and *Hornet*) each displaced approximately 20,000 tons in order to adhere to the weight limits of the applicable treaties. The *Wasp* was in its own class, smaller than the *Yorktown* at approximately 15,000 tons. The *Essex*-class carriers (27,000 tons) were designed after the limits of the treaty were abandoned after 1937.
16. The Bureau of Navigation (BuNav) was renamed the Bureau of Naval Personnel (BuPers) in 1942. The acronyms will be used interchangeably throughout this book.
17. Often found on recruiting posters or in maintenance handbooks, "Keep 'em flying" was the slogan for the Navy's aircraft maintenance force throughout the war.

Chapter 1. Progress and Shortcomings

1. Norman Friedman, *Fighters Over the Fleet* (Annapolis, MD: Naval Institute Press, 2016), 28.
2. Friedman, *Fighters Over the Fleet*, 13–15.
3. Bureau of Naval Personnel, *Navy Wings* (Washington, DC: U.S. Government Printing Office, 1955), 30.
4. Howard Mingos, ed., *The Aircraft Year Book for 1937* (New York: Aeronautical Chamber of Commerce of America, 1937), 88.
5. The USS *Langley* (CV 1) was converted into a seaplane tender in 1937 and saw combat against the Japanese during the first months of the war, On February 27, 1942, she was attacked by Japanese aircraft and suffered irreparable damage. The *Langley* was scuttled by U.S. forces shortly thereafter rather than risking the ship falling into enemy hands.
6. Reeves, an 1894 graduate of the U.S. Naval Academy, is credited with wearing the first football helmet in an 1893 Naval Academy football game. The helmet was made for him by an Annapolis shoemaker who crafted the helmet after Reeves was told by a doctor that if he took one more hit to the head in a game, he risked death or brain damage. Source: Louis Blakely, "History of the Football Helmet," Past Time Sports, http://www.pasttimesports.biz/history.html. Accessed April 17, 2019.
7. Friedman, *Fighters Over the Fleet*, 32.
8. Clark G. Reynolds, *Admiral John H. Towers: The Struggle for Naval Air Supremacy* (Annapolis, MD: Naval Institute Press, 1991), 212–15.
9. William Larkins, *U.S. Navy Aircraft 1921–1941* (Concord, CA: Aviation History Publications, 1961), 23, 44, 341.
10. William F. Trimble, *Wings for the Navy: A History of the Naval Aircraft Factory 1917–1956*, 89–91 (Annapolis, MD: Naval Institute Press, 1990).
11. Reeves, Yarnell, and Mitscher would continue to serve naval aviation interests both operationally and administratively throughout World War II.
12. The Washington Naval Treaty of 1922 put a limit on combined aircraft carrier tonnage at 135,000 and an individual ship limit of 27,000 tons (although the limits were often exceeded during construction as seen in the *Lexington* and *Saratoga* at 36,000 tons each). The *Ranger* was designed in 1925 as a smaller version of the

Lexington class (14,000 tons), similar in size to the *Langley*. The three *Yorktown*-class carriers (*Yorktown, Enterprise, Hornet*) each weighed approximately 20,000 tons in order to adhere to the weight limits of the applicable treaties. The *Wasp* was in its own class, smaller than the Yorktown, but of similar design, weighing approximately 15,000 tons. The *Essex*-class carriers (27,000 tons) were designed after the limits of the treaty were abandoned after 1937.

13. Archibald D. Turnbull and Clifford L. Lord, *History of United States Naval Aviation*, 1972 Reprint by Arno Press (New Haven, CT: Yale University Press, 1949), 260–61.
14. Office of Deputy Chief of Naval Operations (Air), "Aviation Personnel, 1939–45," 211.
15. The three carriers in discussion were based on the design of the USS *Lexington* (CV 2). The number three thousand was most likely associated with an aircraft complement of seventy-eight airplanes per carrier.
16. Turnbull and Lord, *History of United States Naval Aviation*, 264.
17. Bureau of Aeronautics, "BUAER Annual Report 1930" (United States Navy, 1930). "Rated" refers to technicians who are skilled in maintenance of aircraft systems, as any trained mechanic would be. "General service" included support personnel for such duties as administration, flight deck operations, or supply. Essentially, those who were not considered airplane mechanics or ordnance technicians.
18. Turnbull and Lord, *History of United States Naval Aviation*, 265.
19. Larkins, *U.S. Navy Aircraft 1921–1941*, 90, 146.
20. Norman Friedman, *U.S. Aircraft Carriers* (Annapolis, MD: United States Naval Institute, 1983), 389.
21. Friedman, *U.S. Aircraft Carriers*, 391–94.
22. Robert C. Stern, *The* Lexington *Class Carriers* (Annapolis, MD: Naval Institute Press, 1993), 109.
23. Stern, 149.
24. Stern, 109–10; Norman Friedman, *Carrier Air Power* (New York: Rutledge, 1981), 112.
25. Interview of Cdr. Alfred M. Pride, BUSHIPS Correspondence, June 16, 1942. As quoted in Stern, 110.
26. Friedman, *U.S. Aircraft Carriers*, 392–93.
27. Friedman, *U.S. Aircraft Carriers*, 392–93; the *Langley* was decommissioned as an aircraft carrier in 1936 and converted into a seaplane tender in 1937.
28. Airspeed figures are given in knots (kts), not miles per hour (mph).
29. Charles McCarthy, "Naval Aircraft Design in the Mid-1930s," *Technology and Culture* 4, no. 2 (Spring 1963): 173.
30. "Extracts from the Annual Report of the Bureau of Aeronautics as Submitted by Rear Admiral Ernest J. King, U.S. Navy, to the Secretary of the Navy, for Fiscal Year 1934," Dec. 9, 1934.
31. Friedman, *Fighters Over the Fleet*, 444.
32. Friedman, *Fighters Over the Fleet*, 446.
33. Friedman, *Fighters Over the Fleet*, 447; Gordon Swanborough and Peter Bowers, *U.S. Navy Aircraft Since 1911* (New York: Funk & Wagnalls, 1968), 384.

34. Figure 1.1 data is compiled from: Larkins, *U.S. Navy Aircraft 1921–1941* and Friedman, *Fighters Over the Fleet*.
35. U.S. Navy, *Bureau of Aeronautics Annual Report* (Washington, DC: Government Printing Office), 1935–38.

Chapter 2. Expansion, Turf Wars, and Estimates

1. See introduction for more discussion on historiographical shortcomings.
2. Department of the Navy, *Bureau of Aeronautics Manual 1940* (Washington, DC: United States Government Printing Office, 1940), 3.
3. Office of Deputy Chief of Naval Operations (Air), "Aviation Personnel, 1911–1939," in *United States Naval Administration in World War II* (Washington, DC: U.S. Government Printing Office, 1959), 21: 210; DuBose (1893–1967) retired as a full admiral in 1955. Source: https://navy.togetherweserved.com. Accessed July 16, 2018.
4. Headquarters, Naval Air Technical Training Command, *Technicians' War: A Picture Story of U.S. Naval Air Technical Training Command* (Atlanta, GA: Albert Love Enterprises, 1945). This estimate is not based solely on carrier technicians. It included land-based aircraft squadrons which operated much larger, multiengine aircraft that would require more maintenance personnel. The ratio on board aircraft carriers was closer to 10:1, which included nonaircrew aviation maintenance officers. See Friedman, *U.S. Aircraft Carriers*, Appendix E.
5. For a more thorough discussion on the topic of aircraft carrier policy in relation to battleship development during the interwar years, see Charles Melhorn, *Two-Block Fox: The Rise of the Aircraft Carrier, 1911–1929* (Annapolis, MD: Naval Institute Press, 1974).
6. Aircraft complement on board each aircraft carrier would vary throughout the war. The average for an aircraft carriers of *Yorktown* size was between seventy-two and seventy-eight aircraft. As aircraft technology changed and carrier decks increased in size, the number of aircraft on board larger carriers such as the *Essex* would reach ninety to one hundred by 1943. See Friedman, *U.S. Aircraft Carriers*.
7. *Flying and Popular Aviation*, January 1942.
8. Articles and comments within this issue of *Flying and Popular Aviation*, located in USNA's Nimitz Library, were submitted and edited in the fall of 1941 prior to the attack on Pearl Harbor, even though the publication date is January 1942. Articles include "The Power Plant," by Rico Botta; "Radio," by G. B. Hall; "CV–The Carrier," by William Halsey; "The Naval Air Station," by Ben Morelli; "The Naval Aircraft Factory," by E. M. Pace; "Maintenance," by V. H. Schaeffer; and "Naval Operations and Aviation," by Harold M. Stark.
9. V. H. Schaeffer, "Maintenance," *Flying and Popular Aviation*, January 1942, 132.
10. Schaeffer, "Maintenance," 132.
11. "Aviation Maintenance," n.d., Carriers Collection, Box 17, NHHC.
12. Trimble, *Wings for the Navy*, 211.
13. Schaeffer, "Maintenance," 133.
14. E. M. Pace, "The Naval Aircraft Factory," *Flying and Popular Aviation*, January 1942, 208.

15. Bureau of Aeronautics, "Aviation Personnel and Training," in *United States Naval Administration in World War II* (Washington, DC: U.S. Government Printing Office, 1959), 12: 1–2. For clarity, only "Personnel Division" will be used to identify this division, regardless of the time frame being discussed.
16. A "rating" is another term for an enlisted sailor who has qualified as proficient in a specific field of labor or warfare, (i.e., radioman, electrician's mate, or aviation metalsmith).
17. *Bureau of Aeronautics Manual 1940*, 8.
18. *Bureau of Aeronautics Manual 1940*, 7.
19. "Aviation Personnel, 1911–1939," 97.
20. "Aviation Personnel, 1911–1939," 97.
21. The "Two Ocean Navy Act" or "Vinson-Walsh Act" was the largest single procurement bill in U.S. history. It increased the overall size of the Navy by 70 percent, including the requirement for 15,000 naval aircraft. It was enacted into law on July 19, 1940.
22. Frederick J. Horne, "Report of Board Convened to Investigate and Report Upon the Regular and Reserve Aviation Personnel of the Navy and Marine Corps," December 22, 1939.
23. Bureau of Aeronautics, "Aviation Personnel and Training," 99–100.
24. Bureau of Aeronautics, "Aviation Personnel and Training," 99–101.
25. Bureau of Aeronautics, "Aviation Personnel and Training," 102.
26. Bureau of Aeronautics, "Aviation Personnel and Training," 102.
27. Bureau of Aeronautics, "Aviation Personnel and Training," 103.
28. As quoted in Reynolds, *Admiral John H. Towers: The Struggle for Naval Air Supremacy*, 294.
29. Memorandum from Chief, BuAer to Chief, BuNav, Aug. 23, 1940, RG 24, NC 70, Box 610, National Archives and Records Administration, Washington, DC (hereinafter NARA I).
30. Memorandum from Chief, BuAer to Chief, BuNav, Aug. 23, 1940.
31. Bureau of Aeronautics, "Aviation Personnel and Training," 115.
32. Bureau of Aeronautics, "Aviation Personnel and Training," 102.
33. See Memorandum from Towers to Horne, "Personnel in the Naval Aeronautics Organization, Recommendations Concerning," Sept. 27, 1939, RG 72, Box 189, National Archives and Records Administration, College Park (hereinafter NARA II).
34. Second Horne Board report, 19–20, as cited in Bureau of Aeronautics, "Aviation Personnel and Training," 137.
35. "Aviation Personnel Board 1940–1941," para. 50.
36. Bureau of Aeronautics, "Aviation Personnel and Training," 137.
37. "Aviation Personnel Board 1940–1941," para. 246.
38. "Aviation Personnel Board 1940–1941," paras. 261–63.
39. Memorandum from Chief of Naval Operations, to Chief, BuNav, February 12, 1941, as referenced in Bureau of Naval Personnel, "History of Enlisted Personnel Activity," in *United States Naval Administration in World War II* (Washington, DC: U.S. Government Printing Office, 1959), 122.

40. Bureau of Aeronautics, "Aviation Planning," in *United States Naval Administration in World War II* (Washington, DC: U.S. Government Printing Office, 1959) 5: 32–33.
41. W. H. Heiser, *U.S. Naval and Marine Corps Reserve Aviation, Volume I, 1916–1942 Chronology* (McHenry, IL: Dihedral Press, 2006), 134.
42. The Navy had forecast a capability to operate 13,981 carrier-based aircraft by December 31, 1945 according to the current strength of the fleet plus the number of aircraft carriers and aircraft in production per a BuAer briefing given in July 1944. See "The Program for Naval Aviation," July 5, 1944, 5, NAVAIR Collection, Box 120, NHHC.
43. Bureau of Aeronautics, "Aviation Personnel and Training," 104.
44. Bureau of Aeronautics, "Aviation Personnel and Training," 104–105.
45. Bureau of Aeronautics, "Aviation Personnel and Training," 165.
46. Bureau of Aeronautics, "Aviation Personnel and Training," 166.
47. Towers to Nimitz, October 12, 1940, as quoted in Bureau of Aeronautics, "Aviation Personnel and Training," 167.
48. Bureau of Aeronautics, "Aviation Personnel and Training," 168.
49. Bureau of Aeronautics, "Aviation Personnel and Training," 169.
50. Chief, BuNav to All Commandants of Naval Districts, Aug. 20, 1940, as noted in Bureau of Aeronautics, "Aviation Personnel and Training," 170–71.
51. ALNAV 114, November 20, 1940; also noted in Bureau of Aeronautics, "Aviation Personnel and Training," 169.
52. "Bureau of Aeronautics Analysis of Naval Production Airframe Contracts," Aug. 1945, Carriers Collection, Box 13, NHHC.
53. Memorandum for Admiral Towers, May 19, 1942, unsigned, as quoted in Bureau of Aeronautics, "Aviation Personnel and Training," 207.
54. Little else is mentioned about George D. Murray in the administrative histories of the Bureau of Aeronautics. In March 1941, after his tour at BuAer, he was given command of the USS *Enterprise* (CV 6). Murray served as its commanding officer during the Battle of Midway. After Midway he was promoted to rear admiral command and was appointed commander, Carrier Division Three and Task Force 17, which included the *Hornet* until she was sunk. In 1943 he was assigned as chief of the Naval Air Intermediate Training Command in Pensacola. He retired in 1951 as a full admiral. For additional details of his wartime experiences, I recommend William Tuohy, *America's Fighting Admirals: Winning the War at Sea in World War II* (St. Paul, MN: Zenith Press, 2007).
55. See Table 2.1.
56. Bureau of Aeronautics Report, "Summary of Progress," Dec. 1, 1941, 19, RG 72, Stack 470, Row 70, Boxes 1–3, NARA II.
57. This data is found in a memo dated Dec. 7, 1940, from BuNav to BuAer. It reports and is part of enclosure (A) in the Confidential Supplement of the second Horne Board report of 1940. As cited in Bureau of Aeronautics, "Aviation Personnel and Training," 313.
58. The specific number of aviation ratings is listed as 11,213 in *Annual Report of the Chief, BuAer for Fiscal Year 1941*, as cited in Bureau of Aeronautics, "Aviation Personnel and Training," 312–13.

59. "Annual Report of the Secretary of Navy: Fiscal Year 1945," sec. Appendix A.
60. "Annual Report of the Secretary of Navy: Fiscal Year 1945," A-21.
61. Rear Adm. Ben Morelli, "The Naval Air Station," *Flying and Popular Aviation*, Jan. 1942, 194. A careful analysis of the advertisements, articles, and statements by contributing authors (three admirals—Stark, Halsey, and Towers—and others) give no indication that the United States was at war at the time of submission. A hard copy of this periodical can be found at USNA Nimitz Library.

Chapter 3. Establishing the Trade Schools

1. Lt. Cdr. A. W. Wheelock, "Lecture on Duties of Divisions in the Bureau of Aeronautics, Navy Department," January 1942, sec. Training Division, RG 72, Entry 172, Box 1, Stack 470, NARA II.
2. T. B. Haley, "Historical Report of the Technical Training Section through December 1943," Dec. 1943, 2–3, WW II Training, Box 68, Technical Training Reports 1943, NHHC; Bureau of Aeronautics, "Aviation Personnel and Training," 310.
3. The U.S. Army Air Force also had been supplementing the education of its own aircraft technicians with civilian schools at this time. They established the Army Technical Training Command in 1941, prior to Pearl Harbor. By November 1941, the AAF had plans to turn out trained aircraft technicians at a rate of 100,000 per year. Source: Wesley Frank Craven and James Lea Cate, eds., *The Army Air Forces in World War II*, Vol. 1: *Plans and Early Operations, January 1939 to August 1942*, (Chicago, IL: University of Chicago Press, 1955), 111.
4. Haley, 2.
5. Horne, "Aviation Personnel Board 1940–1941."
6. Haley, 3–4.
7. B. W. Patch, "American Naval and Air Bases," CQ Researcher, 1939, http://library.cqpress.com/cqresearcher/document.php?id=cqresrre1939021600; Ben Morelli, "The Naval Air Station," *Flying and Popular Aviation*, January 1942, 151; Naval History and Heritage Command, "Hepburn," https://www.history.navy.mil/research/histories/ship-histories/danfs/h/hepburn.html.
8. "Captain Austin Wadsworth Wheelock, U.S. Navy" (Bureau of Naval Personnel, Jan. 18, 1945), Officer Biography Folder, NHHC.
9. Haley, 2.
10. Haley, 3.
11. House Hearings, Sundry Naval Legislation, 77th Congress, 1st Session, 1941, 2056. As quoted in Bureau of Aeronautics, "Aviation Personnel and Training," 195–96.
12. Haley, 4.
13. Bogan Board Report, September 19, 1941, as referenced in Bureau of Aeronautics, "Aviation Personnel and Training," 274.
14. Bureau of Aeronautics, "Aviation Personnel and Training," 275.
15. Bureau of Aeronautics, "Aviation Personnel and Training," 275.
16. Bureau of Aeronautics, "Aviation Personnel and Training," 276–77.
17. Bureau of Aeronautics, "Aviation Personnel and Training," 277.
18. Bureau of Aeronautics, "Aviation Personnel and Training," 276–77; Haley, 2.

19. Haley, 2.
20. Bureau of Aeronautics, "Aviation Personnel and Training," 333–35.
21. Haley, 4.
22. Haley, 4–5.
23. "What Is the Naval Air Technical Training Command," *Bulletin of Naval Air Technical Training Courses*, 1945, 1, WW II Training, Box 68, NHHC.
24. "What Is the Naval Air Technical Training Command."
25. Junius Cotten, "Letter from J. Cotten to C. P. Mason," August 19, 1940, 1, Aviation Commands, AR/180, Box 230, NHHC, "Prospective" is a term used for an individual who has been selected for a billet, but has not taken the oath of office or executed his or her official orders into such. It is commonly used with commanding officer or executive officer billets, and abbreviated PCO or PXO. Charles P. Mason retired as a vice admiral in 1946.
26. "Letter from J. Cotten to C. P. Mason," 1.
27. "Letter from J. Cotten to C. P. Mason," 2–3.
28. *Florida Times Union*, Oct. 15, 1940, 6. As referenced in "History of Naval Air Technical Training Center Jacksonville, Florida," 9–10.
29. "History of Naval Air Technical Training Center Jacksonville," 22–23.
30. "History of Naval Air Technical Training Center Jacksonville," 23.
31. Haley, 24.
32. Buchanan, 318.
33. "History of Naval Air Technical Training Center Jacksonville," 24.
34. "History of Naval Air Technical Training Center Jacksonville," 25.
35. Memo from BuAer to BuNav regarding AM postgraduate instructors, Aug. 23, 1940.
36. "History of Naval Air Technical Training Center Jacksonville," 26.
37. Bureau of Aeronautics, "Aviation Personnel and Training," 318–19.
38. Daniel J. Brimm and Harry Edward Boggess, *Airplane and Engine Maintenance for the Airplane Mechanic* (New York: Pitman, 1936); Daniel J. Brimm, *Seaplanes Maneuvering, Maintaining, Operating* (New York: Pitman, 1937); Daniel J. Brimm and Harry Edward Boggess, *Aircraft Engine Maintenance* (New York: Pitman, 1939).
39. Bureau of Aeronautics, "Aviation Personnel and Training," 319.
40. Memorandum of observations from Wheelock to Radford, Dec. 1, 1941, also known as the "Wheelock Memo." Referenced in Bureau of Aeronautics, "Aviation Personnel and Training," 1959, 326–46.
41. Bureau of Aeronautics, "Aviation Personnel and Training," 319.
42. The General Classification Test was a general aptitude test that the Army developed in World War I. The Navy adapted it for its own purposes to determine the general aptitude of applicants. The test was revised during the war and minimum score requirements varied. The scores 62 and 70 were based on a previous edition of the test. By 1943, the minimum test scores had been reduced to 52 for these two ratings. It is unclear whether this was due to test revision or a lowering of the minimum standard for trade school applicants. According to the Navy's instruction for GCT interviews, "The object has been to set the minimum scores at a

level that would insure the inclusion of a sufficient number of men to meet the needs of the fleet, and, at the same time, to select those men most likely to meet the school requirements successfully." See "US Navy Interviewer's Classification Guide, NAVPERS 16701," 1943, NHHC, https://www.history.navy.mil/research/library/online-reading-room/title-list-alphabetically/u/us-navy-interviewers-classification-guide.html#mm. Accessed Oct. 4, 2018.
43. "History of Naval Air Technical Training Center Jacksonville," 275, 400.
44. "History of Naval Air Technical Training Center Jacksonville," 29.
45. "US Navy Interviewer's Classification Guide, NAVPERS 16701."
46. "US Navy Interviewer's Classification Guide, NAVPERS 16701."
47. Bureau of Aeronautics, "Analysis of Naval Airframe Production Contracts," Aug. 11, 1945, NAVAIR Collection, Box 69, NHHC.
48. Norman Friedman, *USS* Yorktown *(CV10)*, Ship's Data 7 (Annapolis, MD: Leeward, 1977), 20, 50.
49. A. H. Van Keuren, "Letter from BUSHIP to SECNAV, 'Design of U.S.S. Essex Class,'" Sept. 10, 1940, Carriers Collection, Box 7, NHHC.
50. Bureau of Aeronautics, "Aviation Personnel and Training," 320. In early 1942, the "Trade School" name was dropped in favor of "Service Schools."
51. "History of Naval Air Technical Training Center Jacksonville," 398.
52. Service Schools Memorandums 5–42 and 48–42, Feb. 27, 1942, as referenced in "History of Naval Air Technical Training Center Jacksonville," 56–58.
53. "History of Naval Air Technical Training Center Jacksonville," 405.
54. "History of Naval Air Technical Training Center Jacksonville," 400–401; Bureau of Naval Personnel, "History of Enlisted Personnel Activity," 50.
55. "History of Naval Air Technical Training Center Jacksonville," 407.
56. An in-depth discussion of the CASU is included in chapter 5.
57. Haley, 5; Bureau of Aeronautics, "Aviation Personnel and Training," 320.
58. "Ninth Naval District," Naval History and Heritage Command, https://www.history.navy.mil/research/library/research-guides/lists-of-senior-officers-and-civilian-officials-of-the-us-navy/district-commanders/ninth-naval-district.html. Accessed Oct. 25, 2018.
59. See Table 3.2.
60. Haley, 5.
61. Haley, 8.
62. Haley, 8.
63. See Table 3.3.
64. "The Technical Training Command's Maintenance Program," *Aviation*, July 1942, 236. The twenty-two schools included nonaircraft mechanic subjects such as weather forecasting, photography, parachute rigger, etc.
65. Headquarters, Naval Air Technical Training Command, *Technicians' War: A Picture Story of U.S. Naval Air Technical Training Command*.
66. See Table 3.2.
67. ART rating specialized in maintenance of aircraft radios. AOs were responsible for aviation ordnance including the delivery systems built into the aircraft. Engines and aircraft skin refer to AMM and AM ratings responsibilities.

68. Bureau of Aeronautics, "Aviation Personnel and Training," 323–24.
69. "NATTC Memphis," 1945, 1, Aviation Commands, 1941–52, AR/180, Box 240, NHHC; Haley, 7.
70. Haley, 7; "NATTC Memphis," 2.
71. The figure 37,237 was the maximum student load that BuAer reported to SECNAV in a memo dated Apr. 16, 1942. As referenced in Haley, 7.
72. Data herein contained in a BuAer letter dated Sept. 15, 1942; Haley, 7.
73. Haley, 13.
74. Haley, 13.
75. Haley, 14; Bureau of Aeronautics, "Aviation Personnel and Training," 340–44; pro bono services by companies such as these were not as selfless as they might have appeared. Often manufacturers received such lucrative incentives from the government to expand production and meet wartime demands, that providing factory-run training for the Navy made little impact on the profits of their "cost-plus" contracts. For more or this topic I recommend Eugene E. Wilson's, *Slipstream: The Autobiography of an Air Craftsman* (Palm Beach, FL: Literary Investment Guild), 1967, and *The Grumman Story* by Richard Thruelson (New York: Praeger, 1976).
76. Bureau of Supplies and Accounts, Letter of Sept. 14, 1942. As referenced in Haley, 15.
77. Bureau of Aeronautics, "Aviation Personnel and Training," 343–44.
78. Haley, 14–16; Bureau of Aeronautics, "Aviation Personnel and Training," 353.

Chapter 4. Paradigm Shift

1. Haley, 15.
2. Bureau of Aeronautics, "Aviation Personnel and Training," 353–54.
3. U.S. Congress, House of Naval Affairs Committee, *Sundry Legislation Affecting the Naval Establishment*, 77th Cong., H. Doc. No. 4, 1940 (Washington, DC, 1942), 133.
4. Haley, "Historical Report of the Technical Training Section through December 1943," 18; Bureau of Aeronautics, "Aviation Personnel and Training," 360.
5. Haley, 18–19.
6. Haley, 16. SECNAV letter of September 11, 1942, included two other newly established training commands. The Naval Air Primary Training Command and Naval Air Intermediate Training Command were responsible for pilot flight instruction. All three commands were given the same autonomy to operate independently of the district commandants.
7. "What Is the Naval Air Technical Training Command," VI.
8. For the most informative account of NC-4's crossing and Read's relationship with Towers, see Richard K. Smith, *First Across: The U.S. Navy's Transatlantic Flight of 1919* (Annapolis, MD: Naval Institute Press, 1973) and Clark G. Reynolds, *Admiral John H. Towers: The Struggle for Naval Air Supremacy* (Annapolis, MD: Naval Institute Press, 1991).
9. Haley, 19.

10. Haley, 19. I am indebted to Professor Jon T. Sumida, PhD, for introducing me to the phrase *who pays, how much, and why* in his undergraduate course on the history of early warfare (HIST 224) at University of Maryland, College Park, in 2015.
11. Haley, 20.
12. Haley, 20; "What Is the Naval Air Technical Training Command," VI.
13. Headquarters, Naval Air Technical Training Command, *Technicians' War: A Picture Story of U.S. Naval Air Technical Training Command*, sec. Specialized Training.
14. Headquarters, Naval Air Technical Training Command, *Technicians' War: A Picture Story of U.S. Naval Air Technical Training Command*, sec. Specialized Training; "What Is the Naval Air Technical Training Command," 5–6.
15. *Naval Aviation News*, Dec. 1, 1944, 20.
16. Bureau of Naval Personnel, "Training Activity," in *Administrative History of World War II: Bureau of Personnel* (Department of the Navy, 1959), 287.
17. *Bureau of Aeronautics Manual 1940* (Washington, DC: United States Government Printing Office, 1940), 65.
18. *Bureau of Aeronautics Manual 1940*.
19. Bureau of Naval Personnel, "Training Activity," 287–88.
20. Bureau of Naval Personnel, "Training Activity," 288.
21. Bureau of Naval Personnel, "Training Activity," 290–91.
22. *Aircraft Metal Work* (Washington, DC: Standards and Curriculum Division, Training, Bureau of Naval Personnel, 1945).
23. *Aircraft Propellers* (Washington, DC: Standards and Curriculum Division, Training, Bureau of Naval Personnel, 1945).
24. Bureau of Naval Personnel, "Training Activity," 293.
25. *Naval Aviation News*, June 15, 1945, 27.
26. Bureau of Naval Personnel, "Training Activity," 297–302.
27. Haley, 26.
28. Haley, 26–27.
29. Buchanan, 322–23.
30. *Naval Aviation News*, April 15, 1944, 18–21.
31. Captain Mildred McAffee Horton Oral Transcript, 1969, U.S. Naval Institute, Annapolis, MD. As referenced in Reynolds, *Admiral John H. Towers: The Struggle for Naval Air Supremacy*, 381.
32. *Naval Aviation News*, June 1, 1943, 13. In late 1944, the Navy approved assignment of Waves to a limited number of overseas stations. Locations such as Hawaii, Alaska, and the Panama Canal Zone or Caribbean operating area were authorized. Hawaii took precedence. Selection priority was given to Waves with aviation ratings such as AMM, AM, and control tower operators. Those with the "Specialist X" class rating such as pigeon trainers and time shack operators were also in high demand. *Naval Aviation News*, December 1, 1944, 9.
33. *Naval Aviation News*, June 1, 1943, 13.
34. *Naval Aviation News*, June 1, 1943, 14.
35. *Naval Aviation News*, June 1, 1943, 14.
36. Gladys Marsheck Echols, Veteran's History Project, Oral Histories from Dundalk, Maryland, transcribed Nov. 14, 1988, 7–8.

37. Echols, 8.
38. Echols, 9.
39. Echols, 9.
40. Echols, 11.
41. The petty officer rank is usually modified by first, second, or third class. In U.S. naval terminology, one's rating may be substituted both formally and informally for the title of petty officer, (petty officer second class [PO2] is interchangeable with aviation machinist's mate second class [AMM2]).
42. Echols, 17, 28.
43. Regina T. Akers, "The Waves 75th Birthday," NHHC, last updated May 10, 2019, https://www.history.navy.mil/browse-by-topic/wars-conflicts-and-operations/world-war-ii/1942/manning-the-us-navy/waves_75th.html.
44. In late 1944, the Navy approved assignment of Waves to a limited number of overseas stations. See previous note above.
45. *Naval Aviation News*, June 1, 1943, 15–18.
46. *Naval Aviation News*, September 15, 1943, 18.
47. Lucy Brewer was a young woman who disguised her gendered identity in 1812 in order to serve in the U.S. Marine Corps as a sharpshooter aboard the frigate USS *Constitution*. She served three years on the ship without having her gender revealed. Eventually she was honorably discharged; she is considered by many as the first female Marine, although there is an ongoing debate regarding the legitimacy of her story.
48. *Naval Aviation News*, Jan. 15, 1944, 18.
49. Wilbert Walker, *We Are Men: Memoirs of World War II and the Korean War* (Chicago: Adams Press, 1973), 2–3.
50. Walker, 4.
51. Walker, 16.
52. Walker, 17.
53. Walker, 20.
54. Walker, 21.
55. Walker, 25.
56. Walker, 25.
57. Walker, 26.
58. Walker, 26.
59. Walker, 33.
60. Walker, 33–34.
61. Walker, 36–37.
62. Walker, 38.
63. Walker, 38.
64. Wheelock, "Lecture on Duties of Divisions in the Bureau of Aeronautics, Navy Department."
65. Headquarters, Naval Air Technical Training Command, *Technicians' War: A Picture Story of U.S. Naval Air Technical Training Command*, sec. Naval Air Technical Training Command.

Chapter 5. Specialization of Labor and Timing the Delivery

1. Buchanan, 354.
2. Ship, Commissioning, Aircraft Complement: *Langley* (1920); *Saratoga* (1927), 78; *Lexington* (1927), 78; *Ranger* (1934), 76; *Yorktown* (1937), 90; *Enterprise* (1938), 90; *Wasp* (1940), 100; *Long Island* (1941), 21; *Hornet* (1941), 72. Source: Norman Friedman, *U.S. Aircraft Carriers* (Annapolis, MD: Naval Institute Press, 1983).
3. William Halsey, "CV-The Carrier," *Flying and Popular Aviation*, Jan. 1942, 120.
4. Friedman, *U.S. Aircraft Carriers*, 151–55.
5. Robert Guttman, "Curtiss SB2C Helldiver: The Last Dive Bomber," *Aviation History*, July 2000, 3, https://www.historynet.com/curtiss-sb2c-helldiver-the-last-dive-bomber/. Accessed Jan. 25, 2019.
6. "Aviation Personnel, 1911–1939," 210–11.
7. Bureau of Ships, "U.S.S. *Essex*–Design Of," Sept. 10, 1940, Carriers Collection, Box 7, NHHC.
8. Bureau of Ships.
9. "History of USS *Lexington* (CV-16) from 17 February 1943 through 31 March 1945," June 11, 1945, 47. RG 38 "World War II War Diaries," NARA II, https://www.fold3.com/image/302074535. Accessed Feb. 19, 2019.
10. Wesley Frank Craven and James Lea Cate, eds., *The Army Air Forces in World War II, Plans and Early Operations, January 1939 to August 1942*, Vol. 1 (Chicago: University of Chicago Press, 1955), 747–48.
11. The ratios herein are not exact numbers. Some of the technicians worked in the different aviation shops and some were administrative in nature. But for general comparison, the numbers are based solely on documented personnel. See Friedman, *U.S. Aircraft Carriers*, Appendix E.
12. Blaine Stubblefield, "Carrier Aircraft Maintenance Is Really Tough," *Aviation*, June 1945, 107; Blaine Stubblefield, "It's No Child's Play: Arming and Fueling Carrier Planes," *Aviation*, Aug. 1945, 111. By the end of the war, the division labels had changed slightly, placing Ordnance and Servicing under the direction of V-1, renaming V-3 Operations, and making V-4 the Administration Division.
13. *USS Leyte CV-32 Shakedown Cruise: August–December 1946* (Atlanta: Albert Love, 1946).
14. Details on the varying air department division nomenclature is derived from the "Air Department" section of official Cruise Book of the USS *Lexington* CV-16 from 1943 to 1946. It is an unpublished document found as a bound copy in the Nimitz Library of the U.S. Naval Academy.
15. "Aviation Maintenance," 72.
16. "Aviation Maintenance," 73.
17. *Naval Aviation News*, Jan. 15, 1944, 32.
18. The tradition of painting the name and hometown of the plane captain on naval aircraft is still practiced today.
19. "Aviation Maintenance," 74.
20. *Naval Aviation News*, Nov. 1, 1944, 9.
21. "Aviation Maintenance," 76.

22. Schaeffer, 135.
23. "Aviation Maintenance," 75.
24. Check crew numbers are based on late 1943 to early 1944 data. As numbers of aircraft varied throughout the war, the quantity and division of check crews varied as well. See Table 5.1
25. "Aviation Maintenance," 75.
26. "Aviation Maintenance," 75–76.
27. "Aviation Maintenance," 78.
28. See Table 5.1.
29. "Aviation Maintenance," 78.
30. The overwhelming majority of smaller carriers were of the *Casablanca* class. Fifty were built by the Kaiser Company between November 1942 and July 1944. Other smaller U.S. carriers beyond the *Essex* class included the *Bogue* (10), *Sangamon* (4), *Independence* (9), *Commencement Bay* (4), and *Avenger* (1) classes. See Friedman, *United States Aircraft Carriers* (Annapolis, MD: USNI, 1983).
31. "Aviation Maintenance," 80.
32. "Aviation Maintenance," 80.
33. "Aviation Maintenance," 80–81.
34. "Aviation Maintenance," 80–81.
35. "Aviation Maintenance," 82.
36. Stubblefield, 106.
37. Stubblefield, 108.
38. "Aviation Maintenance," 76.
39. "Saratoga Seeks New Stand," *Naval Aviation News*, Jan. 1, 1944, 28.
40. Stubblefield, 107.
41. Stubblefield, 107.
42. Stubblefield, 107.
43. *Naval Aviation News*, Aug. 15, 1943, 9.
44. Stubblefield, 108.
45. "Aircraft Corrosion: BUAER Develops Preservation Methods for Planes and Parts," *Naval Aviation News*, May 1, 1944, 1–2.
46. "Aviation Maintenance," 77.
47. Stubblefield, 106.
48. Forrest F. Bruner Jr., *Pearl Harbor to Tokyo—36 Months: My Hell in the South Pacific*, n.d., 109.
49. Lloyd M. Gilmore, Personal Diary, entry of August 31, 1944, *America in World War Two: Oral Histories and Personal Accounts*, https://americainworldwartwo.amdigital.co.uk//Documents/Details/2002_025_AM_015. Accessed Oct. 15, 2020.
50. Gilmore Diary, entry of Sept. 10, 1944.
51. Gilmore Diary, entry of Feb. 3, 1944.
52. Bruner, 37.
53. Bruner, 74–75.
54. Bruner, 108.
55. Bruner, 126.

56. Samuel Eliot Morison, *Victory in the Pacific: 1945* (Boston: Little, Brown, 1968), 96–99.
57. Albert Antar Obitutary, https://www.legacy.com/us/obituaries/orlandosentinel/name/albert-antar-obituary?n=albert-antar&pid=163140075. Accessed Oct. 20, 2020.
58. *Naval Aviation News*, Jan. 1, 1944, 4.
59. Franklin Brown, *USS* Lexington (Boston: Burdette, 1965), 29
60. *Naval Aviation News*, June 15, 1945, 28.
61. *Naval Aviation News*, June 15, 1945, 28. Kendall's comments neglect to mention Waves or women technicians at all. This is obviously an oversight on his part.
62. Stern, 116.
63. "CASU Training Manual of the ACORN Assembly and Training Detachment" (Navy Department, February 1945), 1, WWII Aviation Training, Box 64, NHHC; "CASU: Carrier Aircraft Service Unit," *Naval Aviation News*, Sept. 1, 1944, 13.
64. Stern, 116.
65. Robert Olds, *Helldiver Squadron: The Story of Carrier Bombing Squadron 17 with Task Force 58* (New York: Dodd, Mead, 1944).
66. "CASU: Carrier Aircraft Service Unit," 14–15.
67. "CASU: Carrier Aircraft Service Unit," 13.
68. *Naval Aviation News*, Nov. 15, 1944, 29.
69. "CASU: Carrier Aircraft Service Unit," 14–18.
70. "CASU Training Manual of the ACORN Assembly and Training Detachment," 1; "Operational Experience," 36.
71. "Aviation Repair and Overhaul Unit 5," April 17, 1946, 1, RG 38 "World War II War Diaries," NARA II, https://www.fold3.com/image/302084329.
72. As quoted in "Aviation Repair and Overhaul Unit 5," 1.
73. "Aviation Repair and Overhaul Unit 3," April 17, 1946, RG 38 "World War II War Diaries," NARA II, https://www.fold3.com/image/1/302084326.
74. *Two Degrees from the Middle: The History of Aviation Repair and Overhaul Unit Number One in World War II* (St. Paul, MN: Bronson West, 1945). The units were called Major Aircraft Repair Squadrons (MARS), but in late spring 1943 the designation was changed to Aviation Repair and Overhaul Unit (AROU).
75. "History of Aircraft Repair and Overhaul Unit Two," Dec. 1945, 1–2, RG 38 "World War II War Diaries," NARA II, https://www.fold3.com/image/302002819. Accessed Jan. 11, 2019.
76. "Aviation Repair and Overhaul Unit 5," sec. Appendix E.
77. "History of Aircraft Repair and Overhaul Unit Two," 2.
78. "History of Aircraft Repair and Overhaul Unit Two," 1.
79. *Two Degrees from the Middle*.
80. *Two Degrees from the Middle*, section on Engine Overhaul Division.
81. Commander, Air Force Pacific Fleet, "Analysis of Pacific Air Operations, June 1944," July 27, 1944, 60, RG 38 "World War II War Diaries," NARA II, https://www.fold3.com/image/1/280033241. Accessed May 13, 2019.
82. *Two Degrees from the Middle*, section on Aircraft Pool Division.
83. See Table 3.1.

84. In February 1943, Cdr. Austin Wheelock left BuAer and assumed command of the seaplane tender USS *Matagorda* (AVP-22) and would serve a follow-on tour on Towers' staff at commander, Naval Air Forces, Pacific Fleet. See "Captain Austin Wadsworth Wheelock, U.S. Navy," BuPers, 1945.
85. Five hundred hours was the typical allowance before a major overhaul was required, but could vary with aircraft model. See *Bureau of Aeronautics Manuals, 1940–45*.
86. "Aircraft Action Report, Fighter Squadron Thirteen," September 25, 1944, RG 38 "World War II War Diaries," NARA II, https://www.fold3.com/image/1/295408183.
87. "Operational Experience," 51.
88. For a more complete account of the operational and doctrinal history of the Fast Carrier Task Force, see Clark Reynolds, *The Fast Carriers: Forging of an Air Navy* (Annapolis, MD: Naval Institute Press, 1968).
89. "Operational Experience," 51. These numbers do not reflect noncombat training, maintenance, or logistics flights for either period
90. See Table 5.3.
91. *Naval Aviation News*, July 15, 1945, 15.
92. *Naval Aviation News*, July 15, 1945, 16–19

Chapter 6. Supplying a Throwaway Culture

1. "Operational Experience," 9.
2. By 1944, the concept of a fast carrier task force, primarily developed by Vice Adm. Marc "Pete" Mitscher, replaced the traditional, smaller task forces designed around one or two carriers plus a small complement of escort ships for protection. Admiral Nimitz, commander of the U.S. Pacific Fleet, divided his fleet into the two regional fleets: the U.S. 3rd Fleet operating as the South Pacific Force under the command of Adm. William "Bull" Halsey, and 5th Fleet under Adm. Raymond Spruance. When deployed, the fast carrier task force operating under Halsey's 3rd Fleet was identified as TF-38, and when operating under Spruance's 5th Fleet, TF-58. Each TF was under the command of a three-star admiral, such as Vice Admiral Mitscher or John McCain Sr. These task forces consisted of smaller task groups (TG) designated separately, each operating under it's own flag officer. For example TF-38 consisted of TG 38.1, TG 38.2, TG 38.3, and TG 38.4. Thus the makeup of the fast carrier task forces consisted of multiple large fleet carriers and escort carriers, plus dozens of support and escort ships. For a definitive discussion of this subject, see Clark G. Reynolds, *The Fast Carriers: Forging an Air Navy*.
3. "Operational Experience," 10–11.
4. Worrall Reed Carter, *Beans, Bullets, and Black Oil: The Story of Fleet Logistics Afloat in the Pacific During World War II* (Washington, DC: Government Printing Office, 1953), 31.
5. "Operational Experience," 11
6. Majuro was captured from the Japanese during the battle of Kwajalein by the USMC V Amphibious Corps Reconnaissance Company in January 1944.
7. Carter, 145–46.

8. Carter, 145–46.
9. Carter, 145–46; Samuel Eliot Morison, *History of United States Naval Operations in World War II:* Leyte, *June 1944–January 1945* (Boston: Little, Brown, 1966), 12: 92.
10. Morison, Leyte, 93–95.
11. Carter, 140. For a more in-depth study on underway replenishment in general, I recommend a deeper reading of Carter's *Beans, Bullets, and Black Oil* and Thomas Wildenberg, *Gray Steel and Black Oil: Fast Tankers and Replenishment at Sea in the U.S. Navy, 1912–1992.*
12. Carter, 146.
13. Buchanan, 330–31.
14. Buchanan, 334.
15. Buchanan, 334–35.
16. As the war in the Pacific expanded, the Navy recognized the need for another ASD closer to the front. Pearl Harbor gained its own ASD by 1944 and managed the intake and exhaust of aircraft and parts supplies in the Pacific in coordination with Philadelphia.
17. Buchanan, 336.
18. *Naval Aviation News*, May 1, 1944, 34.
19. Buchanan, 336.
20. *Naval Aviation News*, May 1, 1944, 34.
21. *Naval Aviation News*, May 1, 1944, 35.
22. *Naval Aviation News*, Jan. 1, 1944, 6.
23. *Naval Aviation News*, Mar. 15, 1945, 19.
24. *Naval Aviation News*, Mar. 15, 1945, 19.
25. *Naval Aviation News*, June 15, 1944, 21.
26. Ralph Vincent Wilhelm, "Administration of the Beneficial Suggestion Program for Civilian Personnel Employed by the United States Navy," MA thesis (Northwestern University, 1950), 2–4.
27. *Naval Aviation News*, Mar. 15, 1945, 29.
28. *Naval Aviation News*, May 1, 1945, 8.
29. *Naval Aviation News*, Feb. 1, 1945, 46.
30. *Naval Aviation News*, Sept. 15, 1944, 32.
31. *Naval Aviation News*, Sept. 15, 1944, 40.
32. *Naval Aviation News*, Mar. 1, 1945, 36.
33. *Naval Aviation News*, June 15, 1944, 16.
34. See Table 6.1.
35. "Annual Report of the Secretary of Navy: Fiscal Year 1945," 21–22.
36. Haley, "Historical Report of the Technical Training Section through December 1943," 19. See chapter 4 for more details and references to technical schools and the establishment of NATTC.
37. In 1941 $79 million equated to $1.3 billion in 2019 dollars. Price quoted is for airframes only. Calculation based on average inflation rate of 3.71 percent between 1941 and 2019. Source: U.S. Bureau of Labor Statistics. The F4F Wildcat was built by Grumman until 1943. Beginning in 1942, General Motors began a Wildcat

production line based on Grumman's design, but redesignated the airplanes as FM-1 and FM-2 Wildcats. Wildcat manufacturing ended in 1945.
38. Equated to $445,000–$907,000 in 2019 dollars. See "Bureau of Aeronautics Analysis of Naval Production Airframe Contracts."
39. Equated to $633,000–$1,078,000 in 2019 dollars. Prices are for airframe only, spare parts, engines, etc., are not included.
40. "Bureau of Aeronautics Analysis of Naval Production Airframe Contracts."
41. Percentage of spares varied for different versions of each fighter from 15 to 30 on F4F and 9 to 22 on F6F. Source: "Bureau of Aeronautics Analysis of Naval Production Airframe Contracts."
42. "Bureau of Aeronautics Average Unit Contract Prices—Navy Airplanes." See Table 6.2.
43. William Pratt, "Airplane Carriers," Correspondence from President, Naval War College to CNO, April 11, 1927, Carriers Collection, Box 1, NHHC.
44. "Bureau of Aeronautics Analysis of Naval Production Airframe Contracts."
45. Wheelock, "Lecture on Duties of Divisions in the Bureau of Aeronautics, Navy Department," 6.
46. "US Navy Interviewer's Classification Guide, NAVPERS 16701."
47. "US Navy Interviewer's Classification Guide, NAVPERS 16701."
48. "Annual Report of the Secretary of Navy: Fiscal Year 1945," 53.
49. "Bureau of Aeronautics Analysis of Naval Production Airframe Contracts," 1.
50. Stubblefield, "Carrier Aircraft Maintenance," 106.
51. "Harry Ervin Yarnell," Naval History and Heritage Command, accessed April 9, 2019, https://www.history.navy.mil/research/library/research-guides/modern-biographical-files-ndl/modern-bios-y/yarnell-harry-ervin.html.
52. Henry E. Yarnell, "Admiral H. E. Yarnell, USN (Ret.) to the Secretary of the Navy," Memorandum, November 6, 1943, 1, RG 72, Entry 172, Box 1, Stack 470, NARA II.
53. Yarnell, 5–6.
54. "Aviation Repair and Overhaul Unit 5," 1. See chapter 5 for full quote.
55. Yarnell, 18.
56. "Annual Report of the Secretary of Navy: Fiscal Year 1945," 21.
57. Friedman, *Fighters Over the Fleet*, 447.
58. *Naval Aviation News*, Dec. 1, 1944, 9.
59. Bureau of Aeronautics, "Analysis of Naval Airframe Production Contracts," Aug. 11, 1945, 1, NAVAIR Collection, Box 69, NHHC.
60. Using 102 aircraft per CV, and 30 per CVL and CVE, I referenced Table 6.1 and used the following calculation: $(102 \times 20) + (78 \times 30) = 4,380$.
61. "Airplane Carriers," Correspondence from Chief of the Bureau of Aeronautics to the General Board, March 01, 1926, 4, Carriers Collection, Box 1, NHHC, 4.
62. "The Program for Naval Aviation."
63. "Operational Experience," 73.
64. "The Program for Naval Aviation." It is unclear how many months BuAer considered a task force to be actively engaged in combat according to the actual brief, but by 1944 the average carrier task force deployment was six months. Considering two to three weeks transit time on either side, the numbers average out to be

nearly sixteen per month when "on station" in a combat zone. War is never an exact science, and BuAer most likely did its best to take all of these factors into consideration.

65. "Taxes for Navy Personnel," *BUAER News*, Sept. 1, 1943, 23, https://www.history.navy.mil/content/dam/nhhc/research/histories/naval-aviation/Naval%20Aviation%20News/1940/pdf/1sep43.pdf. Accessed April 11, 2019. This equated to approximately $1,683 in 2019.
66. $115.20 month/31 days = $3.72 per day; $3.72/12 hours = $0.31 per hour.
67. "Bureau of Aeronautics Average Unit Contract Prices—Navy Airplanes."
68. Bureau of Ships, "U.S.S. *Essex*—Design Of."
69. "Operational Experience," 12.
70. Bureau of Aeronautics, "Analysis of Naval Airframe Production Contracts."
71. "Annual Report of the Secretary of Navy: Fiscal Year 1945," A-48.
72. "Annual Report of the Secretary of Navy: Fiscal Year 1945," 6–7.
73. James H. Belote and William M. Belote, *Titans of the Seas: The Development and Operations of Japanese and American Carrier Task Forces During World War II* (New York: Harper & Row, 1975), 43–46.
74. Belote, *Titans of the Seas*, 47. Accounts of this event can be found in *Task Force 8 After Action Reports* and USS Enterprise *War Diary* for the period Dec. 7, 1941–Feb. 5, 1942.
75. Buchanan, 354–55.
76. "Chronology of Naval Aviation (Draft Copy)," Aug. 18, 1960, NAVAIR Collection, Box 129, NHHC.
77. Buchanan, 355.
78. *Naval Aviation News*, Feb. 1, 1945, 19.
79. Buchanan, 354–55.
80. "Chronology of Naval Aviation (Draft Copy)," Aug. 18, 1960, NAVAIR Collection, Box 129, NHHC.
81. Buchanan, 355.
82. *Naval Aviation News*, Feb. 1, 1945, 21.
83. *Naval Aviation News*, Feb. 1, 1945, 21.
84. *Naval Aviation News*, Feb. 1, 1945, 20. https://www.history.navy.mil/content/dam/nhhc/research/histories/naval-aviation/Naval%20Aviation%20News/1940/pdf/1feb45.pdf. Accessed July 22, 2021.
85. *Naval Aviation News*, February 15, 1945, 33.
86. *Naval Aviation News*, Feb. 1, 1945, 21.
87. *Naval Aviation News*, Feb. 1, 1945, 21.
88. *Naval Aviation News*, Feb. 1, 1945, 23.
89. *Naval Aviation News*, Feb. 1, 1945, 24.
90. *Naval Aviation News*, Feb. 1, 1945, 26.
91. *Naval Aviation News*, Feb. 1, 1945, 18–27.
92. Friedman, *U.S. Aircraft Carriers*, 87.
93. Friedman, *U.S. Aircraft Carriers*, 111.
94. Bureau of Ships, "U.S.S. *Essex*—Design Of."
95. David A. Anderton, *Hellcat* (New York: Crown, 1981), 16.

96. "Bureau of Aeronautics: Summary of Objectives as of 10–31–42," Oct. 31, 1942, RG 72, Entry 67, Stack 470, Row 63, Box 189, NARA II.
97. Friedman, *USS* Yorktown *(CV10)*, 20.
98. Total operational accidents: 3,937, all others: 2,392. Data extracted from Table 6.6.
99. Combat missions is a loosely defined term. For reporting purposes, Navy aircraft could sortie in support of a combat mission without seeing any actual combat, i.e., no enemy forces are located or engaged. Any flight launched with the possibility of encountering enemy forces (whether on land, sea, or air) would be considered a combat mission, whether or not contact was made. Flights where the intended purpose was for training, proficiency, logistical support, or post-maintenance check flights constituted noncombat sorties and would be notated as such in aircraft and pilot logbooks. During World War II, naval aviators first began notating flight time in support of combat in their logbooks with green ink. As a result, combat missions are routinely referred to as "green time" in aviator jargon.
100. "Operational Experience," 74. Data includes both fighter and attack model aircraft (VF, VT/VB).
101. "Operational Experience," 74.
102. Commander, Carrier Division Twenty-Two, "Report of Capture of Okinawa Gunto, Phases I and II, 27 March to 19 June 1945," July 20, 1945, RG 38, "World War II War Diaries," NARA II, https://www.fold3.com/image/1/296526823.
103. Commander, Air Force Pacific Fleet, "Analysis of Air Operations: Fast Carrier Operations in the China Sea, 10–16 January 1945," April 2, 1945, 4, 12, RG 38, "World War II War Diaries," NARA II, https://www.fold3.com/image/1/295415402.
104. In comparison, the U.S. Army Air Corps reported much lower rates of available aircraft during the War. The 43rd Bombardment Group reported that no more than 50 percent of aircraft assigned were available for missions in the southern Pacific theater in 1942. Some of their shortcomings were due to "shortages of spare parts, trained mechanics, and service units." See Wesley Frank Craven and James Lea Cate, eds., *The Army Air Forces in World War II: The Pacific: Guadalcanal to Saipan, August 1942 to July 1944* (Chicago: University of Chicago Press, 1955), 4: 9.
105. "The Program for Naval Aviation."
106. "Bob Hope's Tribute to Aircrewman," *Bluejacket* 3, no. 11 (Feb. 8, 1945), edition: Aviation Commands 1941-1952, NATTC Memphis, Box 240, NHHC.

Conclusion

1. Headquarters, Naval Air Technical Training Command, *Technicians' War: A Picture Story of U.S. Naval Air Technical Training Command*.
2. For additional details on the current naval aviation maintenance program, see COMNAVAIRFORINST 4790.2 series publication, "The Naval Aviation Maintenance Program (NAMP)."
3. "The Naval Aviation Maintenance Program (NAMP)."

4. For a more thorough discussion on the nature of Soviet military preparedness at the outset of World War II, see David M. Glantz, *Stumbling Colossus: The Red Army on the Eve of World War* (Lawrence, KS: University of Kansas Press, 1998).
5. While the war in Afghanistan entailed two decades of conflict, I do not consider it a protracted war in the same sense as World War II, thanks to its irregular, insurgent nature. World War II in the Pacific was fought between formal nation-states with large, well-organized conventional forces. Due to its brevity, Operation Desert Storm offers a more recent example of a large-scale conflict that required little in the way of extended capital and skilled labor over time—very different than what the United States experienced in World War II.

Bibliography

Archival Sources

America in World War Two: Oral Histories and Personal Accounts, https://www.americainworldwartwo.amdigital.co.uk/.

Aviation Commands Collection, Naval History and Heritage Command (NHHC), Washington, DC.

Carriers Collection, NHHC, Washington, DC.

Naval Air Systems Command (NAVAIR) Collection, NHHC, Washington, DC.

Officer Biography Records Collection, NHHC, Washington, DC.

Records of the Bureau of Aeronautics, RG 72, National Archives II, College Park, Maryland.

Records of the Bureau of Personnel, RG 24, National Archives I, Washington, DC.

Records of the Bureau of Personnel, RG 24, National Archives II, College Park, Maryland.

Records of the Office of the Chief of Naval Operations, "World War II War Diaries," RG 38, National Archives, at https://www.fold3.com/title/750/wwii-war-diaries.

World War II Training Collection, NHHC, Washington, DC.

Veteran's History Project, Department of the Navy Library, Washington Navy Yard, Washington, DC.

Government Publications

Aircraft Metal Work. Washington, DC: Standards and Curriculum Division, Training, Bureau of Naval Personnel, 1945.

Aircraft Propellers. Washington, DC: Standards and Curriculum Division, Training, Bureau of Naval Personnel, 1945.

"Annual Report of the Secretary of Navy: Fiscal Year 1945." Department of the Navy, 1946.

Bruner, Forrest F. Jr. "Pearl Harbor to Tokyo—36 Months: My Hell in the South Pacific." Washington, DC: n.p. [Department of the Navy Library], n.d.

Bureau of Aeronautics. "BUAER Annual Report 1930." U.S. Navy, 1930.

———. *Bureau of Aeronautics Manual 1940*. Washington, DC: U.S. Government Printing Office, 1940.

———. *United States Naval Administration in World War II*. Washington, DC: U.S. Government Printing Office, 1959.

Bureau of Naval Personnel. *Navy Wings*. Washington, DC: U.S. Government Printing Office, 1955.

———. *United States Naval Administration in World War II*. Washington, DC: U.S. Government Printing Office, 1959.

Cruise Book, USS Lexington (CV-16), 1943–46. Annapolis, MD: U.S. Naval Academy Library, January 1946.

Department of the Navy. *Bureau of Aeronautics Manual 1940*. Washington, DC: U.S. Government Printing Office, 1940.

"Extracts from the Annual Report of the Bureau of Aeronautics as Submitted by Rear Admiral A. B. Cook, U.S. Navy, to the Secretary of the Navy, for Fiscal Year 1937," Nov. 12, 1937.

"Extracts from the Annual Report of the Bureau of Aeronautics as Submitted by Rear Admiral Ernest J. King, U.S. Navy, to the Secretary of the Navy, for Fiscal Year 1934," Dec. 9, 1934.

Headquarters, Naval Air Technical Training Command. *Technicians' War: A Picture Story of U.S. Naval Air Technical Training Command*. Atlanta: Albert Love, 1945.

Horne, Frederick J. "Report of Board Convened to Investigate and Report Upon the Regular and Reserve Aviation Personnel of the Navy and Marine Corps," Dec. 22, 1939.

Naval History and Heritage Command. "Harry Ervin Yarnell." https://www.history.navy.mil/research/library/research-guides/modern-biographical-files-ndl/modern-bios-y/yarnell-harry-ervin.html. Accessed Apr. 9, 2019.

———. "Hepburn." https://www.history.navy.mil/research/histories/ship-histories/danfs/h/hepburn.html. Accessed June 23, 2022.

———. "Ninth Naval District." https://www.history.navy.mil/research/library/research-guides/lists-of-senior-officers-and-civilian-officials-of-the-us-navy/district-commanders/ninth-naval-district.html. Accessed May 10, 2019.

Two Degrees from the Middle: The History of Aviation Repair and Overhaul Unit Number One in World War II. St. Paul, MN: Bronson West, 1945.

"US Navy Interviewer's Classification Guide, NAVPERS 16701," 1943, NHHC. https://www.history.navy.mil/research/library/online-reading-room/title-list-alphabetically/u/us-navy-interviewers-classification-guide.html#mm.

U.S. Congress, House. 1940. *Sundry Legislation Affecting the Naval Establishment*, 77th Congress. H. Doc. 4.

USS Leyte CV-32 Shakedown Cruise: August–December 1946. Atlanta: Albert Love, 1946.

Periodicals and Online Sources

"Aircraft Corrosion: BUAER Develops Preservation Methods for Planes and Parts." *Naval Aviation News*, May 1, 1944, 1–2.

Blakely, Louis. "History of the Football Helmet." Past Time Sports. http://www.pasttimesports.biz/history.html. Accessed Apr. 17, 2019.

"CASU: Carrier Aircraft Service Unit." *Naval Aviation News*, Sept. 1, 1944, 12–21.

Guttman, Robert. "Curtiss SB2C Helldiver: The Last Dive Bomber." *Aviation History*, July 2000. https://www.historynet.com/curtiss-sb2c-helldiver-the-last-dive-bomber/.

Halsey, William. "CV—The Carrier." *Flying and Popular Aviation*, Jan. 1942.

McCarthy, Charles. "Naval Aircraft Design in the Mid-1930s." *Technology and Culture* 4, no. 2 (Spring 1963): 165–74.

Morelli, Ben. "The Naval Air Station." *Flying and Popular Aviation*, Jan. 1942.

Pace, E. M. "The Naval Aircraft Factory." *Flying and Popular Aviation*, Jan. 1942.
Patch, B. W. "American Naval and Air Bases." CQ Researcher, 1939. http://library.cqpress.com/cqresearcher/document.php?id=cqresrre1939021600.
"Saratoga Seeks New Stand." *Naval Aviation News*, Jan. 1, 1944.
Schaeffer, V. H. "Maintenance." *Flying and Popular Aviation*, Jan. 1942.
Stubblefield, Blaine. "Carrier Aircraft Maintenance Is Really Tough." *Aviation*, June 1945.
———. "It's No Child's Play: Arming and Fueling Carrier Planes." *Aviation*, Aug. 1945.
"Taxes for Navy Personnel." *BUAER News*, Sept. 1, 1943.
"The Technical Training Command's Maintenance Program." *Aviation*, July 1942.
"Training Technicians." *BUAER News*, Sept. 1, 1943. https://www.history.navy.mil/content/dam/nhhc/research/histories/naval-aviation/Naval%20Aviation%20News/1940/pdf/1sep43.pdf.

Secondary Sources

Anderton, David A. *Hellcat*. New York: Crown, 1981.
Belote, James H., and William M. Belote. *Titans of the Seas: The Development and Operations of Japanese and American Carrier Task Forces During World War II*. New York: Harper & Row, 1975.
Brimm, Daniel J. *Seaplanes Maneuvering, Maintaining, Operating*. New York: Pitman, 1937.
Brimm, Daniel J., and Harry Edward Boggess. *Aircraft Engine Maintenance*. New York: Pitman, 1939.
———. *Airplane and Engine Maintenance for the Airplane Mechanic*. New York: Pitman, 1936.
Brown, Franklin. USS *Lexington*. Boston: Burdette, 1965.
Buchanan, A. R., ed. *The Navy's Air War*. New York: Harper, 1947.
Carter, Worrall, R. *Beans, Bullets, and Black Oil: The Story of Fleet Logistics Afloat in the Pacific During World War II*. Washington, DC: Government Printing Office, 1953.
Craven, Wesley Frank, and James Lea Cate, eds. *The Army Air Forces in World War II: Plans and Early Operations, January 1939 to August 1942*. Vol. 1. Chicago: University of Chicago Press, 1955.
———, eds. *The Army Air Forces in World War II: The Pacific: Guadalcanal to Saipan, August 1942 to July 1944*. Vol. 4. Chicago: University of Chicago Press, 1955.
Friedman, Norman. *Carrier Air Power*. New York: Rutledge, 1981.
———. *Fighters over the Fleet*. Annapolis, MD: Naval Institute Press, 2016.
———. *U.S. Aircraft Carriers*. Annapolis, MD: United States Naval Institute, 1983.
———. USS *Yorktown (CV-10)*. Ship's Data 7. Annapolis, MD: Leeward Publications, 1977.
Friedman, Norman, Thomas C. Hone, and Mark D. Mandeles. *American and British Aircraft Carrier Development 1919–1941*. Annapolis, MD: Naval Institute Press, 1999.
Glantz, David M. *Stumbling Colossus: The Red Army on the Eve of World War*. Lawrence, KS: University of Kansas Press., 1998.
Goodspeed, M. Hill, and Rick Burgess, eds. *U.S. Naval Aviation*. Pensacola, FL: Naval Aviation Museum Foundation, 2001.

Heiser, W. H. *U.S. Naval and Marine Corps Reserve Aviation, Volume I, 1916–1942 Chronology*. McHenry, IL: Dihedral Press, 2006.

Keegan, John. *The Face of Battle*. London: Penguin Books, 1978.

Larkins, William. *U.S. Navy Aircraft 1921–1941*. Concord, CA: Aviation History Publications, 1961.

Melhorn, Charles. *Two-Block Fox: The Rise of the Aircraft Carrier, 1911–1929*. Annapolis, MD: Naval Institute Press, 1974.

Mingos, Howard, ed. *The Aircraft Year Book for 1937*. New York: Aeronautical Chamber of Commerce of America, 1937.

Morison, Samuel Eliot. *History of United States Naval Operations in World War II*. Vol. I. Boston: Little, Brown, 1960.

Olds, Robert. *Helldiver Squadron: The Story of Carrier Bombing Squadron 17 with Task Force 58*. New York: Dodd, Mead, 1944.

Polmar, Norman. *Aircraft Carriers: A History of Carrier Aviation and Its Influence on World Events*. Dulles, VA: Potomac Books, 2006.

Reynolds, Clark G. *Admiral John H. Towers: The Struggle for Naval Air Supremacy*. Annapolis, MD: Naval Institute Press, 1991.

———. *The Fast Carriers: The Forging of an Air Navy*. Annapolis, MD: Naval Institute Press, 1968.

Smith, Douglas V., ed. *One Hundred Years of Airpower*. Annapolis, MD: Naval Institute Press, 2010.

Stern, Robert C. *The* Lexington *Class Carriers*. Annapolis, MD: Naval Institute Press, 1993.

Sumida, Jon T., and David A. Rosenberg. "Machines, Men, Manufacturing, Management, and Money: The Study of Navies as Complex Organizations and the Transformation of Twentieth Century Naval History." In *Doing Naval History: Essays Toward Improvement*, edited by John B. Hattendorf. Newport, RI: Naval War College Press, 1995.

Swanborough, Gordon, and Peter Bowers. *U.S. Navy Aircraft Since 1911*. New York: Funk & Wagnalls, 1968.

Trimble, William. *Admiral William A. Moffett: Architect of Naval Aviation*. Washington, DC: Smithsonian Institution Press, 1994.

Trimble, William F. *Wings for the Navy: A History of the Naval Aircraft Factory 1917–1956*. Annapolis, MD: Naval Institute Press, 1990.

Turnbull, Archibald D., and Clifford L. Lord. *History of United States Naval Aviation*. 1972 Reprint by Arno Press Inc. New Haven, CT: Yale University Press, 1949.

Walker, Wilbert. *We Are Men: Memoirs of World War II and the Korean War*. Chicago: Adams Press, 1973.

Wildenberg, Thomas. *Gray Steel and Black Oil: Fast Tankers and Replenishment at Sea in the U.S. Navy, 1912–1992*. Annapolis, MD: Naval Institute Press, 1996.

Wilhelm, Ralph Vincent. "Administration of the Beneficial Suggestion Program for Civilian Personnel Employed by the United States Navy." Master's thesis, Northwestern University, 1950.

Index

NOTE: page numbers with italicized *f* or *t* indicate figures or tables respectively.

A&R (assembly and repair) facilities: amphibious landing ships as, 148; apprentices, 48; *ASO Catalog* and, 159; BuAer on training AMMs by, 50; cost accounting system for, 23; Echols as AMM in, 98–99; as informal training venues, 19; Jacksonville AMM graduates and, 66; labor shortage (1941) in, 38; Navy's aircraft overhaul program and, 31
Accessories Division, AROU Assembly and Repair Department, 143
ACORN units, 139, 149
Admiralty Islands, AROU in, 142
AEMs (aviation electronics mates), 94*t*, 124, 137
aerographer's mates, 94*t*, 97, 117
Aerographers' School, 78*t*, 84
Afghanistan, 235n5
air compressors, on ARVs, 150
air department, of ships: aircraft maintenance division and, 208; responsibilities, 114–5, 116, 117–23; on smaller escort and light carriers, 123–5; subdepartments, 117, 227nn11, 14; tricing procedure in hangars and, 22
air groups. *See* Carrier Air Groups
aircraft, land-based, CASU maintenance of, 141
aircraft, naval: combat, service life factors, 191, 194; design modifications for carriers, 115; early procurement program, 18–19; FDR on increased numbers of, 10, 32, 40, 44, 48–49, 183; as flyable duds, 154; increased size of, carriers and, 23; interwar role of, 3; low inventory before 1939 of, 25; Monthly Reporting of Operating Aircraft on, 192–3; name and hometown painted on, 119, 227n18; new or repaired, escort carriers' delivery of, 153; newly delivered to the Pacific theater, 144; outbreak of World War II and, 22; pools sitting on Pacific land bases, 153; ratio of men to, 29, 116, 218n4; representative, for technician training, 58; spare parts supply chain and, 157; standardized carrier inventory for, 29, 218n6; technical advances in, 23–24. *See also* aircraft carriers; carrier aircraft; flying hours
aircraft carriers: aircraft complement on, 29, 197, 218n6; aviation personnel over time vs., 171*f*; changing views on role of, 14; daily maintenance operations on, 125; increased inventory of, 168–9; maintenance, matériel expenditure factors and, 172; maintenance shops aboard, 122; production, trade school students and, 61, 63; projecting personnel requirements for, 28–29; Royal Navy's compared with U.S. Navy's, 15; ship's company duties on, 116–7; supporting role during interwar period for, 3; underway replenishment of, 155–6; before World War II, 1; World War II flight hours from, 147, 192, 209, 230n89; World War II increase in, 114. *See also* air department, of ships; aircraft, naval; Carrier Air Groups; carrier aircraft; escort carriers; fleet carriers; light carriers
Aircraft Engine Maintenance (Brimm), 58
aircraft instruments repair technicians, 37. *See also* instruments
aircraft machinist mates. *See* AMMs
aircraft maintenance: abandoning broken planes vs., 174–6; as afterthought until two-ocean naval war, 207; *ASO Catalog* and, 159; carrier air departments and, 117; carrier aviation and, 1, 2, 112–3, 114–5; carrier warfare and,

241

183; combat operations and, 198–9; enlisted schools for, 78t; on the flight deck, 16–17; further study potential on, 212–3; imbalance of logistical support capacity for, 49; matériel expenditure factors and, 172; *Naval Aviation News* articles on, 162; naval leadership concerns on, 144; negligence, mishaps or damage and, 127; overnight performance of, 128–9; preventive, on carriers, 30; pre-World War II, 30; Radford Board on, 190; safe positioning for, 165; shade-tree, 195; specialized labor force for, 11–12, 211; status at end of interwar period, 9–10; studies of, 7–8, 215n11; supplies and parts specific to, 158; Wrens and, 103–4; Yarnell's naval aviation survey and, 177. *See also* A&R (assembly and repair) facilities; AROUs; CASUs; specialists

aircraft manufacturing industry: abandoning broken planes and, 174–5; *ASO Catalog* of parts and, 159; aviation maintenance and increased production by, 209; Class C2 schools and, 81; increased production, trade school students and, 61; increased production of aircraft and parts by, 156; mass production and technology used by, 56; numbering and nomenclature issues and, 158–9; production capability waning, 189–90; replacement engines contracted by, 176; spare parts supply chain and, 157; training arrangements with, 72. *See also* factory schools; manufacturers' plants

Aircraft Metal Work (1945 edition), 89
aircraft painters (PTRVs), 37, 93t. *See also* painter V
Aircraft Pool Division, AROU Assembly and Repair Department, 143, 144
Aircraft Propellers textbook, 89
aircraft torpedomen (TMVs), 93t, 94t
aircraft-engine overhaul experts, 37. *See also* AROUs; CASUs; overhauls, aircraft
aircrew gunners, 93, 95, 123
airframes: aviation mechanics' knowledge of, 30; F4F vs. F6F average unit aircraft prices, 173t; Hellcat improvements, 180; increased deliveries of, 168–9; Joint Aircraft Committee and, 156; maintenance, matériel expenditure factors and, 172, 232nn32–33; repair and maintenance, ARVs and, 149–50
Airplane and Engine Maintenance for the Airplane Mechanic (Brimm), 58
airship riggers, 94t
Akron, 20
Alameda Naval Air Station, 64t, 67, 69t, 70, 160
alcohol poisoning, 132–3
Allied unit, maintenance of, 141
aluminum alloys, 18
American Bridge Company, 148
AMMCs (aviation carburetor mechanics), 93t
AMMFs (aviation flight engineers), 93t
AMMHs (aviation hydraulic mechanics), 93t
AMMIs (aviation instrument mechanics), 93t
AMMPs (aviation propeller mechanics), 93t
AMMs (aviation machinist's mates): additional schools for, 66; check crews and, 121–2; Echols on training as, 97–98; Ford's curriculum in Dearborn for, 67; at Jacksonville trade school, 55, 65–66; length of school for, 69t; Marine Corps Women's Reserves as, 102–3, 104, 210; Memphis and Norman NTCs and, 70; minimum required GCT scores for, 59–60, 222–3n42; minimum score for entry into, 176; Nimitz on activating from Reserve of, 40; postwar jobs for, 137; responsibilities, 69, 223n67; on smaller escort and light carriers, 124; specialist ratings, 94t; technological advances in aircraft and, 92; training, 48, 53–54, 65; Walker in first class of Black sailors as, 106–7; WAVES as, 96–97; workload of, 68. *See also* maintainers
ammunition ships, service squadrons and, 152
amphibious landing ships (LSTs), 148
amphibious operations, 148

Index

AMs (aviation metalsmiths): at Jacksonville trade school, 55; length of school for, 69t; new texts published for, 88; Nimitz on activating from Reserve of, 40; postwar jobs for, 137; responsibilities, 69, 223n67; on smaller escort and light carriers, 124; specialist ratings, 94t; training, 48, 53–54; Walker's training and service as, 106, 108–9; WAVES as, 96. *See also* maintainers
Anderson, Norman O., 143
Antar, Albert, 135
AOMBs (aviation bombsight mechanics), 93t
AOMTs (aviation turret mechanics), 93t, 94t
AOs (aviation ordnancemen): at Jacksonville trade school, 55; length of school for, 69t; minimum required GCT scores for, 59–60, 222–3n42; minimum score for entry into, 176; new texts published for, 88; postwar jobs for, 137; responsibilities, 223n67; specialist ratings, 94t; specialized tasks for, 92; training, 48, 54
apprentice technicians (prior to 1940), 24, 47, 48
Ark Royal, 15
armaments: F4F vs. F6F average unit aircraft prices, 173t; maintenance, matériel expenditure factors and, 172
ARMs (aviation radiomen), 54, 55, 69t, 94t
Army, U.S., 81, 156, 157
Army Air Corps, later Army Air Force, U.S., 116, 141, 156–7, 221n1, 234n104
Army Technical Training Command, 68, 221n1, 223n64
AROUs (aviation repair and overhaul units): Assembly and Repair Department subdivisions, 143–4; cannibalization of spare parts at, 192; division of labor concept and, 209; engine overhauls by month, 145t; engine replacements by, 176; IAMMSP and workload reduction for, 189, 190–1; labor intensive repairs at, 208; major overhauls by, 146–7; planning and implementation, 142–3, 146; spare parts, labor-intensive work and, 178; supply and logistics and, 210. *See also* A&R (assembly and repair) facilities

arresting gear, 15, 118, 131
ARTs (aviation radio technicians), 68, 94t, 124, 223n67
ARVs (assembly and repair vessels), 148–50, 151
ASD (Aviation Supply Depot), 158–9, 231n16
ASO (Aviation Supply Office), 157, 158
ASO Catalog, 159, 160, 161
Assembly and Hoist Detail, 124–5
Assembly and Repair Department, AROU, 143
assembly and repair facilities. *See* A&R (assembly and repair) facilities
assembly and repair vessels. *See* ARVs
Atlanta Naval Air Station, formerly Atlanta Naval Reserve Aviation Base, 78t, 97
attack aircraft (VB/VT), 200–201, 200t, 201t
automatic-pilot technicians, 37
Avenger-class carriers, 228n30
Aventinus (LST), 148, 149–50
aviation boatswain's mates, 94t
aviation bombsight mechanics (AOMBs), 93t
aviation carburetor mechanics (AMMCs), 93t
aviation carpenter's mates, 40
aviation electrician's mate, 94t, 124, 137
Aviation Engineering Officers' School, 84, 87
aviation fire controlman, 94t
aviation flight engineers (AMMFs), 93t
aviation hydraulic mechanics (AMMHs), 93t
aviation instrument mechanics (AMMIs), 93t
aviation machinist mates. *See* AMMs
aviation machinist's mate, chief petty officer (AMMC), 121
aviation mechanics and technicians: A&R facilities as training sites for, 50; *ASO Catalog* instructions for, 159; availability, aircraft availability and, 12; better trained, spare parts needed and, 175; Bob Hope's praise for, 204; BuAer on increases needed for war, 25–26; civilian, Navy aircraft buildup and, 41; dedication of, 136–7; expanded course offerings

for, 68; Horne Board on need for, 33, 37–38; increased, increased carriers and aircraft and, 169; increased, numbers of new aircraft and, 167–8; Japanese defeat and, 205; labor costs for repairs made by, 182; learning curve in 1930s for, 24–25; life on aircraft carriers for, 129–30; Moffett congressional testimony on need for, 19; Navy's success in the air war and, 203–4; new engine and aircraft systems and, 23; new texts published for, 88; number of, by 1943, 5; planes available to fly and, 29; postwar jobs for, 138; primary tasks for, 30; rated, 20, 217n17; ratio to planes, 29, 116, 218n4; recruitment policies for, 10; specific number of ratings (1941), 220n58; training, carrier aviation and, 1; training problems, 38–39; U.S. carrier forces and, 14; WAVES as, 96–97; work conditions for, 125–6; work schedule, 128–9; World War II role, 27; Wrens as, 103–4. *See also* AMMs; AMs; AOs; enlisted aviation personnel; maintainers; schools, naval aircraft maintenance

aviation metalsmiths. *See* AMs

Aviation Navy, 80

aviation ordnancemen. *See* AOs

aviation personnel: aircraft carriers over time vs., 171*f*; matériel on hand, 1940–45, and, 170*t*, 232n60. *See also* enlisted aviation personnel; rate or ratings

Aviation Personnel Board of 1939, 33. *See also* Horne, Frederick J. and the Horne Board

aviation propeller mechanics (AMMPs), 93*t*

Aviation Radar School, Ward Island, TX, 78*t*

aviation radio technician (ARTs), 68, 94*t*, 124, 223n67

aviation repair and overhaul units. *See* AROUs

aviation supply clerks (SKVs), 93*t*, 94*t*, 160–1

Aviation Supply Depot (ASD), 158–9, 231n16

Aviation Supply Office (ASO), 157, 158

aviation turret mechanics (AOMTs), 93*t*, 94*t*

aviation welders, 37

barges, self-propelled, 153
Barker, Joseph W., 59
baseball caps, CASU operations and, 140
Basic Electricity (BuPers Training Unit), 91
Basic Machines (BuPers Training Unit), 91
Bataan, 154
battleships, 1, 3, 14
Belleau Wood, 154
Beneficial Suggestion Program (Benny Suggs): clamping plastics, 166; dolly for removing crashed airplanes, 164–5; dope application and refrigeration unit, 164; hydraulic system failure temporary fix, 166; rim jack for Hellcat flat tires, 165–6; St. Johns' tail jack, 163; tailwheel locking procedure, 165; value of, 167
billets, determining number of where to assign, 38–39
Black men, 11, 105–10, 208, 210–1
Black women, 100
boats (thirty-six foot), as ferries for ARVs, 150
Bogan, G. F., 51
Bogue-class carriers, 228n30
Bombsight Maintenance Schools, 78*t*
bomb-sight mechanics, 37
Brewer, Lucy, 102–3, 226n47
Brimm, Daniel J., Jr.: on current and planned trade schools' capacities, 63, 64*t*; curriculum development and, 58–59, 87–89, 91; Jacksonville Trade Schools and, 66; trailblazing efforts of, 212
Britain, Great. *See* Royal Navy
Bruner, Forest F., Jr., 132–4, 137
Buchanan, A. R., 8
Bureau of Aeronautics (BuAer): administrative histories of, 8; aircraft requirements estimates by, 197–8; aircraft technician apprentices and, 48; annual wartime budget for, 184; on average carrier air group and replacements, 181; Aviation Supply Office and, 158; aviation technical training revisions by, 168; aviation technicians for war needed by, 25–26; aviation

training program moved to, 51–52; on corrosion and aircraft maintenance, 17, 18; creation of, 10; enlisted aviation personnel estimate (1937), 43–44, 43*t*; on enlisted aviation technicians, 19; failure to anticipate aircraft mechanics' importance, 14–15; hiring and training challenge for, 27–28, 207; increased manning and training requirements and, 34–35; industry partners and, 10–11; intensified operational activity (1942) and, 74; interwar aircraft on hand, 4; NATTC and, 79–80; not comprehending airplane maintenance required, 39; technician planning shortfalls criticized, 42; on training by wartime manufacturers, 72–73; training publications (manuals), 87–88; Training Section, 54; tricing procedure in hangars and, 21–22; WAVES as aviation technicians for, 96; Wheelock as liaison between NATTC and, 76

Bureau of Aeronautics Manual (1940 ed.), 31, 87–88, 89

Bureau of Construction and Repair (BUCON), 21–22

Bureau of Medicine's training program, 52

Bureau of Navigation (BuNav), later Bureau of Naval Personnel (BuPers): aviation technical training revisions by, 168; aviation technical training schools consolidated by, 70; aviation training publications and, 88–90; defaulting to BuAer requests, 32; factory schools and, 71; hiring and training challenge for, 27–28; intensified operational activity (1942) and, 74; little concern with meeting skilled labor requirement by, 4; lowering minimum GCT scores for entry into ratings, 175–6; Murray on administration of aviation personnel and, 33–34; NATTC and, 76, 79–80; not comprehending airplane maintenance required, 39; Personnel Division and, 33–34; ratings for AMM graduates from Jacksonville school, 65; renaming of, 68, 215n16; Standards and Curriculum Section, 91; on training with wartime manufacturers, 72–73; Wheelock on airmen training under, 50; World War II challenges for, 11

Bureau of Ordnance (BuOrd), 74, 183–4

Bureau of Ships (BuShips), 74, 183–4

Bureau of Supplies and Accounts (BuSandA), 23, 158

Bureau of Yards and Docks, 70, 74

Butler, Henry V., 66

C1 schools, 81, 84
C2 schools, 81
C3, 199*t*
CAP (carrier air patrol), 186, 187, 188
carburetor test shops, 150
cargo ships, service squadrons and, 152, 155
cargo trucks, on ARVs, 150
Carrier Air Groups (CAGs) (V-5): as air department subdivision, 117; components (1934), 21; cost of equipping, 1929 and 1944, 184*t*; ship's company and, 114; technician-to-plane ratio design for, 116
carrier aircraft: ARVs as support for, 151; average *Essex*-class complement of, 115*t*; crashed, dolly for flight line removal of, 164–5; daily availability reports on, 125; distribution, 199*t*; as end-of-war throwaways, 167; folded-wings issues with, 126; forecast capability by 1945 of, 220n42; IAMMSP and replacements for, 189; jumping chocks, 136; labor costs for repairs on, 182; landing mishaps, 126–7; life-expectancies of, 12, 209; losses, by type of loss, 199–201, 200*t*; maintenance, matériel expenditure factors and, 172; Monthly Reporting of Operating Aircraft on, 192–3; naval aviation maintenance and, 206; Navy inventory increases during Pacific war, 6, 147, 215n7; Pacific Fleet AROUs and, 143; Radford Board on retirement schedule for, 190–1; routine flight hour inspections for, 120–1; safe for flight, check crews and, 121–2; saltwater corrosion of, 127–8; service life factors, 191, 194; spare, allocations for, 197–8; spotting, 118, 125, 130–2; World War II increase in, 113–4, 114*t*.

See also fighter aircraft; flying hours; scout bombers; scouting aircraft; torpedo bombers
carrier aircraft service divisions (CASDs), 139. *See also* air department, of ships
carrier aviation: aircraft maintenance and, 1, 2, 112–3; tire blowouts and prop strikes, 126–7. *See also* air department, of ships; aircraft, naval
carrier fleet, 4, 5. *See also* aircraft carriers; Fast Carrier Task Force; Royal Navy
Casablanca-class carriers, 228n30
CASUs (carrier aircraft service units): aviation engineering officers and, 84; division of labor concept and, 209; engine replacements by, 176; IAMMSP and workload reduction for, 189, 190–1; Jacksonville AMM graduates and, 66; labor intensive repairs at, 208; service squadrons and, 153; as shore-based air group service outfits, 139–41; spare parts, labor-intensive work and, 178; spare parts' cannibalization at, 192; supply and logistics and, 210
catapults, 15, 118
cautionary notes, in *Naval Aviation News*, 163–4
ceiling, for naval aircraft, 193–4
Celler, F. A., 142
check crews, 121–2, 124, 228n24
Chicago, Navy Pier: Butler's plans for, 66–67; current and planned capacity of trade school, 64t; enlisted technical school at, 78t; increased student matriculations for, 63; length of school at, 69t; as major aviation technical training center, 70
Chicago Vocational School, 66, 78t
Chloris (LST), 148, 149–50
chock pullers, 133
chocks, aircraft jumping, 136
Civil Aviation Administration (CAA) schools, 77
civilian Teacher Training Program, 80
Class A maintenance, 129
Class A schools: Black sailors attending, 106; Group III schools as, 84; NATTC consolidation and, 81; SKV schools for storekeeper graduates of, 160–1; standard time frame for classes at, 68; technical aviation training at, 54, 110; Towers on additions to supplement, 70
Class B maintenance, 129
Class B schools (advanced training), 54, 81, 110
Class C maintenance, 129
Class C schools (specialized skills training), 54, 81, 110
Class D maintenance, 129, 176
Class I, II, or III strikes of aircraft, 193
Class P schools, 81
Claude fighters, Mitsubishi A5M, 186–7
combat aircraft service unit (forward) [CASU (F)], 141
combat information and control division (V-3), 117
combat missions, use of term, 234n99
combat operations: aircraft maintenance and, 198–9; carrier aircraft losses by type of loss, 201, 201t; carrier aircraft losses due to, 200–201, 200t; daily, flight deck division and, 119–20; replacement planes to support, 181; task force active engagement in, 230–1n64
Commencement Bay-class carriers, 228n30
commercial airline schools, 77
commercial aviation industry, 40–41
communications, 30, 95, 150
Congress, 36, 80
control tower operators, 84, 97
Cooley, A. D., 190
Copahee, 153–5
Corpus Christi, TX, Parachute Materials School, 78t
corrosion, 17–18, 23, 127–8, 211
Cotton, Junius L., 54–55
Cowpens, 154
cranes, off-loading new airplanes using, 153
curriculum: Brimm and development of, 58–59, 87–89; Ford's, in Dearborn, 67; limited petty officer training at factories and, 71; standardized, for aviation technicians, 68, 207
Curtiss electric pitch propellers, Henriques' compression wrench for, 163
Curtiss-Wright Corporation, 72–73, 224n75

Index 247

CVBs (heavy carriers), 119, 165, 199t
CVEs (escort carriers): aircraft distribution for, 199t; aircraft maintenance on board, 123–5; aircraft strength during World War II, 114t; aviation personnel on hand, 1940–45, and, 170t, 232n60; blown tires on flight deck of, 165; changes in sailors' uniforms on, 119; *Copahee* as aircraft transport, 153–5; daily maintenance operations on, 125; enlisted aviation personnel complement for, 20; introduction of, 169; number of, by V-J day, 6; number of airplanes on board, 15; service squadrons and, 152; spare parts transported by, 153; wing jack storage on, 165
CVLs (light carriers): aircraft distribution for, 199t; aircraft maintenance on board, 123; aircraft strength during World War II, 114t; aviation personnel on hand, 1940–45, and, 170t, 232n60; changes in sailors' uniforms on, 119; enlisted aviation personnel complement for, 20; service squadrons and, 152; wing jack storage on, 165
CVs (fleet or medium carriers): aircraft distribution for, 199t; aircraft strength during World War II, 114t; aviation personnel on hand, 1940–45, and, 170t, 232n60; enlisted aviation personnel complement for, 20; number of, by V-J day, 6. *See also* aircraft carriers

Dahlgren, VA, Bombsight Maintenance School, 78t
damage: battle-caused, 30; maintenance department negligence and, 127
Dearborn, MI: current and planned capacity of trade school, 64t; naval training school, 67, 69t, 78t
Deputy Chief of Naval Operations for Air (DCNO, Air), 8, 28
Desert Storm, Operation, 235n5
destroyers, 152
Detroit, MI. *See* Dearborn, MI
Devaney, Charles W., 119–20
distilling ships, service squadrons and, 152
dive-bombers, 6, 121
dolly for removing crashed airplanes from flight line, 164–5

dope (plasticized lacquer) application tip, 164
Douglas Aircraft Corporation, 72
"down" aircraft (down for repair): *ASO Catalog* and, 159; flat tires and, 165; implications of, 210; readiness percentages and, 202; specialists reducing time as, 208; as unavailable to fly, 125
DuBose, Laurence T., 28–29, 116, 218n3

Echols, Gladys Marsheck, 97–98
education: effective modern military and, 211–2. *See also* schools, naval aircraft maintenance
Education, U. S. Office of, 56–57, 80
electronics: aviation mechanics' knowledge of, 30; on smaller escort and light carriers, 124
electronics subdivision (V2R), of engineering-maintenance division, 121
elevators, aircraft, 16, 21
Ellyson, Theodore G., 19
Ely, Eugene, 17
Emery, H. C., 42
Engine Overhaul Division, AROU Assembly and Repair Department, 143–4
engine test stands, 150
engine transportation stands, 150
engineering subdivision (V2-E), of engineering-maintenance division, 121–2
engineering-maintenance division (V-2): as air department subdivision, 117; repair and preventive maintenance by, 118; responsibilities, 120–1; subdivisions, 121–2
engines, aircraft: air-cooled compared with liquid-cooled, 22–23; changes by carrier technicians, 176; disassembly/reassembly of, 30; escort carriers' delivery of, 153; F4F vs. F6F average unit aircraft prices for, 173t; Ford-manufactured Pratt & Whitney R-2800 series, 67; increased horsepower, 23–24, 25f, 179–80; Joint Aircraft Committee and, 156; maintenance, matériel expenditure factors and, 172; Monthly Reporting of Operating Aircraft on, 193; numbering interchangeable parts for, 159;

248

Index

overhauled at AROUs, 143–4; repair and maintenance, ARVs and, 149–50. *See also* overhauls, aircraft

enlisted aviation personnel: on active duty (1940–41), 44*t*; BuAer estimated requirement (1937), 43*t*; for Carrier Air Groups, 21; Horne Board Report on, 37; Horne updating requirements for, 44–45; number of, 1940 and 1945, 6; Personnel Division and various ratings of, 31–32; skilled and unskilled, estimates for, 45, 220n57; WAVES as, 96. *See also* aviation mechanics and technicians; rate or ratings; trade schools

enlisted aviation technicians: aerial combat training for, 93, 95–96; BuAer's interwar lack of attention to, 4; Pacific War victory and, 2

Enterprise: air squadron complement on, 29; construction, 22; displacement, 216n15, 217n12; Gilmore as AMM on, 130–2; Murray as commander of, 187–8, 220n54

equipment, miscellaneous, 87–88, 163, 172, 173*t*

escort carriers. *See* CVEs

Essex: commissioning, trade school students and, 61, 63; cost of equipping air group for, 184*t*; Navy's carrier aircraft capacity and, 6; pre-World War II design, 115; technician-to-plane ratio design for, 116

Essex-class carriers: air group configurations for, 198; air squadron complement on, 29; engineering division on, 120; ordnance and servicing division on, 122–3; production, enlisted personnel assigned to, 61, 63; spare or reserve aircraft allowance for, 197; standard aircraft complement aboard, 182–3; technician-to-plane ratio design for, 116

F2A Buffalo monoplane fighter, Brewster, 24, 42, 179

F3B-1 fighters, Vought, 23, 24, 25*f*

F3F biplane fighter, Grumman, 24, 42, 176, 179

F4B fighter, 184*t*

F4B-4 fighter, Boeing, 23

F4F Wildcats, Grumman: airframe cost range for, 172; aviation engineering officers and, 84; F6F average unit aircraft prices vs., 173*t*; horsepower, 25*f*; increased procurement of, 169, 231–2n37; Marshall Islands campaign and, 186, 187; Navy contract for, 61; Navy takes first delivery of (1940), 42; Navy's monthly contract for, 176; percentage of spares for, 232n41; Pratt & Whitney R-1800 engines in, 67; production of, 231–2n37; spare parts in contracts for, 183; as standard fighter, 24

F4U Corsair, Vought, 24, 25*f*

F6F Hellcats, Grumman: airframe improvements, 180; aviation engineering officers and, 84; delivery rate for, 191; Devaney as plane captain for, 119–20; F4F average unit aircraft prices vs., 173*t*; George's rim jack for flat tires on, 165–6; massive deliveries for, maintenance practices and, 172; modified as multi-role fighter-bomber, 115–6; Navy's monthly contract for, 176; number ordered outweighing flight deck space for, 181; percentage of spares for, 232n41; Pratt & Whitney R-2800 engines in, 67, 180; spare parts in contracts for, 183; specifications, 24; wing guns' servicing for, 126

Fabius (LST), 148–50

factory schools, 11, 71, 81. *See also* aircraft manufacturing industry; manufacturers' plants; schools, naval aircraft maintenance; trade schools

Fast Carrier Task Force: flying hours reports from, 146; Japanese defeat and, 205, 211; Mitscher and, 230n2; service squadrons and, 152–3; technical training, flight hours tempo and, 147–8, 151; underway replenishment of, 156

FF-2, Grumman, 23–24, 25*f*, 217n27

fighter aircraft (VFs): average *Essex*-class complement of, 115*t*; aviation personnel on hand, 1940–45, and, 170*t*, 232n60; aviation personnel over time vs., 171*f*; broken, abandon or fix? 174–6; early Carrier Air Groups and, 21;

increased inventory of, 115; increased procurement of, 169; losses, by type of loss, 200*t*, 201*t*; Navy inventory (1940 and 1945), 6; readiness, maintenance policies and, 202; replacements, 181; semiannual value of deliveries, 176, 176*t*; on smaller escort and light carriers, 123; technicians assigned to, 121; VE-7S bi-wing, 22; Vought VE-7 Bluebird as first, 17

Fighting Squadron Two (VF-2), 16

Five-Year Program for naval aviation, 19

fleet carriers. *See* CVs

fleet tugs, service squadrons and, 152

Fletcher, Frank "Jack," 186, 188

flight deck: blown tires on, 165; crash landings on, dolly for removing, 164–5; hazards or vulnerabilities, 134–6; Reeves on parking aircraft on, 16; space limitations, major repairs and, 129; spotters on, 118, 125, 130–2; technicians required for parking aircraft on, 21; Towers and Reeves on, 17; unflyable aircraft on, 182

flight deck division (V-1): as air department subdivision, 117; daily combat operations and, 119–20; Gilmore on *Enterprise* in, 130–2; sailors' uniforms, 118–9

Flight Division, of BuAer, 31. *See also* Personnel Division, of BuAer

floodlight (portable) trailers, on ARVs, 150

Florida State Department of Education, 57

Flying and Popular Aviation (January 1942 issue), 29, 46, 218n8, 221n61

flying boats, 15

flying hours: aircraft condition and, 147, 192, 209, 230n89; limited, prior to 1944, 212

FM-1 and FM-2 Wildcats, General Motors, 231–2n37

Ford, Henry, 67

forklift trucks, on ARVs, 150

Fortune (cargo ship), 155

Fox, C. W., 190

Franklin, Japanese bombing of, 134–5

friendly fire, aircraft losses due to, 200*t*

fuel, aviation: air department and, 114; on *Essex*-class carriers, 123; exhaustion, aircraft losses due to, 201*t*; gasoline crews responsible for, 118; Marine Corps' WR training on, 102; officer schools' training on, 87; ordnance and servicing division and, 122; plane captains and, 119; purchases (1940 and 1945), 6; replenishment, 152; running rich and, 127; on smaller carriers, 124; underway replenishment of, 155–6; *Yorktown* bombing and, 135–6

Gates, Artemus, 51, 52

general cargo trucks, on ARVs, 150

General Classification Test (GCT), 59–61, 222–3n42

general service personnel, 20, 217n17

George, E. W., 165–6

Gilmore, Lloyd M., 130–2

Goodyear Tire and Rubber Company, 72

Government Printing Office, 90

Great Lakes Naval Training School, 69*t*, 84

green time, use of term, 234n99

ground school training, 53

Group I centers, 80, 82*f*

Group II centers, 81, 83*f*

Group III schools, 81, 84, 85*f*, 92, 159

Group IV schools, 81, 84, 86*f*, 92, 159

Grumman: aircraft deliveries per month by, 172; mass production and technology used by, 56; Pratt & Whitney engines used by, 179–80; training included in new equipment delivery by, 72–3, 224n75. *See also* F3F biplane fighter; F4F Wildcats; F6F Hellcats; FF-2

Guadalcanal campaign, carrier operations an, 151

"Guide for Expansion of Peacetime Shore Establishments, A" (Hepburn), 49

Guinn, Thomas D., 142

gunners, aircrew, 93, 95, 123

Hale, Frederick, 28

Halsey, William, Jr. "Bull," 185, 186–7, 188, 230n2

Hancock, 202–3

Hangar Operations (V-2) Division, on smaller carriers, 123, 124

hangars, carrier: airplane crashes under tow in, 126; "hangar queens" in, 30; IAMMSP and space in, 196–7; Reeves

and use of, 16; tricing spare or damaged aircraft in, 21–22; uses for, 20–21
Harris, Dale, 153–4
heavy carriers (CVBs), 119, 165
Henriques, David, 163
Hepburn, Arthur J., 49
Hermes, 15
Higgins, Ronald D., 63
histories and historical analysis: administrative, of World War II, 8–9, 215n11; further, of aviation maintenance, 212–3; of logistics and matériel, 5, 6
Hitler, Adolf, 157
Hollywood, FL, air gunner's school at, 93, 95
Hope, Bob, 204
Horne, Frederick J. and the Horne Board, 33, 36–37, 38, 44–45, 48
Hornet: aircraft availability, 202–3; commissioning, trade school students and, 61; construction, 22; *Copahee* as aircraft transport to, 154; displacement, 216n15, 217n12; loss of, 114t; technician-to-plane ratio design for, 116
hydraulics, 30, 166

Independence-class carriers, 228n30
innovative ideas, *Naval Aviation News* dissemination of, 162–3
Instruction Navy, 80
instructors: civilian Teacher Training Program and, 80; civilian versus military, 57; at Jacksonville trade school, 55, 56, 63; for pilot and technical schools, 37–38; for SKV schools, 160–1
Instrument Schools, 78t
instruments: aircraft instruments repair technicians, 37; AMMIs (aviation instrument mechanics), 93t; F4F vs. F6F average unit aircraft prices, 173t; maintenance, matériel expenditure factors and, 172
Integrated Aeronautic Maintenance, Materiel, and Supply Program (IAMMSP): aircraft availability and, 191–2, 202–3; aircraft striking guidelines, 193–4; aviation supply and maintenance culture and, 209; carrier aircraft losses and, 201–2; nature of repair and, 195; new aircraft deliveries and, 194–5; operating aircraft status reports and, 192–3; publicity regarding, 195–6; shifting maintenance to continental U.S., 189, 190–1; tempo of, 196; on using newest combat airplanes, 191
interwar period: early, labor demands on carriers during, 20; growth in squadrons and air groups size during, 21; naval aviation during, 3–4
Intrepid, 61, 115

Jacksonville, FL, Naval Air Technical Training Center, 160
Jacksonville Naval Air Station: aviation technical training at, 49, 53; enlisted technical schools at, 78t; officer school at, 79t
Jacksonville Trade School: Aviation Machinist's Mate School, 65–66, 132; capacity to deliver technicians by, 61; Cotton as head at, 55; current and planned capacity of, 64t; curriculum for, 58–59; inadequate facilities for fleet requirement numbers, 66; increased student matriculations for, 63; instructors, 57, 66; length of school at, 69t; local newspaper on, 55–56; as major aviation technical training center, 70; Material Department, 58; Navy and Marine enlisted students by month at, 62t; recruitment and rating model of, 60; two-class-shifts per day schedule, 63, 65, 168; Wheelock on increased student load at, 71
jeeps and jeep trailers, on ARVs, 150
Jennings, R. S., 142
Joint Aircraft Committee (JAC), 156
Jupiter, 15. See also *Langley*

Kaiser Company, 228n30
Kaiser-class carriers, 199t
Kasaan Bay, 164–5
Keegan, John, 9
"keep 'em flying," 12, 138, 157, 195, 209, 216n17
Kendall, H. S., 138, 229n61
King, Ernest J., 23, 190
Knox, Frank, 39, 40, 41
Koch, F. R., 165–6

Index

Koch, J. V., 142
Kwajalein Atoll, 143, 230n6

labor force: buildup, of aircraft technicians, 8; for naval aircraft, 9–10; shortage, engine overhauls (1941) and, 38; specialized, for carrier aircraft maintenance, 11–12, 211; trained and sized to sustain Pacific air war, 147–8. *See also* aviation mechanics and technicians; pilots; skilled labor; specialists
Lakehurst, NJ: Aerographers' School in, 78*t*; WAVES training at, 97
Langley: aircraft operations from, 5; in combat against Japan (1942), 216n5; conversion and commissioning of, 15–16; decommissioning and seaplane tender conversion, 217n27; as first aircraft carrier, 9, 215n14; operational personnel complement for, 20; Reeves and flight deck enlargement on, 17; research and development operations of, 113
Lexington (CV 2): airplanes on board (1934), 21; construction, aircraft procurement and, 18–19; *Langley* dimensions compared with, 16; loss of, 114*t*; operational personnel complement for, 20; as reconfigured battle cruiser, 9; technician-to-plane ratio design for, 116, Washington Naval Treaty and, 215–6n15, 216–7n12; working during bombing of, 136–7
Lexington (CV 16): air department on, 116, 117–8, 227n14; aircraft availability, 202–3; Bruner as AMM on, 132–3; typical day on, 130
Lexington-class carriers, 21–22, 138–9, 217n12
Leyte Gulf, Battle of, 155
light carriers. *See* CVLs
line maintenance power supply jeeps, on ARVs, 150
Link Trainer (flight simulator) operators, 78*t*, 97
Lockheed Aircraft Corporation, 72
logistics: cargo ships and, 155; carrier war in the Pacific and, 198–9; naval aviation's supply chain and, 177–8, 210; for Pacific fleet, historical literature on, 5. *See also* service squadrons; spare parts

London Naval Treaty, 9
Long Island, 22
LSTs. *See* ARVs

Maas, Melvin J., 75
Magara (LST), 148–50
maintainers: as behind-the-scenes aircraft technicians, 2; daily routines, 30; *Enterprise* in Marshall Islands campaign and, 187–8; growing ranks of, 168–9; learning new planes on the fly, 180–1; NATTC and, 5, 68; on-board responsibilities, 118; on smaller escort and light carriers, 123. *See also* ordnance and servicing division; plane captains
Maintenance and Plans Division, of BuAer, 32
Major Aircraft Repair Squadrons (MARS), 229n74. *See also* AROUs
Majuro, capture of, 154, 230n6
manufacturers' plants: aviation technician training at, 77. *See also* aircraft manufacturing industry; factory schools
Marianas campaign (1944), 153–4, 156
Marine Corps, U.S.: enlisted, as Jacksonville Trade School students, 61, 62*t*, 63; Women's Reserve (WR), 102–3, 104, 210
marksmanship, aircrew gunners and, 95
Marshall Islands, 186–9
Martin (Glen L.) Aviation Company, 56, 105
Mason, Charles P., 55, 222n25
Matagorda, 230n84
matériel, for Pacific fleet, historical literature on, 5
Mathematics (BuPers Training Unit), 91
McAfee, Mildred, 96
McCain, John S., Sr., 89, 230n2
mechanical failures, aircraft loss and, 201–2, 201*t*
mechanics. *See* aviation mechanics and technicians
medium carriers. *See* CVs
Memphis Naval Training Center: commissioning as aviation maintenance center, 70; construction completed, 168; Echols on training as AMM at, 98; enlisted technical school at, 78*t*; skilled labor for AROUs and CASUs

and, 146; Wheelock on increased student load at, 71
Midway Island, Towers on technical training at, 36
Minneapolis Naval Air Station, Turbo-Supercharger Regulator Course, 84
Mitscher, Marc A. "Pete": fast carrier task force concept and, 230n2; first naval aviation board and, 19; manning BuAer discussions and, 185; Murray on Personnel Division staffing to, 33, 34; naval aviation and, 216n11; service squadrons and, 155; touring Navy's shore aviation training facilities, 75
mobile machine truck and trailer, on ARVs, 150
Moffett, William A.: on aviation technician complement, 19–20, 217n15; congressional testimony on personnel requirements by, 28–29; first naval aviation board and, 19; labor force for naval aircraft and, 9–10; Towers' lessons on bureaucracy from, 35
Monthly Reporting of Operating Aircraft, 192–3
Mott, E. B., 188
Murray, George D.: on distribution of fleet aviators and technicians, 41–42; as *Enterprise* commander, 185; on FDR's increases in personnel and aircraft, 32–34; Marshall Islands campaign and, 187; plan for sharp increase in personnel by, 50; on Reserve component of Personnel Division, 32; on three-thousand-plane navy, 43, 220n54

Nakai, Kazuo, 187–8
National Defense Act (1942), 70
National Defense Training Program, 57
NAVAER 1872 form, 192–3
Naval Air Intermediate Training Command, 224n6
Naval Air Primary Training Command, 224n6
Naval Air Technical Training Command (NATTC): aerial combat training, 93, 95–96; consolidation of schools, 80–81, 168; creation of, 11, 76, 207; curricula for, 87–89; decrease in spare parts and, 175; financing and budgeting for, 79–80; graduation rates, increased Pacific flight operations and, 146–7; Group I activities, 82, 82*f*; Group II activities, 82, 83*f*; Group III activities, 84, 85*f*; Group IV activities, 84, 86*f*; impact of, 110–1; officer schools, 84, 87; Pacific War victory and, 5; postwar job guidance by, 137; Read as first chief of, 79, 80; revised rating structure recognizing specialists, 92–93, 93*t*, 94*t*; segregation and, 84, 106–10; technological advances in aircraft and, 91–92; training publications (manuals), 88–91; WAVES training with, 96–98; on World War II as "The Technician's War," 211. *See also* Black men; WAVES
Naval Aircraft Factory (NAF), U.S.: aviation technicians' training at, 31; on corrosion costs, 17–18; as informal technician training venue, 19; major repairs or overhauls at, 30, 112; school for aircraft instruments at, 48
Naval Appropriations Bill (1926), 28–29
Naval Armory, Chicago Vocational School and, 66
naval aviation: annual wartime budget for, 183–4; rating manuals, 90–91
Naval Aviation News: Beneficial Suggestion Program (Benny Suggs), 163–7; BuAer books and manuals advertised in, 90; as BuAer publication, 161–2; cautionary notes by, 163–4; WAVES survey, 99–100
naval aviators. *See* pilots
Naval Districts: NATTC creation and, 76; supervision of physical facilities by, 74–75
Naval Expansion Act (1938), 26
Naval History and Heritage Command, 8
Naval History Office, individual unit histories at, 8
Naval Reserve: activations for aviation personnel, 10, 40–41, 114, 207; enlisted personnel, Horne on naval aviation needs and, 38; Personnel Division and, 32; recruiting aviation technicians for, 37
Naval Reserve air bases (NRABs), 38
Naval War College's fleet problems (wargames), 3–4

Navy, U.S.: administrative leadership, 5–6, 207; aircraft technician labor force buildup and training, 8; contracts for spare parts delivery, 157, 172, 174, 183; enlisted, as Jacksonville Trade School students, 61, 62*t*; FDR's Germany First policy and, 156–7; Ford's curriculum in Dearborn and, 67; hiring and training challenge for, 27–28; industrial base at start of war, 212; institutional changes during World War II, 206–7; Joint Aircraft Committee and, 156; NATTC, BuAer, BuPers and, 79; segregation in, 105–10; standardized aviation technician instruction and, 68; unable to meet fleet's aviation technician requirements, 66, 70–71. *See also specific bureaus*

Navy Interviewer's Classification Guide, U.S., 60

Navy's Air War, The (Buchanan), 8

Nell bombers, Mitsubishi G3M, 187

night fighter groups, aircraft distribution for, 199*t*

Nimitz, Chester: activating Reservists with naval aviation ratings, 40–41; manning BuAer discussions and, 185; Pacific Fleet Command and, 89; shore-based aviation facility staff shortages and, 34; on South Pacific aviation repair and overhaul unit, 142–3; technician planning shortfalls criticism and, 42–43; on Towers handling aviation personnel and training, 52; Towers relationship with, 35; two regional fleets under, 230n2. *See also* Bureau of Navigation (BuNav), later Bureau of Naval Personnel (BuPers)

nomenclature: SKV school graduates and, 161; for spare parts by multiple manufacturers, 158–9

nonflying aviation personnel. *See* aviation mechanics and technicians; rate or ratings

Norden Factory, New York, Bombsight Maintenance School, 78*t*

Norfolk Naval Air Station: A&R facilities in, 48; BuAer on training aviation machinist's mates at, 50

Norfolk Naval Training Center (NTC) or Training Station: aircraft maintenance schools at, 48; aircraft technician training at, 53, 54; AMM course length at, 69*t*; AMM school moves to Memphis, 70; Cotton's study of schools at, 55; current and planned capacity of, 64*t*; officer schools at, 79*t*

Norman Naval Training Center, Oklahoma: commissioning as aviation maintenance center, 70; construction completed, 168; enlisted technical school at, 78*t*; skilled labor for AROUs and CASUs and, 146; Wheelock on increased student load at, 71

numbering, of spare parts by multiple manufacturers, 158–9

O2U Corsair, Vought, 184*t*

Office of the Chief of Naval Operations, 162

officer in charge (OIC), of Group III schools, 81

officer schools, 76, 79*t*, 84, 87

officers: aviation, Towers on need for, 10; Yarnell's naval aviation survey and, 177–8. *See also* petty officers

oilers, service squadrons and, 152

Okinawa campaign, service squadrons and, 153

operational accidents, 200–201, 200*t*, 201*t*

operational loss, definition of, 181

ordnance: aviation mechanics' knowledge of, 30. *See also* AOs

ordnance and servicing division (V-4): as air department subdivision, 117; management and responsibilities, 122–3; on smaller escort and light carriers, 124–5

Ordnance Division, AROU Assembly and Repair Department, 143

Organized Reserve, 40–41

Overhaul Division, AROU Assembly and Repair Department, 143

overhauls, aircraft: aircraft technician training and, 48; by AROUs, 143–4, 145*t*; flights per aircraft and, 146–7, 230nn85, 89; IAMMSP on, 209; increased naval aircraft inventory and, 147; Jacksonville AMM graduates and, 66; labor shortage (1941) and, 38; lack of skilled labor for, 212; Nimitz on sources of technicians to be trained in, 38; routine flight hour inspections and, 120–1; at sea, pre-World War II, 30; in the South Pacific, 141–2; by specialists, 208; Towers on technical training at facilities for, 36. *See also* CASUs

overseas military service jobs, for Wrens, 104

Pacific fleet, Richardson on lack of technical ratings for aviation units, 35–36
paint, on F6F-5 Hellcats, 180
painter V (aviation): specialist ratings, 94*t*. *See also* PTRVs
Parachute Loft Division, AROU Assembly and Repair Department, 143
Parachute Materials Schools, 78*t*
parachute riggers (PRs), 84, 97, 124
patrol squadrons, Jacksonville AMM graduates and, 66
Pearl Harbor, as new aircraft hub, 153
Pearl Harbor attack, 1, 3, 27, 46, 68
Pensacola Naval Air Station: aircraft technician training at, 48, 53, 54; current and planned capacity of trade school, 64*t*; enlisted technical schools at, 78*t*; as flight training center, 68
Perreault, Seraphin B., 142
Personnel Division, of BuAer: Mitscher on reorganization of, 34; Murray on administrative staff of, 32–33; nomenclature for, 219n15; responsibilities, 31–32. *See also* Bureau of Navigation (BuNav), later Bureau of Naval Personnel (BuPers)
petty officers: limited, streamlined technical training for, 71; use of, rating substituted for, 226n41
Phelps, 136
Philadelphia Naval Air Station, A&R facilities in, 48
photographer's mates, 94*t*, 117–8
Photographers' School, 78*t*, 84
pigeon trainers, 225n32
pilots: aircraft losses due to, 200, 201*t*; aircrewmen and, 95–96; available pool of, spare aircraft and, 115; flight instruction for, 224n6; increased aircraft and pool of, 38–39; planes available to fly and, 29; Towers on need for, 10

plane captains (PCs), 118–20, 227n18
Planning and Matériel Division, AROU Assembly and Repair Department, 143
Planning Division, BuAer, 181
plastics, Koch's clamp for, 166
PN-9 flying boat, 18
power units, on ARVs, 150
Pratt, William V., 174
Pratt & Whitney: Engineering Officers' School at, 79*t*; mass production and technology used by, 56; R-1800 engines, 67; R-1830 engines, 179; R-2800 engines, 67, 180; technical training at, 71
private colleges, aviation technician training at, 77
Production Planning Division (BuAer), 198
Propeller and CO2 Division, AROU Assembly and Repair Department, 143
propeller overhaul specialists, 37
propeller trailers, on ARVs, 150
propellers, 163, 172, 173*t*
PTRVs (aircraft painters), 37, 93*t*. *See also* painter V
public universities, aviation technician training at, 77
Purcell, OK, air gunner's school, 93, 95

Quonset Point Naval Air Station, RI, officer schools, 79*t*

racism in the military, 84, 105–10
radar training schools, 53
radars, Joint Aircraft Committee and, 156
Radford, Arthur W.: as first director of aviation training, 53; growing number of small training courses and, 73; Radford Board and, 189, 190–1; revised aircraft maintenance policies of, 203; on technical training and aviation maintenance, 176; trailblazing efforts of, 212
radio technicians (RTs), 60
radiomen (qualified in aircraft), 37, 40
radio/radar, F4F vs. F6F average unit aircraft prices, 173*t*
Radio-Radar Division, AROU Assembly and Repair Department, 143

radio/radar maintenance, matériel expenditure factors and, 172
radio/radar maintenance truck, on ARVs, 150
radios, Joint Aircraft Committee and, 156
range of opposing aircraft, estimating, 95
Ranger: authorization for, 29; operational personnel complement for, 20; spare or reserve aircraft allowance for, 197; Washington Naval Treaty and, 19, 22, 215–6n15, 216–7n12
rate or ratings: aircrew safety and, 68; aircrewman, 93, 95–96; Aviation Machinist's Mate School at Jacksonville and, 65; Class A schools and, 54; Horne Board Report focus and, 36–37; naval aviation, subject manuals for, 88–91; revised structure recognizing specialists, 92–93, 93t, 94t; use of term, 219n16; variations in length of school for, 69. *See also* enlisted aviation personnel
Read, Albert Cushing, 79, 80, 168, 212
readiness: of carrier aircraft squadrons, 7; *Flying and Popular Aviation* on, 29; revised maintenance policies and, 202; stock numbering, inventories, and forecasting requirements for, 158
rearming boats, on ARVs, 150
reconnaissance aircraft, British, 15
Reeves, Joseph M. "Bull," 16–17, 19, 216n6, 216n11
refrigeration unit, carrier, dope application and, 164
Regular Navy Section, in Personnel Division, 32
Repair Division, AROU Assembly and Repair Department, 143
replacements: engines, 176; fighter aircraft, 181; IAMMSP and, 189. *See also* throwaway culture
replenishment, aircraft-specific, 152. *See also* underway replenishment
"Report on Naval Aviation" (Yarnell), 176–7
Reserve, in Personnel Division, 32
Richardson, James O., 35
Richardson, L. B., 190
Roosevelt, Franklin D.: Germany First policy, 156–7; increased naval aircraft inventory and, 10, 32, 40, 44, 48–49, 183; Naval Expansion Act signed by, 26; on Navy increasing enlisted men (1939), 32; technician training for war on Japan and, 167
Rosenberg, David A., 8, 9
Rosenkranz, J. W., 166
Royal Navy (RN), 15, 103–4

saltwater corrosion, 17–18, 23, 127–8, 211
San Diego Naval Air Station: aircraft technician training at, 48, 53–54; AMM and AO schools move to Memphis from, 70; BuAer on training aviation machinist's mates at, 50; current and planned capacity of trade school, 64t; enlisted technical schools at, 78t; length of school at, 69t; officer schools at, 79t
Sangamon-class carriers, 199t, 228n30
Saratoga: airplanes on board (1934), 21; construction, aircraft procurement and, 18–19; cost of equipping air group for, 184t; *Langley* dimensions compared with, 16; as reconfigured battle cruiser, 9; torpedo in the side of, 186; Washington Naval Treaty and, 215–6n15, 216–7n12
SB2C Helldiver, 84, 115
SBD Dauntless dive-bombers, 115, 186, 188
schools, naval aircraft maintenance: *ASO Catalog* and, 159; lack of funding (1920s) for, 19; pre–World War II, 4; prior to 1940, 47; two-class-shifts per day schedule, 63, 65, 208. *See also* factory schools; trade schools; training facilities and schools
scout bombers, 115, 115t, 123
scouting aircraft (scouts), 3, 15, 21, 121
seaplanes, 15, 79
Seaplanes Maneuvering, Maintaining, Operating (Brimm), 58
Seattle Naval Air Station trade school, 64t, 67, 69t, 70
Secretary of the Navy: Annual Report (1945), 45; aviation training program and, 52–53; establishes NATTC as command under, 76, 77; NATTC funds allocation and, 79–80; revised rating structure recognizing specialists and, 92; training schools and, 70. *See also* Knox, Frank
segregation, 84, 105, 106–10

service squadrons, 152, 153–5, 159
shops subdivision (V2-S), of engineering-maintenance division, 121
skilled labor: for AROUs and CASUs, 146; BuNav and requirement for, 4; requirements for, 45; studies of protracted wars and, 213. *See also* aviation mechanics and technicians
SKVs (aviation supply clerks or storekeepers), 93*t*, 94*t*, 160–1
SO3C Seamew observation seaplane, 72
sorties, use of term, 234n99
Soviet Union, military preparedness for World War II, 212
spare parts: abandoning broken planes and, 174–5; aircraft contracts for, 157, 172, 174, 183; for ARVs, 150; *ASO Catalog* of, 159–60; cannibalization of, 190, 192; carrier air groups, 1929 and 1944 costs for, 184*t*; on carriers, IAMMSP and, 196; CASUs as forward staging area for, 140–1; corrosion prevention on, 128; cost of equipping air groups with, 184*t*, 185; F4F vs. F6F average unit aircraft prices, 173*t*; at forward stations, IAMMSP and, 192; matériel expenditure factors and, 172; NATTC training and, 175; procurement policies and, 12; for repairs, cost of replacement compared with, 182; shortage, Yarnell's survey and, 177–8; supply surge in, numbers of new aircraft and, 168; technology improvements and, 174; transported by escort carriers, 153. *See also* Aviation Supply Office
specialists: aviation supply clerks or storekeepers and, 160; carrier aircraft maintenance and, 11–12, 208, 212; Class C schools and, 54, 110; Group III schools for, 92; Group IV schools for, 81, 84, 92; rate or ratings structural revisions recognizing, 92–93, 93*t*, 94*t*
Sperry Gyroscope Company, Instrument Schools and, 78*t*
spotting airplanes, 118, 125, 130–2
Spruance, Raymond, 230n2
St. Johns, Charles R., 163
standard stock, bulk purchases of material designated, 158
Stark, Harold, 34, 38, 40, 45–46, 52–53

storekeeper V (aviation), SKVs, 93*t*, 94*t*, 160–1
strike (air-to-ground) capability, carrier aircraft and, 3
strikers, use of term, 48
striking an aircraft, methods for, 193
Sumida, Jon T., 8, 9
Summary of Objectives (BuAer), 197–8
supplies, aircraft maintenance, 158. *See also* spare parts
supply depots, 159. *See also* spare parts
supply system, mission-capable aircraft and, 12
support equipment, Joint Aircraft Committee and, 156

T4M torpedo bomber, Martin, 184*t*
tactics: aviation strides and, 5; fleet battle experiments and, 15–16; improvements, 2; interwar period and, 207; Pacific War victory and, 3, 206; studies of, 7; Young on Marshalls campaing and, 188
tailhooks, running, 131
tailwheels: dolly for removing crashed airplanes and, 165; locking procedure, 163–4
Task Force 38 (TF 38), 155, 202–3, 230n2
Task Force 58 (TF 58), 230n2
task groups, in task forces, 230n2
Taylor, Montgomery Meigs, 19
TBD Devastators, 186, 188
TBF Avengers, 126, 163
TBM Avengers, 84
technical training. *See* trade schools; training facilities and schools
Technical Training Section, of BuAer, 53, 91–93, 146
"Technically Speaking," in *Naval Aviation News*, 162
Technicians' War, The, 29
technology: advancements, maintenance personnel shortage and, 40; changing missions from defensive to offensive, 191; frontline fighters and, 195; improvements, 2; improvements, spare parts and, 174; Japanese defeat and, 205; Pacific War victory and, 3; training in, 212. *See also* F6F Hellcats, Grumman
tenant commands, 81

Index

throwaway culture: abandoning broken planes and, 174–6; buying airplanes in bulk and, 182; cost of equipping air groups and, 184t, 185; as Navy's best course, 209–10; Radford's naval aviation maintenance recommendations and, 203; reduced spare parts in aircraft contracts and, 183; replacements and, 181; transition in last phase of war to, 167; wartime budgets and, 183–4

time shack operators, 225n32

tires: blown, controlled crashes and, 126–7; changing, on a carrier, 165; flat, on F6Fs, George's rim jack for, 165–6

TMVs (aircraft torpedomen), 93t, 94t

torpedo bombers: average *Essex*-class complement of, 115t; early Carrier Air Groups and, 21; losses, by type of loss, 200t; Navy inventory (1940 and 1945), 6; readiness, maintenance policies and, 202; replacements, 181; on smaller escort and light carriers, 123; technicians assigned to, 121

torpedoes, air-launched, aircrew gunners and, 123

torpedoman's mate V (aviation), 93t, 94t

torpedo-topping compressors, on ARVs, 150

Towers, John H.: on aircraft on the flight deck, 17; on aviation technician shortage (1940), 4; on Bogan Board recommendations, 51–52; as BuAer chief (1939–1942), 10; on centralizing training under BuAer, 39; as commander, Pacific Fleet Air Forces, 89; enlisted aviation personnel estimate (1937), 43t, 44; factory schools and, 71–72; maintenance infrastructure concerns of, 144; manning BuAer discussions and, 185; on mobilizing Organized Reserve, 40; Murray on Personnel Division staffing to, 33, 34; on naval aviation's supply chain, 177; on Navy's aviation training program, 50; Navy's technical training program under, 36; Nimitz relationship with, 35; on personnel operations as sufficient, 45; Read and, 79; on south Pacific overhaul facility, 141–2; on technical training and aviation maintenance, 176; technician planning shortfalls criticized, 42–43; on timeline for adding aviation technicians, 26; welcoming the WAVES, 96, 104. *See also* Bureau of Aeronautics

tractors, on ARVs, 150

trade schools: *ASO Catalog* and, 159; complete restructuring of, 12; Cotton on Jacksonville school inadequacy, 55; current and planned capacity of, 64t; factory technicians and equipment for, 56; graduates, in AROUs and CASUs, 146; instruction facilities expansion and, 75; instructors for, 57; locations, 78t; making room for pilot and general aviation training, 68; NAS Jacksonville as first, 54; NATTC and, 76; problems with, 11; recruiting students for, 59–61; separated from A&R facilities, 50; for training aviation technicians, 10–11, 30–31, 207; training equipment for, 57–58; WAVES attendance at, 96; Wheelock on separate command for, 75–76. *See also* factory schools; officer schools; schools, naval aircraft maintenance; training facilities and schools; *specific schools*

training facilities and schools: CASUs as, 140–1; Horne Board Report on need for, 37; IAMMSP on aircraft for, 194; institutional changes in U.S. Navy and, 206–7; NATTC consolidation of, 80–81, 168; wartime manufacturers and, 72–73, 224n75. *See also* factory schools; schools, naval aircraft maintenance; trade schools; *specific schools*

training manuals, 87–91

training policies: budgets and, 80; changes before entering war, 4, 10; for enlisted aviation mechanics, 7; logistics and, 3; NATTC and, 80–81

tricing procedure in hangars, spare or damaged aircraft and, 21–22

Two Ocean Navy Act (1940), 219n21. *See also* Vinson-Walsh Act

underway replenishment, 155
unskilled labor requirements, 45
"up" aircraft, 166, 211. *See also* "down" aircraft

Use of Blueprints (BuPers Training Unit), 91
Use of Tools (BuPers Training Unit), 91

VE-7 Bluebird, Vought, 17, 25*f*
VF-2 (Fighting Squadron Two), 16
VFs. *See* fighter aircraft
Vinson-Trammel Act (1934), 29
Vinson-Walsh Act (1940), 44, 219n21
Volunteer Reserve, 40, 41
Vought. *See* F3B-1 fighters; F4U Corsair; O2U Corsair; VE-7 Bluebird
Vought-Sikorsky, training included in new equipment delivery by, 72–73, 224n75
VTs. *See* torpedo bombers

Walker, Wilbert, 105–10
Ward Island, TX, Aviation Radar School, 78*t*
wars, protracted, 213, 235n5
Washington Naval Conference and Treaty (1922), 9, 15, 215–6n15, 216–7n12
Wasp, 22, 114*t*, 197
water purification units, on ARVs, 150–1
WAVES (Women Accepted for Volunteer Emergency Service): as aviation technicians, 96–97, 104, 210; Echols at A&R facilities, 98–99; Echols training as AMM with, 97–98; *Naval Aviation News* survey on, 99–100; Navy regulations on, 100–102; overseas assignments, 225n32, 226n42; postwar jobs for, 229n61
weapon carriers, on ARVs, 150
welding shop truck, on ARVs, 150
Wheelock, Austin W.: Brimm's assessment of technical training and, 58; as BuAer–NATTC liaison, 76–77; BuNav training system and, 49–51; growing number of small training courses and, 73; manufacturing output of Navy fighters and, 61; as *Matagorda* commander, 230n84; on naval barracks built at factories, 71; paying for aviation technical training and, 80; on separate command for technical schools, 75–76; skilled labor for AROUs and CASUs and, 146; student load recommendations by, 71; on technical training and aviation maintenance, 175, 176; technical training under, 53; textual material for naval technical training and, 91; trailblazing efforts of, 212; on wartime technical training inadequacy, 70
Whiting Field Naval Air Station, 106
wing jacks, tire changing on a carrier and, 165
wing shop, on ARVs, 150
women: aviation technical ratings and, 207–8; naval air war and, 11. *See also* WAVES
Women's Reserve (WR), U.S. Marine Corps, 102–3, 104, 210
Women's Royal Naval Service (Wrens), 103–4
World War II: administrative naval histories of, 8–9, 215n11; aviation supply clerks or storekeepers and, 161; CASUs in the Pacific during, 140; institutional changes in U.S. Navy during, 206–7; naval aircraft proliferation during, 113, 114*t*; Navy shipbuilding and, 9; as "The Technician's War," 211
Wright-1820 engines, 179

Yarnell, Henry E., 19, 176–7, 216n11
Yellow Water, FL, air gunner's school at, 93, 95
yeomen (YN), 117
Yorktown: air squadron complement, 29; commissioning, trade school students and, 61; construction, 22; *Copahee* as aircraft transport to, 154; displacement, 216n15, 217n12; flight deck bombed, 135; loss of, 114*t*; Marshall Islands campaign and, 186–9; pre-World War II design, 115; spare or reserve aircraft allowance for, 197
Yorktown-class carriers, 216n15, 217n12
Young, Howard L., 186, 188

Zeroes, Japanese, 95, 134, 191

About the Author

Stan Fisher, a commander in the U.S. Navy, is a permanent military professor of naval and American history at the United States Naval Academy. Before transitioning to the classroom, he accumulated more than 2,500 flight hours as a Navy pilot, mainly in SH-60B and MH-60R Seahawk helicopters. He earned a commission through the Naval Reserve Officer Training Corps in 1997 and has deployed on frigates, cruisers, and aircraft carriers. Fisher is also a qualified operational test pilot, Seahawk weapons and tactics instructor, and maintenance officer; he has also completed tours of duty in engineering and acquisitions at the Naval Air Systems Command. He is a past recipient of the Samuel Eliot Morison Naval History Scholarship and was awarded a PhD from the University of Maryland in 2019. When not teaching or researching, he enjoys spending time boating on the Chesapeake Bay with his family and friends. This is his first book.

The Naval Institute Press is the book-publishing arm of the U.S. Naval Institute, a private, nonprofit, membership society for sea service professionals and others who share an interest in naval and maritime affairs. Established in 1873 at the U.S. Naval Academy in Annapolis, Maryland, where its offices remain today, the Naval Institute has members worldwide.

Members of the Naval Institute support the education programs of the society and receive the influential monthly magazine *Proceedings* or the colorful bimonthly magazine *Naval History* and discounts on fine nautical prints and on ship and aircraft photos. They also have access to the transcripts of the Institute's Oral History Program and get discounted admission to any of the Institute-sponsored seminars offered around the country.

The Naval Institute's book-publishing program, begun in 1898 with basic guides to naval practices, has broadened its scope to include books of more general interest. Now the Naval Institute Press publishes about seventy titles each year, ranging from how-to books on boating and navigation to battle histories, biographies, ship and aircraft guides, and novels. Institute members receive significant discounts on the Press' more than eight hundred books in print.

Full-time students are eligible for special half-price membership rates. Life memberships are also available.

For more information about Naval Institute Press books that are currently available, visit www.usni.org/press/books. To learn about joining the U.S. Naval Institute, please write to:

Member Services
U.S. Naval Institute
291 Wood Road
Annapolis, MD 21402-5034
Telephone: (800) 233-8764
Fax: (410) 571-1703
Web address: www.usni.org